9ØTSI

Property in Securities

Eva Micheler analyses the English, German and Austrian law of securities, addressing the rules governing transfers of securities, including unauthorised transfers, equities arising out of defective issues and the holding of securities through intermediaries. The book presents an account of the current English, German and Austrian legal regimes. It has been written with a view to explaining the German and Austrian regime to readers with a common law background and to explaining the English regime to readers with a civil law background.

The book also aims to determine whether globalisation will cause the two different approaches to converge. It concludes that the respective rules in all three jurisdictions have historically evolved consistently with incumbent legal doctrine. This pattern of change is likely to continue. Convergence will occur on a functional rather than on a doctrinal level. Moreover recent reform initiatives advanced by the UNIDROIT and the EU will lead to functional rather than doctrinal convergence.

DR EVA MICHELER is a Senior Lecturer at the London School of Economics and an ao Universitätsprofessor at the University of Economics in Vienna.

Cambridge Studies in Corporate Law

Series Editor

Professor Barry Rider,
University of London

Corporate or Company Law encompasses the law relating to the creation, operation and management of corporations and their relationships with other legal persons. **Cambridge Studies in Corporate Law** offers an academic platform for discussion of these issues. The series is international in its choice of both authors and subjects, and aims to publish the best original scholarship on topics ranging from labour law to capital regulation.

Books in the series

Janet Dine, *The Governance of Corporate Groups*
A. J. Boyle, *Minority Shareholders' Remedies*
Gerard McCormack, *Secured Credit under English and American Law*
Janet Dine, *Companies, International Trade and Human Rights*
Charlotte Villiers, *Corporate Reporting and Company Law*

Property in Securities

A Comparative Study

Eva Micheler

CAMBRIDGE
UNIVERSITY PRESS

CAMBRIDGE UNIVERSITY PRESS
Cambridge, New York, Melbourne, Madrid, Cape Town, Singapore, São Paulo

Cambridge University Press
The Edinburgh Building, Cambridge CB2 8RU, UK

Published in the United States of America by Cambridge University Press,
New York

www.cambridge.org
Information on this title: www.cambridge.org/9780521832656

First published 2007

Printed in the United Kingdom at the University Press, Cambridge

A catalogue record for this publication is available from the British Library

ISBN 978-0-521-83265-6 hardback

For Aurelia, Paul and Theodore

Contents

Preface

This book is the product of research carried out over the last nine years. I began researching property rights in securities in 1997 when I first arrived in England to study at the University of Oxford.

I have since then completed my Habilitation on this topic which was published in German in 2004. In that book, I advance a theory seeking to explain the proprietary dimensions of securities in German and Austrian law.

In this book, I approach the topic from a comparative perspective. The book has three aims. First, it aims to explain the relevant English law to readers with a civil law background, and the relevant German and Austrian law to readers with a common law background. Second, it aims to make a novel contribution to the debate as to whether legal systems are converging or developing in a path-dependent manner. Third, it expresses a view on how the law relating to property rights in securities can be harmonised across jurisdictions.

I am much indebted to my academic mentors, Paul L. Davies and Peter Doralt, without the support of whom this book and the earlier German volume would have never been written. I am also very grateful to Joanna Benjamin who knows more about the subject than I ever shall and who is an inspiring and very personable colleague at the London School of Economics.

I would also like to thank my other colleagues and those who are responsible for running the Law Department at the London School of Economics and the Institut für Bürgerliches Recht, Handels- und Wertpapierrecht at the Wirtschaftsuniversität Wien for providing me with environments that are so conducive to legal research.

Last but not least I would like to thank my husband, Steven, for encouraging me to write this book, for being prepared to discuss the fine points of securities law over the last nine years and for being a wonderful companion through the highs and lows of my academic work.

London, 11 August 2006   EVA MICHELER

Table of legislation

Table of cases

Introduction

This book contains an analysis of the English, German and Austrian law of securities. The term 'securities' is used in the context of this book to refer to shares, bonds and other financial instruments which are issued to the capital market with a view for them to circulate among market participants. The analysis presented in the book addresses the rules governing transfers of securities, including unauthorised transfers, equities arising out of defective issues and the holding of securities through intermediaries. The book does not contain an examination of the regulatory regime associated with securities and their issue. It does not, for example, provide an analysis of the disclosure requirements that apply to securities on their being first issued, or throughout the period during which they are listed on a public market.

The boundaries of this area of the law can be defined by reference to the two steps that are taken when securities are bought and sold. The first step is the conclusion of a contract for the sale of securities. Such contracts can be made on the stock exchange, through an electronic trading system, or directly between buyer and seller. The conclusion of a sales contract is referred to in the financial markets industry as 'trading'.[1] This book is not concerned with this first step.

The second step, and the focus of this book, is the performance of the contract for the sale of securities. This step is referred to in the financial markets industry as 'settlement'. The analysis presented in the book concerns the rules governing the completion of transactions relating to securities and also the rules that regulate the relationship between

---

[1] P. Moles and N. Terry *The Handbook of International Financial Terms* (Oxford: Oxford University Press, 1997) define trade at 558 as 'colloquial term for a transaction' and transaction at 560 as 'a purchase or sale made in the markets'.

intermediaries who hold securities on behalf of investors and their clients. This involves complicated questions of company and property law which have been the subject of significant academic work in the past few years.[2]

Several approaches to settlement exist, which differ in legal as well as in institutional terms. In this book, two approaches will be analysed. The first is the system adopted by English law; the second is that adopted by German and Austrian law. The jurisdictions which have adopted the respective approaches are members of the European Union (EU) and represent equally advanced economies. There nevertheless exist significant differences between them: England is a common law jurisdiction, Germany and Austria are civil law countries.

In England, securities are almost exclusively issued in the form of *registered instruments*. Their transfer involves an amendment of a register of holders: the name of the transferor on the register is replaced by the name of the transferee. The register is maintained by or on behalf of the issuer; as a result, issuers frequently know the names and particulars of their investors.[3] If paper certificates are issued for securities, these certificates are documents of evidence only and do not constitute negotiable instruments. The financial service providers operating in this context in England are registrars who maintain registers on behalf of companies. To eliminate paper from the transfer process, England has opted for *dematerialisation*. Instead of issuing paper certificates, issuers are able to issue uncertificated securities that are transferred electronically through a central service provider named CRESTCo Ltd. English law will be analysed in part I of the book.

In Germany and in Austria, securities are almost exclusively issued in the form of *bearer instruments*. These instruments are classified as tangible movables: Transfers are effected by the physical delivery of the paper documents. Issuers are, traditionally, not involved in the administration of transfers and do not know the identity of their investors.

---

[2] See in particular: A. O. Austen-Peters, *Custody of Investments, Law and Practice* (Oxford: Oxford University Press 2000); Joanna Benjamin, *Interests in Securities* (Oxford: Oxford University Press 2000); Joanna Benjamin and Madelaine Yates, *The Law of Global Custody* (London: Butterworth 2003); Maisie Ooi, *Shares and Other Securities in the Conflict of Laws* (Oxford: Oxford University Press 2003); Arianna Pretto, *Boundaries of Personal Property Law: Shares and Sub-Shares* (Oxford: Hart Publishing 2005).

[3] This is, however, only the case if the investor chooses to hold the securities directly. An investor may also chose to hold securities indirectly, in which case the name of a nominee appears on the register and the nominee receives issuer information on behalf of the investor.

The financial service providers operating in this context in Germany and in Austria are banks with whom securities are deposited and a central depository which stores most of the certificates relating to listed securities. To eliminate paper from the transfer process, Germany and Austria have opted for *immobilisation*. Certificates continue to exist; they are, however, put out of circulation and stored in a central depository. Transfers are effected by way of book entry on client accounts and without the need physically to move paper certificates. German law and Austrian law will be examined in part II of the book.

The book has three aims. The first is to present an account of the current English, German and Austrian legal regime governing the transfer and holding of securities and to compare the two approaches adopted by English law, on the one hand, and German and Austrian law, on the other. The book has been written with a view to explaining the English regime to readers with a civil law background and to explaining the German and Austrian regime to readers with a common law background. In order to enhance the understanding of the respective legal frameworks, the two approaches will be compared throughout the book.

The second aim is to analyse the law of securities against the background of a recent debate in the area of comparative law. In recent years, comparative legal scholars have focused on studying the effect of globalisation on legal systems. The focus of the debate is corporate governance, in particular the question whether globalisation will cause the corporate governance regimes represented around the globe to become more like each other. Some scholars predict that global competition will lead to the emergence of a single model of corporate governance. Others propound the view that there exist significant obstacles in the way of any convergence of legal rules: politics, economics, culture, social and commercial norms and legal mentalities.

The book contributes to this debate. Like corporate governance, the law of securities has been subject to the pressures created by a globalised economy. The book contains an analysis of how English, German and Austrian law have historically responded to change. It will be shown that, historically, all three jurisdictions have adapted to new challenges by refining the legal doctrinal concepts already in place. Whenever they have been faced with a need for reform, neither of the legal systems analysed in the book has created law from scratch, drafted to suit the requirements dictated by politics, economics, culture, or other forces, and it is likely that this pattern of legal change will continue in the face of globalisation. This leads to the conclusion that globalisation is unlikely to cause jurisdictions across the globe to adopt rules with identical wording, or of identical doctrinal background. Convergence will occur only at a functional rather than at a formal level, leaving the underlying doctrinal rules already in place largely intact.

Another conclusion presented in the book is that the institutional framework of a particular jurisdiction is determined by legal doctrine. The book does not claim that legal doctrine is the only factor explaining why certain institutions are present in certain markets. Nevertheless, it will be shown that the type of market infrastructure currently in place in England, Germany and Austria can be explained as a function of the legal rules that govern securities and their transfers.

The third aim of the book is related to the second. The book also intends to make a contribution to the question whether it is possible to harmonise the law governing securities. This harmonisation is currently being discussed by two international organisations. The UNIDROIT, an international organisation promoting the harmonisation of laws across the globe, presented in March 2006 a draft for a Convention on the substantive rules regarding intermediated securities. The EU is in the process of determining whether there exists a need to harmonise securities law across its member states (the EU Legal Certainty Project, see chapter 17). A group of legal experts has been appointed to give advice on whether the differences currently existing between the securities laws of the member states of the EU provide an obstacle capable of preventing the emergence of a single European financial market. If differences in the law are to be found to operate as a hindrance to a single market, the members of the group have been instructed to make suggestions for the harmonisation of this area of the law.

The book also aims to contribute to the question of what form a harmonised law of securities should take. The conclusion from the analysis contained in the book is that no attempt should be made to harmonise the legal doctrinal rules governing securities across Europe: harmonisation is possible, but only consistent with incumbent legal doctrine. The analysis presented in the book shows that notwithstanding the different legal tools applied in the different legal systems, the underlying explanation for these legal rules and the practical outcomes produced by them are similar. The legal systems share a common understanding of the theory underlying the law of securities; rather than interfering with domestic legal doctrine, law can be most effectively harmonised across Europe at a functional level by determining the outcomes which are to be achieved by the different jurisdictions.

Chapter 1 of the book contains an analysis of the arguments advanced in the current debate on convergence and path-dependence of legal development. English law will be examined in part I of the book, and German and Austrian law in part II. Part III of the book contains the conclusions following from the analysis presented. It will also examine the implications of these conclusions for the convergence and path dependence-debate and for the current plan to harmonise securities law across Europe.

1   Convergence and path-dependence

Modern comparative law scholarship has been concerned with determining the effects of globalisation on legal development. One of the current discussion topics in the field is whether, with globalising economies, legal systems converge. The focus of this discussion is corporate governance.

The debate starts from the premise that there currently exist, roughly speaking, two types of corporate governance models. The two models differ in the way in which firms are owned and in the way in which the law allocates influence between shareholders, the board of directors, employees, creditors and the general public.

Scholars distinguish between jurisdictions with relative dispersion of ownership of public companies (such as the US and the UK) and jurisdictions with relative concentrated ownership of public companies (such as Germany). In the US and UK, public companies have a large number of shareholders who each hold small fractions of the company's capital. Company law tends to favour shareholder interests. In Germany, public companies have one shareholder (or a small group of shareholders) who holds a significant stake in the company.[1] German company law looks after shareholders, but also protects the interests of employees, creditors and the general public.

The question that scholars are trying to solve is whether globalisation has an effect on these governance models. The starting point of the analysis is the assumption that the regime under which companies are governed is a cost factor in production: the assumption is that companies

---

[1] Lucian A. Bebchuk and Mark J. Roe, 'A Theory of Path Dependence in Corporate Ownership and Governance', (1999) 52 *Stan. L. Rev.* 127 at 133.

with better governance are more likely to operate at lower cost and therefore more able to succeed in global competition. This will lead to a change in the governance of companies world wide. The pressure of a global world economy will force jurisdictions and companies to reform their governance models to become more efficient. Will this cause differences between existing governance models to disappear, with the result that a global corporate governance model will emerge? Different scholars have given different answers.

Some argue that the existing corporate governance models will converge; they predict that different jurisdictions will adopt similar rules of company law and corporate practice. Others propound the view that there are significant obstacles that stand in the way of such convergence: politics, economics, culture, social and commercial norms and legal mentality. There is also a point of view which predicts that functional convergence will occur prior to formal convergence. In sections 1.1–1.3 the views advanced in this debate will be analysed; the arguments in favour of convergence will be presented first.

1.1 Convergence

Henry Hansmann and Reinier Kraakman predict the end of history for corporate law.[2] They observe convergence of corporate law towards an Anglo-Saxon style model of corporate law caused by 'a widespread normative consensus that corporate managers should act exclusively in the interests of shareholders, including non-controlling shareholders'.[3] Hansmann and Kraakman believe that all jurisdictions will move to similar rules of corporate law and practice. Differences may persist as a result of institutional and historical contingencies, but the bulk of

---

[2] Henry Hansmann and Reinier Kraakman, 'The End of History for Corporate Law', (2001) *Geo. L. J.* 439; John C. Coffee, Jr., 'The Future as History: The Prospects for Global Convergence in Corporate Governance and Its Implications', (1998–1999) 93 *Nw. U. L. Rev.* 641, Columbia University. Center for Law and Economics Working Paper 144 (November 11, 1998); see also Klaus J. Hopt, 'Common Principles of Corporate Governance in Europe?', in Joseph A. McCahery, Piet Moerland, Theo Raaijmakers and Luc Renneboog, *Corporate Governance Regimes, Convergence and Diversity* (Oxford: Oxford University Press 2002) 175, who concedes that there are path-dependent differences between corporate governance regimes. These differences are deeply embedded in a country's tradition, history and culture. Hopt concludes, however, that market forces can be expected to be stronger in the long run (at 193).

[3] In the abstract to Hansmann and Kraakman, 'The End of History'.

legal development worldwide will be towards a standard model of the corporation.

A view also exists that convergence of corporate laws will occur because cross-border mergers, which have increased in recent years, will bring investors insisting that companies should promote shareholder interests to countries that are stakeholder oriented. This will cause stakeholder oriented jurisdictions to adopt a more shareholder-friendly approach.[4]

Another argument supporting the prediction for convergence is that there is an increase in listings of foreign companies on the New York and London stock exchanges. Listings of this type cause firms to adopt the Anglo-American legal model. To attract investors, firms opt to become subject to higher regulatory and disclosure standards,[5] bringing firms around the globe under the head of the same law and thus achieving convergence of legal rules.

Moreover, even without formal convergence of corporate law, securities law will become global either because of harmonisation or because of migration towards the US and the UK. Securities law will take over the role of protecting shareholders, and there will be a set of securities law rules that apply globally.[6]

All proponents of convergence share the vision that global competition is a strong enough force to trigger change in the laws that govern companies around the globe. In reaching this conclusion, they assume that it is possible for a jurisdiction to amend existing legal norms to any desired degree: there is no mention of limitations to such change. These scholars base their work on the assumption that legal systems are able to choose from an open-ended menu of legal rules.

---

[4] Jeffrey N. Gordon, 'Pathways to Corporate Convergence? Two Steps on the Road to Shareholder Capitalism in Germany: Deutsche Telekom and DaimlerChrysler', (1999) 5 *Colum. J. Eur. L.* 219.

[5] Coffee, Jr., 'The Future as History' 673–679; see also Bernard S. Black, 'The Legal and Institutional Preconditions for Strong Securities Markets', (2001) 48 *UCLA L. Rev.* 781, 816; for a critical view, see Amir N. Licht, 'Cross-Listing and Corporate Governance: Bonding or Avoiding?', (2003) 4 *Chi. J. Int'l L.* 1.

[6] Coffee, Jr., 'The Future as History' 699–704; for a view that securities regulation has proven more susceptible to convergence, see also Amir N. Licht, 'International Diversity in Securities Regulation: Roadblocks on the Way to Convergence', (1998) 20 *Cardozo L. Rev.* 227. It will be shown later in this chapter that listings in the US and the UK can cause change in the jurisdictions from which foreign companies originate. This change is, however, subject to the constraints imposed by the legal doctrine prevailing in the foreign jurisdiction concerned. See chapter 15.

1.2 Path-dependence

The prediction of convergence has been challenged by a number of academic contributors who, as we have been, point to obstacles that stand in the way of a global model for corporate law. Subsections 1.2.1–1.2.5 will analyse these barriers in turn.

1.2.1 Politics

Prominent legal scholars have propounded the view that political forces cause legal systems to develop path-dependently. Mark Roe points out that there are still significant differences between the corporate governance in different jurisdictions, caused by differences in their political orientation. He shows that there is a correlation between a social democratic form of government and certain corporate governance patterns.[7] Roe's view is, in principle, also endorsed by Peter Gourevitch, who refines it by pointing to the fact that it is not so much the form of present government, but the type of government that was in place when corporate governance structures established themselves, that matters. Gourevitch also stresses the fact that a distinction between left- and right-wing politics is too simplistic to account for the relevant political forces, in particular the influence of political interest groups that cut across the left/right political divide on corporate governance patterns.[8]

---

[7] For a comprehensive statement of this theory, see Mark J. Roe, *Political Determinants of Corporate Governance* (Oxford: Oxford University Press, 2003); for a discussion of Roe's central political thesis of corporate governance, see Peter A. Gourevitch, 'The Politics of Corporate Governance Regulation', (2003) 112 *Yale L. J.* 1864; for an international relations perspective, see Jeffrey N. Gordon, 'An International Relations Perspective on the Convergence of Corporate Governance: German Shareholder Capitalism and the European Union, 1990–2000' (February 2003), European Corporate Governance Institute (ECGI), Finance Research Paper Series, http://ssrn.com/abstract=374620.

[8] The same point was made by Otto Kahn-Freund in the mid-1970s (Otto Kahn-Freund, 'On Uses and Misuses of Comparative Law', [1974] *MLR* 1–27). Notwithstanding differences in the terminology used, Kahn-Freund's view is similar to that put forward by Roe and Gourevitch, in that all three think that politics determines if convergence is possible. Otto Kahn-Freund argues that differences in the respective political systems determine whether or not legal rules can be transplanted from one legal system into another. Unlike Roe, Kahn-Freund does not point to a path-dependent form of legal development. He nevertheless stresses the importance of political factors. Kahn-Freund also anticipates the refinement of Roe's theory suggested by Gourevitch, pointing to the division of power between different interest groups as an influential factor which operates as a determinant of whether the transplantation of legal rules will be successful.

Having identified the political orientation of a jurisdiction as a factor that influences corporate governance Roe, in an article written jointly with Lucian Bebchuk, criticises the convergence thesis.[9] Bebchuk and Roe do not say that convergence is impossible; they also do not say that convergence will occur. They point out only that there is one important obstacle that global forces driving towards convergence need to overcome: path-dependence. They distinguish between structure-driven and rule-driven path-dependence.

Structure-driven path-dependence occurs because the present relative distribution of power is a function of the distribution of power that existed at earlier times. To give an example, a jurisdiction in which companies were originally dominated by large shareholders has a tendency to continue to have concentrated ownership structures. There are two reasons for this. The first is that it may be cost-efficient to maintain a division of power; change costs money and, assuming that efficiency is what drives development, change will occur only when its benefit outweighs its cost. The other reason is politics. Incumbent power holders tend to have the ability to influence the political process in their favour. By influencing the political process, large German stakeholders, for example, are able to prevent a change to a structure with dispersed ownership even if such a change were efficient.

The concept of rule-driven path-dependence assumes that law influences ownership structures. If the law succeeds in effectively preventing majority shareholders from taking advantage of their influence, for example, concentrated ownership structures will not arise. Bebchuk and Roe refer to law as 'an additional, indirect (but important) channel through which the initial corporate structure might affect subsequent structures'.[10] Again, change will occur only when lawmakers conclude that the benefits of the change outweigh its cost. Moreover, the political pressure exercised by interest groups who disproportionately benefit from the current legal regime may prevent changes of legal rules, even if these changes were efficient and therefore in the public interest.[11]

It is important to note that in Bebchuk and Roe's analysis, ownership structure comes first and is in itself a function of politics or even 'historical accidents'.[12] Ownership structure then influences the

---

[9] Bebchuk and Roe, 'A Theory of Path Dependence' 127.
[10] Bebchuk and Roe, 'A Theory of Path Dependence' 138, 153–154.
[11] Bebchuk and Roe, 'A Theory of Path Dependence' 154–162.
[12] Bebchuk and Roe, 'A Theory of Path Dependence' 129.

law – which in turn, and alongside other factors – influences future ownership structure. Law is only a secondary force that facilitates the influence of institutions. It shapes institutions, but only as a function of the original institutional setup and also a function of politics. Moreover, there do not seem to be limitations on the degree to which law can be changed.[13] Law appears to be changeable in any desired way. Leaving efficiency, politics and other forces aside, the assumption underlying the Bebchuk–Roe thesis is that the rules of one legal system can be changed to become identical to the rules of another.

1.2.2 Economics

There also exists a view that economic reasons, by themselves, prevent convergence. William Bratton and Joseph McCahery argue that all existing governance models are based on trade-offs. A system such as the German one tolerates influential shareholders obtaining more than their pro rata share of the company's assets, but achieves a high level of shareholder monitoring. The US and the UK governance model prevents asset diversion into the pockets of some shareholders, but at the price of discouraging shareholder monitoring. Built into each of these governance systems is an incentive structure supported by legal rules. This means that the legal rules conductive to blockholding may be ill-equipped to foster dispersed share ownership and liquid markets and the legal rules conductive to liquid markets may have the effect of discouraging blockholding. In a blockholder system, for example, the rules against self-dealing, if they exist at all, are not as sophisticated as they are in a market system. Blockholders monitor management because the cost of doing so is compensated by the private benefits they are able to obtain. If the law intervenes to prevent private rent seeking in a blockholder system, this can prevent blockholders from seeking benefits and may cause the system to transform itself into a market system. There is, however, no guarantee that the removal of the opportunity for rent seeking will in itself create incentives sufficient to facilitate the emergence of a liquid market. The conclusion of the argument put forward by Bratton and McCahery is that the introduction of

---

[13] Bebchuk and Roe, 'A Theory of Path Dependence' 164–165; see also Reinhard H. Schmidt and Gerald Spindler, 'Path Dependence, Corporate Governance, and Complementarity', *International Finance* 5 (3) 311–333; Schmidt and Spindler, 'Path Dependence and Complementarity in Corporate Governance', in Jeffrey N. Gordon and Mark J. Roe, *Convergence and Persistence in Corporate Governance* (Cambridge: Cambridge University Press, 2004) 114.

the legal rules of one system into another (i.e. convergence of legal rules) could perversely destabilise workable (if imperfect) arrangements without assuring the appearance of more effective alternatives.[14]

Bratton and McCahery warn against disturbing the existing balance of influence between players. Legal intervention may backfire, by causing actors who currently monitor management to end their involvement while at the same time not stimulating other actors to take on a monitoring role. They do not suggest that there is anything inherent in the law that would prevent jurisdictions from amending their rules.

1.2.3 Culture

A third possible obstacle to convergence is culture.[15] The argument that culture influences legal systems was notably propounded by Charles Montesquieu.[16] In the context of the recent convergence and path-dependence debate, Amir Licht floats the idea that differences in corporate governance systems may be due to cultural differences.[17] He uses work published in the field of cross-cultural psychology to determine whether there is a correlation between different corporate governance systems and cultural values predominant in the respective jurisdictions.[18] He views law as a function of cultural values, and seems to suggest that, dependent on the degree of importance of such influences, legal rules can be selected indiscriminately 'from a larger menu'.[19]

---

[14] William Bratton and Joseph A. McCahery, 'Comparative Corporate Governance and the Theory of the Firm: The Case against Global Cross Reference', (1999) 38 *Colum. J. Eur. L.* 213; Edward B. Rock, 'America's Shifting Fascination with Comparative Corporate Governance', (1996) 74 *Wash. U. L. Q.* 392; on the efficiency of legal transplants, see also Ugo Mattei, 'Efficiency in Legal Transplants: An Essay in Comparative Law and Economics', (1994) 14 *Int'l Rev. L. & E.* 3.

[15] Amir N. Licht, 'The Mother of All Path Dependencies: Towards a Cross-Cultural Theory of Corporate Governance Systems', (2001) 26 *Del. J. Corp. L.* 147; see also Peter A. Gourevitch, 'The Politics of Corporate Governance Regulation', (2003) 112 *Yale L. J.* 1834, Mark J. Roe, 'Can Culture Constrain the Economic Model of Corporate Law?', (2002) 69 *U. Chi. L. Rev.* 1251 and Martin Krygier, 'Institutional Optimism, Cultural Pessimism, and the Rule of Law', in Martin Krygier and Adam W. Czarnota (eds.), *The Rule of Law after Communism: Problems and Prospects in East-Central Europe* (Aldershot: Ashgate, 1999) 39, on cultural hindrances to the convergence of legal rules.

[16] Charles Montesquieu, *De l'Esprit des Loix* (Amsterdam, 1784).

[17] Amir N. Licht, 'The Mother of All Path Dependencies' 147, 149.

[18] Amir N. Licht, Chanan Goldschmidt and Shalom H. Schwartz, 'Culture, Law, and Corporate Governance', (2005) 25 *Int'l Rev. L. & Econ.* 229; Amir N. Licht, 'Legal Plug-Ins: Cultural Distance, Cross-Listing, and Corporate Governance Reform', (2004) 22 *Berkeley J. Int'l L.* 195.

[19] Amir N. Licht, 'The Mother of All Path Dependencies' 186–187.

1.2.4 Social and commercial norms

Social and commercial norms are also said to cause path-dependent legal development. Gunther Teubner does not use the term 'path-dependence' in his work, but nevertheless propounds a view that supports the path-dependence thesis. He writes that legal rules can be understood only against the background of the society in which they were created. Rules differ according to how deeply rooted they are in the sociological, but also the political, economic, technological and cultural framework of the jurisdiction from which they originate. He gives the example of a rule requiring contractual parties to act in good faith, which originates from German law and is a function of how production is organised in German society. Teubner concludes that the rule will not generate the same results in the UK, where it has been transplanted as a result of the implementation of an EU directive, because British society organises production differently from German society. Teubner distinguishes between 'tight' and 'loose' coupling. Rules that are tightly coupled with a particular society are more difficult to transplant into another legal system than rules that are only loosely coupled with that society. If this rationale is applied to the path-dependence and convergence debate, the conclusion will be that we need to make a distinction. Convergence will be more likely to occur in an area of the law that is loosely coupled with its respective sociological background than it will in relation to rules that are tightly coupled with their sociological background.[20]

The idea that social and commercial norms determine the extent to which convergence occurs can also be found in David Charny's analysis.[21] Charny stresses that social and commercial standards of conduct determine corporate governance alongside legal rules. A given norm can be enforced by either a legal or a non-legal standard. Convergence of norms may be achieved despite the persistence of wide variations of the law on the books. Charny puts forward the idea that the convergence and path-dependence debate should examine more than the evolution of legal rules and take into account social and commercial norms. If social and commercial norms vary between jurisdictions, legal rules

---

[20] Gunther Teubner, 'Legal Irritants: Good Faith in British Law or How Unifying Law Ends Up in New Divergences', [1998] *MLR* 11–32.

[21] David Charny, 'The Politics of Corporate Governance', in Jeffrey N. Gordon and Mark J. Roe, *Convergence and Persistence in Corporate Governance* (Cambridge: Cambridge University Press, 2004) 293.

should continue to differ because of the way they support the operation of non-legal sanctions. Convergence would be achieved if the combined set of legal and non-legal norms converged to a single best-practice standard. Neither Teubner nor Charny point to limitations other than social and commercial norms which would restrict a legislature's ability to reform law.

1.2.5 Legal mentalities

Another obstacle to convergence is said to be the differences in legal mentalities. Pierre Legrand argues that European legal systems are not converging.[22] His main argument is that because there is no common European tradition of legal thinking – or, in his terminology, no common European legal 'mentality' – European legal systems will not converge. The thinking process applied by civil lawyers, on the one hand, and common lawyers, on the other, is so different that even if there existed an identical set of rules in both legal systems these rules would nevertheless be interpreted in different ways, with the result that convergence would not occur.

Legrand writes that different legal communities will interpret identical norms differently. He does not suggest that there exist factors that would prevent a jurisdiction from abandoning a set of rules and replacing them with a entirely different set of rules, but he gives a stern warning that rules imposed on a system which originate from another system will not behave in the same way in the recipient jurisdiction as they did in the donor jurisdiction. He does not say, however, that any of the jurisdictions concerned are subject to limitations in carrying out law reform.

1.3 Functional convergence

There also exists a school of thought mediating between the position that there will be convergence and the position that there exist obstacles that may ultimately prevent it. Ronald Gilson argues that the effect of globalisation is to produce a more varied response than just either convergence, on the one hand, or path-dependence, on the other. Gilson observes that even though corporate law may differ, management is judged against the same performance indicators in all developed corporate systems. Irrespective of whether a jurisdiction

---

[22] Pierre Legrand, 'European Legal Systems are not Converging', (1996) 45 *ICLQ* 52.

is shareholder- or stakeholder-focused, performance standards have become global; Gilson refers to this phenomenon as 'functional convergence'. At the same time, very little convergence of form can be observed. 'Form' in this context constitutes 'strong financial intermediaries' in the German and Japanese system and a strong 'stock market' in the US system.[23] Another example Gilson gives addresses ways in which minority shareholders can be protected. It is, for example, possible to protect them either through a mandatory bid rule under takeover regulations or by a strict rule against self-dealing by management. If both of these approaches provide adequate protection, functional convergence will have occurred despite their quite different institutional features – one protecting minority shareholders by assuring them an exit route from their position, the other protecting them in the continuation of their position.[24] *Functional* convergence occurs when existing governance institutions are flexible enough to respond to the demands of changed circumstances without altering the institutions' formal characteristics. *Formal* convergence occurs when an effective response requires legislative action to alter the basic structure of existing governance institutions.[25] Convergence of function will occur first because convergence of form is more costly; new institutions require new investment, and existing institutions will be supported by related interest groups that render more difficult any necessary political action.[26] Gilson predicts that globalisation will create a mixed bag of formal, functional and hybrid convergence, with the particular outcome being quite sensitive to local conditions.[27]

1.4 Summary of the analysis

The contributors to the debate presented in sections 1.1–1.3 try to ascertain whether the forces of globalisation are stronger than politics, economics, culture, social and commercial norms, or legal mentality.

---

[23] Gilson, 'Globalizing Corporate Governance: Convergence of Form or Function', (2001) 49 *Am. J. Comp. L.* 337–338.

[24] Gilson, 'Globalizing Corporate Governance' 336–337.

[25] Gilson, 'Globalizing Corporate Governance' 356.

[26] Gilson, 'Globalizing Corporate Governance' 338.

[27] Gilson, 'Globalizing Corporate Governance' 332 fn. 14; see also John C. Coffee, Jr., 'Convergence and its Critics: What are the Preconditions to the Separation of Ownership and Control?', (September 2000), Columbia Law and Economics Working Paper 179, http://ssrn.com/abstract=241782.

There is a common theme underlying both the convergence and the path-dependence theories. Both sides of the argument view legal rules as a variable that may be subject to external forces but can otherwise be changed to any desired degree.

The prediction made in the debate is based upon the analysis of different modern company law regimes. No attempt has been made by the participants to determine how different legal systems have historically responded to change. Globalisation is not the first challenge with which legal systems have had to come to terms. The law has adapted to change in the past and the way in which change has occurred previously serves as a basis on which a prediction can be made as to how it will respond to globalisation.

In chapters 2–14, the English, German and Austrian law of securities will be analysed. In all three legal systems, securities law has adapted to significant change, from their inception to the present day.

The first challenge the law had to overcome was the emergence of securities as instruments that were issued to the general public with a view to their circulating among investors. The emergence of these instruments was an international phenomenon. Securities appeared at around roughly the same time in different jurisdictions – including England, Germany and Austria. The instruments served the same principled purposed in all those jurisdictions, and the law supported this purpose. This did not, however, lead to identical rules across jurisdictions; the law adapted domestic legal doctrine to facilitate the needs of both issuers and investors.

When securities first appeared, paper documents were used to carry out transfers. All the jurisdictions analysed in this book experienced the need to eliminate paper at some point in time in their legal development; they all adapted by creating a transfer method that did not require paper to be physically moved. The way in which this reform was carried out was, again, determined by the legal doctrinal rules that were already in place.

In the following chapters, the English, German and Austrian securities law will be analysed in order to provide a comparative account of the legal rules currently in place in the three jurisdictions. The book will also examine the historical legal background from which the current law has evolved, to show that whenever the law adapted to a new challenge, incumbent legal doctrine determined the form in which law reform was carried out. New law is not created from scratch, but by way of revising and modifying existing legal rules.

English law will be examined in part I. German and Austrian law will be analysed in part II. Based on the comparative analysis of the three jurisdictions, some conclusions will be drawn in part III, which will also contain an analysis of the implications of these conclusions for the convergence versus path-dependence debate and also for the possible creation of a harmonised European legal regime.

PART I

English law

In England securities are predominantly issued in the form of registered instruments. Shares and bonds issued by companies are traditionally issued almost exclusively as registered instruments, as are Government bonds or gilts. Money market instruments were issued in the form of bearer securities until 2003 and are now also issued as uncertificated registered securities within CREST.[1]

---

[1] http://www.crestco.co.uk/home/home.html#/bulletins/cmo/cmo_intro.html.

2 Paper transfers

2.1 The historic starting point

English law does not classify securities as tangibles but as *intangibles*: they are choses in action. Historically, choses in action constituted a personal obligation and could therefore not be transferred by the creditor by way of assignment. A transfer was, however, possible with the consent of the debtor.[1] The debtor would agree to terminate the relationship with the transferor and to enter into a new relationship with the transferee. This method of transferring debt has come to be referred to in English law as novation.[2]

Before incorporation became freely available, businesses were set up in the form of deed of settlement companies. The deeds setting up the company usually contained a rule enabling shareholders to transfer their interest by deed. Shares in companies that had a clause to that effect were considered transferable even though choses in action had not yet become generally transferable.[3] It is possible that the rules on transfers of shares and of other securities, which originate from that time, were shaped around the idea that a transfer involves the termination of one obligation and the creation of a new one.[4]

Moreover, the rules on share transfers developed at a time when companies such as the deed of settlement company of the late eighteenth

---

[1] Guenter Treitel, *The Law of Contract*, 11th edn. (London: Sweet & Maxwell, 2003) 672–673.
[2] Treitel, *The Law of Contract* 672–673.
[3] W. S. Holdsworth, *A History of English Law, Volume VIII* (London: Methuen, 1925) 202–203; Robert Pennington, *Company Law*, 8th edn. (London: Butterworths, 2001) 398.
[4] See also Pennington, *Company Law*, 8th edn. (London: Butterworths, 2001) 398–399; Joanna Benjamin, *Interests in Securities* (Oxford: Oxford University Press, 2001) 3.05.

and early nineteenth century[5] resembled modern partnerships more than they resembled modern companies.[6] The default position in partnership law is that a new partner may be introduced only with the consent of all existing partners.[7]

Although there is little authority on the point, this analysis is supported by language used in older case law. Northington LC spoke of a transfer of shares in a joint stock company in the following terms: 'The title is the admission into the company as a partner pro tanto.'[8] Similar language can be found in *Simm*'s case, that concerned a transfer of shares in a company incorporated under the Companies Act 1862. Bramwell LJ referred to the company's processing the transfer documents and said: '[T]hey [the company] admitted him [the transferee] as a partner.'[9] When incorporation had become generally possible in 1744, the new law nevertheless preserved the rule that shares were transferable only when the companies' articles contained a provision enabling shareholders to transfer shares.[10]

Robert Pennington rightly points out that limited liability was, at the time, not yet available to companies[11] (Limited liability was introduced in 1756).[12] Limited liability absent, a change of shareholder can result in a change in the funds available to the company and its creditors, which may have potential effects on the company's ability to continue to do business. In those circumstances, it can be assumed that shareholders would want to reserve a right with the company to approve of transfers and would agree to a transfer only if the new shareholder was of, at least, equal financial standing as her predecessor. It seems logical, therefore, that the Companies Act would adopt as a default rule that shares are not freely transferable and leave it to the shareholders to decide if they preferred, nevertheless, to issue freely transferable shares.

Since the starting point of the analysis was that the issuer would upon every share transfer decide if the proposed transferee was a suitable person to have as a member, it became practice for every share transfer to be presented to, and processed by, the company. The practice that

---

[5] P. L. Davies, *Principles of Modern Company Law*, 6th edn. (London: Sweet & Maxwell, 1997) 29–31; on a transfer of shares in such a company see, for example, *Duncan* v. *Luntley* (1849) 2 Ha & Tw 78, 47 ER 1604.
[6] For an overview, see Davies, *Principles of Modern Company Law* 18–48.
[7] Partnership Act 1890, s. 24 (6).
[8] *Ashby* v. *Blackwell* (1765) 2 Eden 299 at 302–303; 28 ER 913 at 914.
[9] *Simm* v. *Anglo-American Telegraph Company* (1879) 5 QBD 188 at 204.
[10] Pennington, *Company Law* 398.   [11] Pennington, *Company Law* 399.   [12] C 47 (Vic).

developed was that the company would issue certificates to every share-holder. The shares, however, were not transferred by the delivery of the certificates; certificates were not considered to be negotiable instruments but rather documents evidencing the shareholder's entitlement.[13] To effect a transfer, the seller had to provide the buyer with a transfer form and had to hand it over together with the certificates to the buyer.[14] This is reflected, for example, Companies Act 1948 (CA 1975, s. 75), which stated that the registration of a transfer required 'a proper instrument of transfer'.[15]

What amounted to a proper instrument of transfer would be regulated in the articles of association. In practice, the instrument of transfer was a paper document which stated the number of shares passing to the transferee as well as the consideration, and was signed before a witness by the transferor and the transferee. This method continued to apply until the early 1960s, when it was perceived as being too cumbersome 'in modern share dealing'.[16] To make share dealings more straightforward, the Stock Transfer Act 1963 was enacted.[17] All it did, however, was to simplify the requirements relating to the transfer form. The new formal requirements will be discussed below.[18] Having received both the transfer form and the share certificate from the seller, the buyer would lodge both documents with the company to have his name entered on the shareholders' register.[19]

The current default rule is that shares are transferable without the issuer's consent. Companies can refuse to register a transfer only if they can point to a provision in their articles empowering them to do so.[20] Companies can adopt articles making share transfers subject to, for example, the approval of the board of directors or the shareholders' meeting. The model articles annexed to the Companies Act 1985 contain a provision (Table A, reg. 24) which empowers directors to refuse to

---

[13] *Colonial Bank* v. *Hepworth* (1887) 36 ChD 36; *Williams* v. *The Colonial Bank* (1888) 38 ChD 388 (CA); *The Colonial Bank* v. *Cady (Inspector of Taxes)* (1890) 15 App Cas 267; *Shropshire Union Railways and Canal Co* v. *R.* (1875) LR 7 HL 496.

[14] *Skinner* v. *The City of London Marine Insurance Corporation* (1885) 14 QBD 882 at 887 (CA) per Brett MR; *London Founders Association Limited* v. *Clarke* (1888) 20 QBD 576 (CA) at 582 per Esher MR; *Stray* v. *Russell* (1859) 1 El&El 888, 120 ER 1144; *Stevenson* v. *Wilson* 1907 SC 445 at 455 (CS).

[15] CA 1948 s. 74 corresponds to CA 1985, s. 183.

[16] Hansard, HC (series 5) vol. 679, col. 848 (21 June 1963).   [17] 1963, s. 18.   [18] Pp. 24–25.

[19] *Hichens, Harrison Woolston & Co* v. *Jackson & Sons* [1943] AC 266.

[20] *Re Smith, Knight, Co* (1868) LR 4 Ch App 20.

register a transfer if the shares concerned are not fully paid or are shares on which the company has a lien.

In practice, however, transfer restrictions occur only with private companies or unlisted public companies. The Stock Exchange Listing Rules require listed shares to be freely transferable.[21] Exceptional circumstances aside, listed companies do not normally have articles containing restrictions on share transfers.

Although much of the early roots of securities transfers is a matter of speculation, it is possible that the unavailability of a general law of assignment at the time when securities became a popular instrument for arranging finance for large-scale projects caused English law to revert to novation to achieve transferability. The fact that novation was very likely the only method by which securities could be made transferable when securities first became widely used sent English law on a path along which it has continued to develop ever since.

When shares became freely transferable, it would have been possible for companies to discontinue their involvement in the administration of share transfers. They could have done so, for example, by issuing bearer shares which are transferred by way of delivery of the document and do not require the company to keep and administer a register of shareholders. Nevertheless companies continued to issue registered shares and securities; transfers continued to be effected through a register kept by, or on behalf of, the issuing company. Another way of simplifying the transfer process would have been to abolish transfer forms as a separate formal requirement. It would have been possible to have registered securities transferred through endorsement on the back of the certificate.

None of this happened. The law continues to have a transfer procedure that reflects its historic origin. Ignoring dematerialisation for the moment, the standard procedure is that every investor has her name entered on the issuer's register and receives a certificate issued in her name evidencing her entire holding of that type of security.

Unlike, for example, German or Austrian companies, English issuers still do not issue certificates for each individual share. Every investor receives one certificate for all securities of each class held by her and, upon transferring a part of her holding of securities of any class, a

---

[21] Rule 3.15. Stock Exchange Listing Rules as of June 2006, http://www.fsa.gov.uk/pubs/ ukla/chapt03-3.pdf (last visited 4 July 2006).

certificate for the balance of her holding.[22] Every certificate specifies the number and class of the securities to which it relates.

Certificates continue to be documents of evidence only. They do not constitute negotiable instruments. This is reflected in CA 1985, s. 186, which states that a share certificate specifying any shares held by a member is prima facie evidence of her title to the shares.

Transfers also still require the seller to sign a transfer form which, since the Stock Transfer Act 1963 was enacted, has to comply with the model form set out in Schedule 1 to the Act. It is executed by the transferor only and specifies the particulars of the consideration, of the securities and of the person by whom the transfer is made, and the full name and address of the transferee.[23] The execution of the transfer form does not need to be attested.[24] A transfer form is valid even though it has additional features – required, for example, by the company's articles – as long as it satisfies the requirements set out in the Stock Transfer Act.[25]

The transfer form still needs to be delivered, together with the certificate, to the buyer, who usually lodges the documents with the company. It is also possible for the transferor to lodge the respective documents and apply to the company to have the register amended. CA 1985, s. 183 (4) explicitly states that on the application of the transferor of any shares, the company shall enter in its register the name of the transferee in the same manner and subject to the same conditions as if the application had been made by the transferee.

It can be seen that, notwithstanding the fact that securities have become freely transferable, a transfer still requires the issuer's involvement. The issuer is not normally required to approve the transfer, but it needs to receive transfer forms and certificates, satisfy itself as to the authenticity of the documents, enter the name of the transferee on the register and issue new certificates to the transferee.

The legal environment that existed when securities first became widespread shaped the formalities of the transfer process, and these formalities continued to develop in a path-dependent manner. Neither the fact that other instruments of transfer existed, nor that securities and also other choses in action became generally transferable, caused practice to change the transfer procedure that was already in place.

---

[22] Table A, reg. 6.   [23] Stock Transfer Act 1963, s. 1 (1).
[24] Stock Transfer Act 1963, s. 1 (2).   [25] Stock Transfer Act 1963, s. 1 (3).

2.2 Law and equity

Like the rules governing transfer procedure, the rules regulating the transfer of proprietary interests in securities have been shaped by the path adopted by English private law. English private law is predominantly case-based law. Unlike the rules on the sale of goods, which are codified in the Sale of Goods Act 1979, the law relating to the sale of other assets has not been subject to codification.

Moreover, the structure of the English courts and their procedural rules have crucially determined the content of modern substantive property law. English property law exists in its current form only because England at one time operated two different and independent branches of the judiciary that had jurisdiction over the rules governing the transfer of property. These branches were the courts at common law and the court in equity. Both courts gave decisions in cases involving transactions in securities and other property, and each court created its own independent body of law. The English method of organising the administration of justice around a set of two independent courts resulted in what can be termed a 'dualistic model' of property law. English law does not have one, but two concepts of ownership. It distinguishes between ownership at law and ownership in equity. The rules on ownership at law were developed by the common law courts, the rules on ownership in equity were developed by the equity court.

From the point of view of a common lawyer, there would be no need to explain the difference between the courts at law and in equity and their jurisprudence in a book on securities. This book, however, addresses an audience concerned with comparative law. It is also written for the benefit of readers who have their background in a legal system that does not work around a distinction between law and equity. It is therefore useful to explain, in a few paragraphs, the relationship between the law and equity courts and the case law developed by them. In doing so, no attempt will be made to contribute to the English discussion on the nature of equity.

Historically, the courts at common law operated long before the court in equity came into existence. The jurisdiction of the equity court began at a point in time when the common law had become too rigid. It would, theoretically, have been possible for the law courts to change the rules created by them to do justice in cases where the law was considered to be too harsh. This, however, did not happen. What happened instead was that parties who felt that the law courts were unable to assist their rightful complaint petitioned to the Chancellor for relief; the Chancellor would give special remedies to prevent or stop unconscionable conduct. Over time, the office of the Chancellor administering petitions on his behalf became transformed into a special court, the court of equity.

For some time the courts of law and the court in equity operated independently. The courts at law continued to develop the body of case law already established by them, which came to be referred to as 'law'.

The equity court developed rules providing exceptions to or supplementing this pre-existing 'law'. As time moved on, the equity court developed its own body of case law by relying on its own precedent and by distinguishing previous authority on the basis of fact. This body of case law became to be referred to as 'equity'.

One advantage available to the equity court was that it was subject to less rigid procedural rules and was, for example, able to grant injunctive relief or specific performance of contracts. The law courts did not have procedural rules that would enable them to grant injunctions and they could give monetary awards only in the form of damages for breach of contract.

The courts of law and equity were fused in 1873 and 1875 and both branches of English law are now administered by the same courts. Nevertheless, the distinction between law and equity has survived in legal terminology. The case law that goes back to cases decided by the courts of law is still commonly termed 'law'. The case law that goes back to cases decided by the court of equity is still referred to as 'equity'.

Civil lawyers are used to distinguishing legal rules exclusively according to their content. Property law, for example, is the branch of private law determining ownership and other rights in rem. Company law is the branch of law governing the formation and organisation of certain legal entities. The distinction between law and equity does not operate under such subject headings: whether a rule belongs to law or equity is solely determined by whether it evolved out of case law created by the law courts or by the court of equity, respectively.

The distinction between law and equity cuts across a number of private law fields. In terms of scope, equity could be characterised as an eclectic collection of exceptions to legal rules. Equity also exclusively governs whole areas of the law that have not been developed by law, for example trust law. The English trust is a legal institution that was invented by the court of equity.

A civil lawyer would be forgiven for asking why, given that the separate jurisdictions merged 130 years ago and equity consists only of exceptions to other legal rules, the distinction between law and equity continues to exist. Would it not be more logical to think of English private law as being organised by content rather than according to the historic origin of the rules? This would be consistent with having special subject headings for areas of law, such as trust law, that have their historic starting point entirely in the court of equity.

There is, of course, some benefit in analysing current legal rules in terms of their historic origins, but whether or not this justifies a principled separation between law and equity is open to discussion. The significance of the distinction between law and equity, and the nature of equity itself, are issues that are hotly debated in the common law world.

One school of thought argues that law and equity are different in nature. On that view, rules that go back to case law decided by the equity court need to be interpreted with a view to enforcing conscionability.[26] Another school of thought argues that the rules in equity do not justify a different approach and should be developed through the same methods as law.[27]

This book is not the place to contribute to the debate on this issue. It suffices to note here that the distinction between law and equity is based on the historic origin of rules and that that historic origin continues to be of significance in modern English law. The path adopted by English law – and, in particular, the method chosen by English law to administer justice – caused property law to develop rules on ownership at law and rules on ownership in equity. English securities law developed path-consistently within this framework. The result of this is that English law does not approach securities transfers in terms of defining the circumstances in which a transferee acquires ownership in the securities. It rather contains rules according to which, at law, the transferee acquires what is called 'legal ownership'. In addition, equity gives the transferee in certain circumstances an interest in the securities sold. This interest is termed 'equitable' or 'beneficial' ownership.

---

[26] R. P. Meagher, J. D. Heydon and M. J. Leeming (eds.), *Meagher, Gummow, and Lehane's, Equity: Doctrines and Remedies*, 4th edn. (Sydney: Butterworths Lexis Nexis, 2003) [3.005–3.260] 85–121.

[27] Birks, P. 'Equity in the Modern Law: An Exercise in Taxonomy' (1996) 25 *U Western Australia L. Rev.* 1; A. Burrows, 'We Do This at Common Law But That in Equity' (2002) 22 *OJLS* 1.

The interest does not arise in all cases; if it arises, it is vested in the buyer before she becomes the legal owner.

In section 2.3 the instances in which ownership at law vests in the transferee will now be analysed. In section 2.4, the rules governing the acquisition of equitable or beneficial ownership by the transferee will be discussed. Both sections will show that the English rules on ownership rights in securities are a function of the path historically adopted by English property law.

2.3 Legal title and registration

In England, the securities register is the focus point for the acquisition of legal title to securities. The position in modern English law is that legal title is vested in the buyer when her name is registered on the shareholder register. Nourse LJ, for example, held in *J. Sainsbury plc* v. *O'Connor (Inspector of Taxes)* that there 'is no difficulty in ascertaining the legal ownership of shares, which is invariably vested in the registered holder'.[28] Another case is *Re Rose*, where Jenkins LJ wrote:[29] 'In my view, a transfer under seal in the form appropriate under the company's regulations, coupled with delivery of the transfer and certificate to the transferee, does suffice, as between transferor and transferee, to constitute the transferee the equitable owner of the shares ... [But,] the transferee must do a further act in the form of applying for and obtaining registration in order to get in and perfect his legal title.'

These cases are consistent with CA 1985, s. 22, according to which a person who agrees to become a member of a company and whose name is entered in its register of members is a member of the company.

The view that registration is needed to perfect the legal title of the transferee to the securities is not uncontested. Robert Pennington writes that it seems historically more likely that title to shares passed at common law prior to registration when the transferor delivered the executed instrument of transfer to the transferee.[30] In Pennington's view, the requirement for registration was embodied as a condition in the deeds of settlement simply as a measure for the issuer's own

---

[28] [1991] 1 WLR 963 at 977 (CA).

[29] *Re Rose, Rose* v. *Inland Revenue Commissioners* [1952] Ch 499, at 518–519 (CA); *Sahota* v. *Bains* [2006] EWHC 131 (Ch).

[30] Pennington, *Company Law* 416–417; see also Brenda Hannigan [186.53] in Justice Arden and D. Prentice (eds.), *Buckley on the Companies Acts*, 15th edn. (London: Butterworths, 2006).

protection. Pennington propounds the view that the registration requirement has only contractual effect and has no bearing on the question when legal title to the shares vests in the transferee.[31]

Pennington's remarks are expressed in terms of a historical observation which, presumably, goes back to the times when securities, like other choses in action, were not transferable at law. It has already been mentioned that securities and the rules governing their transfers developed at a time when the assignment of choses in action was generally prohibited; choses in action were transferable only by novation. Novation requires the consent of the issuer; the issuer, however, could waive the right to object to transfers by adapting articles to that effect. Pennington's analysis receives support from the fact that if the issuer waived the right to approve every transfer, it seems logical that title to the securities would pass as between buyer and seller irrespective of the issuer's involvement.

On the other hand, it is possible that the historical novation-based analysis also shaped the rules governing perfection of title to the securities between buyer and seller. If it is true that the starting point of the rules governing securities transfers was that a transfer could be effected only with the explicit consent of the issuer, it follows that the consent was also necessary to perfect title to the securities as between buyer and seller. If the law is based on the notion that the issuer needs to approve of a transfer for it to be possible, some involvement of the issuer would, conceivably, continue to be necessary even if transfers become possible by means of special clauses inserted in the issuing documentation, or by way of a general exception in the law. As the rule on the availability of transfers relaxes, the requirement for the issuer to participate in the transfer process relaxes accordingly. The issuer no longer has to approve of every transfer individually, but the requirement for registration in order for legal title to pass to the buyer continues to exist.

In any event, in light of CA 1985, s. 22 and in light of the dictum in J. Sainsbury, the more prudent view is to conclude that a buyer becomes the legal owner upon registration of her name in the securities register.[32]

Moreover, whichever view one prefers to adopt in relation to perfection of title to the securities as between buyer and seller, registration provides the transferee with a stronger position than she has prior to registration. Upon registration, the buyer becomes the issuer's

---

[31] Pennington, *Company Law* 417.   [32] [1991] 1 WLR 963 at 977 (CA).

shareholder or debtor. In the case of shares, the legal owner receives dividends and scrip, enjoys the right to vote at general meetings and is liable to pay for contributions. In other words, she is recognised as a shareholder of the company by the company itself. In the case of debt securities, the legal owner becomes entitled to receive payment of interest and capital.

Another implication of registration is that a transferee whose name has been registered has a better title then a transferee who bought her shares before the registered transferee had bought hers. This is true even if the second transferee to register was provided with a forged certificate, but obtained registration before the first transferee. It is irrelevant that the first transferee received a certificate with a blank transfer before the second transferee had bought her shares.[33] If the second transferee is registered before the first transferee, she becomes the legal owner of the shares.[34]

Registration causes the buyer's entitlement to be enforceable against the issuer and gives her priority over any other transferee who may have concluded a sales contract with the transferor earlier than the transferee. The orthodox view is that legal title as between buyer and seller vests in the buyer when her name is registered on the securities' register.

The title of the buyer is, of course, subject to one important qualification. The transferee will become the legal owner of registered securities only if the transferor of the shares either had legal title herself or if she was authorised by the legal owner to transfer the securities. When the transferor of the securities is not the legal owner, the transferee will not acquire legal title to the securities even if her name has been entered on the register. An entry in the register does not provide the transferee with a title which is good against the securities' legal owner. If securities are transferred without authority of the securities' legal owner, she can enforce her claim and have the register rectified.[35]

It is possible that the fact that registration gives the transferee significant certainty as to her entitlement in English law is a function of English securities law having originated in the law of novation. This

---

[33] *Colonial Bank v. Hepworth* (1887) 36 ChD 36; *Guy v. Waterlow Brothers and Layton (Limited)* (1909) 25 TLR 515.

[34] *Colonial Bank v. Hepworth* (1887) 36 ChD 36 at 43 and 54 per Chitty J.

[35] *Re Bahia and San Francisco Rly Co.* (1868) LR 3 QB 584.

caused English law to develop a regime where transfers of securities required the registration of the transferee's name by the issuer and where registration provided the transferee with more certainty as to her entitlement than the delivery of the transfer documents. The legal environment prevailing when securities first emerged sent English law on a path which has had an impact on all later legal developments.

2.4 Equitable title

In the previous sections the rules governing the acquisition of legal title were analysed. The conclusion was that, provided that the seller was authorised to sell securities, legal title was transferred to the buyer upon registration of her name on the securities register. In this section, the rules governing the acquisition of equitable title to securities will be considered.

2.4.1 Equity and transfers of registered securities

From the point of view of this book, it is important to note that the rules on securities transfers are firmly embedded in the general English private law framework. England approaches securities transfers within the context of the historically determined dualistic jurisprudence of the law and equity courts. The rules on transfers of securities fit squarely into this two-headed model and evolved from the division between law and equity.

When securities first became widely used it must have stimulated legal questions that had not been considered before. The English legal system did not solve these new questions by creating a completely new set of rules, but rather took advantage of the network of rules already in place: it adapted existing legal techniques to solve new legal problems and caused English securities law to stay within the path previously adopted by English private law.

The technique used by English law in order to confer an equitable or beneficial interest on the transferee is trust law. Trust law is, as has already been noted, a body of law created by the court of equity. Trusts are created by express declaration or by law. If a trust arises in the context of a securities transfer, the transferor becomes a trustee. In that capacity, the transferor holds the securities on trust for the benefit of the transferee. The transferee is referred to as the 'beneficiary' of the trust: as a beneficiary, a transferee holds equitable or beneficial title.

This point can be further illustrated by reference to a dictum by Lord Diplock in *Ayerst* v. *C&K (Construction) Ltd*[36]: 'The "legal ownership" of the trust property is in the trustee, but he holds it not for his own benefit but for the benefit of . . . beneficiaries. Upon the creation of a trust in the strict sense as it was developed by equity, the full ownership in the trust property was split into two constituent elements, which became vested in different persons: the "legal ownership" in the trustee, what came to be called the "beneficial ownership" in the cestui que trust.'[37]

If the requirements discussed below are met,[38] a trust arises. The seller becomes a trustee for the benefit of the buyer; this causes the buyer to acquire equitable title to the securities. The seller still remains the legal owner of the securities until the buyer's name is registered on the issuer's register. Because the seller still has legal title to the securities, she can transfer them at law; this means that it is possible for the seller to transfer the securities to a second buyer. If the name of the second buyer is registered, the second buyer will acquire legal title to the securities.

The transfer of legal title to the second buyer, however, does not affect the rights of the first buyer. The general rule is that the first buyer's equitable rights are as enforceable against the second buyer as they were against the seller. This is also achieved through the means of trust law: the second buyer is classified as a 'constructive trustee' holding the securities on trust for the first buyer in the same way as the seller was also classified as a trustee. There is only one exception to this: the second buyer is not considered to be a constructive trustee if she bought the securities in good faith and for value.

The detail of this analysis is crucial from the point of view of this book. English law approaches the parties' proprietary rights in a somewhat cumbersome way which can be explained only by the eccentricities of the operation of the dual jurisdiction at law and in equity, respectively. One might be forgiven for asking why the rules do not simply state that, notwithstanding registration, title to the securities does not pass to a second buyer in certain circumstances unless she is a good faith buyer for value.

The answer is path-dependence. The original starting point was that a buyer whose name was registered had title to the securities. This was

---

[36] [1976] AC 167 at 177.   [37] 'Cestui que trust' is a synonym for 'beneficiary'.
[38] See subsections 2.4.4, 2.4.5, 2.4.6 and 2.4.7.

considered to be harsh in certain circumstances, which will be analysed below.[39] Instead of changing the rules at law, England dealt with the problem in a path-consistent fashion. The court of equity intervened. Equity cannot change law; it can only supplement it. The equity court, therefore, could not take legal title away from the second buyer, but it could subject her to a set of rights that were created in favour of the first buyer. Equity could force the second buyer to respect the first buyer's equitable title. This is how securities transfers became to be analysed through the lens of trust law.

The rule that the second buyer is bound by the equitable rights of the first buyer developed over centuries and the instances in which the second buyer was considered to be bound by the first buyer's equitable title were continuously expanded. In other words, the legal position of the equitable owner became stronger over time.

R. J. Smith writes,[40] that the court of equity, at first, considered only that conscience dictated that the buyer (in our example, the second buyer) should be bound by the trust if she was aware of the trust (actual notice), or would have been aware of it if proper investigations had been made (constructive notice). At the beginning of the twentieth century, the circumstances in which the second buyer would be bound were extended. It was held that every transferee will be bound, unless she is a buyer without notice.[41] The original basis of the enforcement, that of unconscionable conduct by the second buyer, has long since given way to the rule that everybody except the buyer of the legal estate without notice is bound.[42]

The current position is that a buyer who has become the equitable owner of securities is not recognised by the company as a shareholder but has priority over any other buyer except for the bona fide buyer for value. This means that when the second buyer's name is registered, the second buyer and any subsequent transferee needs to hand over any benefits she receives to the first buyer who is the equitable owner.[43] The first buyer's claim will not be successful if the second buyer has

---

[39] See subsections 2.4.4, 2.4.5, 2.4.6 and 2.4.7.

[40] Smith, *Property Law*, 5th edn. (London: Longman, 2006) 24; see also A. P. Bell, *Modern Law of Personal Property in England and Ireland* (London: Butterworths, 1989) 154.

[41] Smith, *Property Law*, 5th edn. (London: Longman, 2006) 24 referring to *Re Nisbet and Pott's Contract* [1906] 1 Ch 386 (CA).

[42] Smith, *Property Law* at 24.

[43] For a detailed analysis of the claims available to the owner in equity, see Richard Nolan, 'Equitable Property', 122 (2006) *LQR* 232–265.

acquired her title to the shares without notice of the buyer's claim and for value. In a case of this sort, the buyer may either sue the seller in contract for damages or trace her proprietary interest into the proceeds of the second sale and assert a claim over them.[44]

Another important consequence of the acquisition of equitable title is that the buyer can enforce her claim against the seller's or the second buyer's unsecured creditors.[45] This is particularly valuable in the seller's insolvency. The equitable owner's title may also be enforced in scenarios that do not involve the seller being insolvent. One example is that an equitable owner's title will prevail against a creditor of the seller who has obtained a charging order on the securities after the equitable owner's title arose.[46] Another legal consequence of the transfer of equitable ownership is a change in the attribution of tax benefits.[47]

Before we examine the circumstances in which equitable title is vested in the buyer, we need to examine the legal nature of equitable title. It is important to determine, from the point of view of this book, whether equitable rights can be classified as proprietary.

2.4.2 Legal nature of an equitable (beneficial) interest

In England, there is debate on whether or not equitable title is a right in rem. F. W. Maitland said that equitable ownership is not a right in rem, but a right in personam because it is not enforceable against the bona fide buyer for value.[48] Maitland's view has never been uncontroversial; it has been criticised in recent academic literature and has not found favour in the courts.[49]

The majority of the House of Lords in *Baker* v. *Archer-Shee*,[50] for example, did not adhere to the view that equitable rights are rights in personam. It held that the beneficiary was the 'sole beneficial owner of the interest and dividends of all the securities, stocks and shares forming part of the trust fund'.[51] This argument was confirmed by

---

[44] *Lake* v. *Bayliss* [1974] 1 WLR 1073.

[45] A. J. Oakley, *Parker and Mellows: The Modern Law of Trusts*, 8th edn. (London: Sweet & Maxwell, 2003) 315–316.

[46] *Hawks* v. *McArthur* [1951] 1 All ER 22.

[47] *J. Sainsbury plc* v. *O'Connor (Inspector of Taxes)* [1991] 1 WLR 963 (CA).

[48] F. W. Maitland, *Equity – A Course of Lectures*, rev. edn. J. Brunyate (Cambridge: Cambridge University Press, 1936) 106–116.

[49] For example, Smith, *Property Law* 24; P. H. Pettit, *Equity and the Law of Trusts*, 10th edn. (Oxford: Oxford University Press, 2006) 81–84.

[50] [1927] AC 844.   [51] At 870 per Lord Carson.

their Lordships four years later in *Archer-Shee* v. *Garland* and in *Tinsley* v. *Milligan*.[52]

Contrary to what these cases might suggest, the controversy as to the nature of equitable rights in property is not yet settled. Some modern writers doubt whether equitable rights can be classified as purely proprietary. These writers agree with Maitland in that they find it difficult to describe a right as proprietary where it cannot be enforced against the bona fide buyer for value. Unlike Maitland, however, these writers do not classify equitable rights as personal because they can be enforced against everybody else except the bona fide buyer for value and are therefore not merely rights between contractual partners. They describe equitable rights as 'hybrid' or sui generis.[53] Some writers refrain from labelling equitable rights altogether.[54] Pettit, for example, writes that:[55] 'It may seem strange, though it is perhaps not untypical of English law, that although the trust is so highly developed an institution, it is impossible to say with assurance what is the juristic nature of the interest of a cestui que trust.'

Observing this discussion from the outsider's perspective, it is striking that the concept of a property right receives comparatively narrow construction. An important focus of the English debate is the question of whether a right that is subject to a bona fide acquisition rule can rightfully be classified as proprietary. The difficulty is that equitable title is not good against the world at large because it is inferior to the claim of a good faith buyer for value.

This book attempts to take a comparative approach to the law of transfers of securities. When analysing equitable title through the eyes of a comparative lawyer, we need to observe that the concept of property rights has received a broader construction in jurisdictions other than England. German and Austrian law, for example, classify ownership as a right in rem despite the fact that their codes contain rules whose result is that these rights are not enforceable against a bona fide buyer for value in a large class of circumstances.[56]

---

[52] *Archer-Shee* v. *Garland* [1931] AC 212 per Lord Tomlin at 222; *Tinsley* v. *Milligan* [1994] 1 AC 340 per Lord Browne-Wilkinson at 371.

[53] See reference in Pettit, *Equity and the Law of Trusts*, 8th edn. (Oxford: Oxford University Press, 1997) 81–84.

[54] See, for example, Nolan, 'Equitable Property' 232–265.

[55] *Equity and the Law of Trusts* 81.

[56] SS. 135, 136, 883, German Civil Code (BGB); s. 365, Austrian Civil Code (ABGB); see also Arts. 9, 900, 931, 937, Swiss Civil Code; J. H. Beekhuis, 'Civil Law', in F. H. Lawson (ed.), *International Encyclopedia of Comparative Law, Volume VI: Property and Trust* (Amsterdam: Martinus Nijhoff, 1972) 8.

There are good reasons to continue debating the legal nature of equitable title in a jurisdiction like England where legal title cannot be acquired in good faith. Because in English law the legal owner's position is stronger than the position of an owner in German or Austrian law, English doctrine needs to be careful about placing legal title, for which there is no good faith rule, and equitable title, for which there is a good faith rule, into the same pigeonhole. When comparing English with German and Austrian law, however, we should not fall into the trap of replicating the English debate on the differences in the nature of legal and equitable title. It is possible to classify the entitlement of a buyer arising out of the constructive trust in the context of a sales transaction as proprietary in the same way as the entitlement of an owner under German or Austrian law.

The buyer's right as a beneficial owner can be considered as proprietary in the context of a comparative legal analysis because the rights of a beneficial owner are good against the seller's general creditors unless they have acquired an overriding interest in good faith and for value. The equitable owner's claim has priority over the seller's judgement creditor and in the seller's insolvency.

2.4.3 Acquisition of an equitable (beneficial) interest

The conclusion of subsection 2.4.2 was that equitable ownership is a proprietary right. In this subsection we shall analyse the circumstances in which equitable ownership arises when securities are sold.

To conduct this enquiry, we need to proceed in a path-consistent manner; the question we need to ask is indirect. We do not start our enquiry by asking about the point in time at which equitable title to the securities passes to the buyer. We have rather to examine the rules governing the creation of a trust to identify the point in time when the seller becomes a trustee and the buyer becomes the beneficiary. At this point, the buyer will be considered to have equitable title in the securities.

A trust arises either as a result of an express declaration or by operation of law. Trusts that are created by a declaration to that effect are referred to as 'express trusts'. Trusts that arise by operation of law are called 'constructive trusts'. Both types of trusts are used in English law to regulate property rights in the context of sales of registered securities. This subsection will begin by analysing constructive trusts, before addressing the use of express trusts in relation to transactions involving registered securities.

The circumstances in which a constructive trust arises in the context of sales transactions are not entirely settled. Commentators agree that a constructive trust arises when a sales contract is enforceable by an order for specific performance. There is disagreement, however, on the question whether a constructive trust will also arise in other circumstances. In addition to the law that developed in relation to sales transactions, we need to take note of a third rule relating to gifts of registered securities. In the context of gifts, a constructive trust arises for the benefit of the donee when the donor has done everything in her power to divest herself of her interest in the securities.[57] This is said to be the case when the donor has executed and delivered the transfer forms and the securities certificates to the buyer.

Subsection 2.4.4 discusses the circumstances in which specific performance is granted. This rule is analysed first because it is the least controversial: there is agreement that a constructive trust arises in those circumstances. What follows in subsection 2.4.5 is a discussion of the question as to whether there are instances in which a constructive trust arises when a contract is entered into that cannot be enforced by an order for specific performance. In subsection 2.4.6 the rule giving rise to a constructive trust upon delivery of the transfer documents will be addressed.

2.4.4 *Equitable title and specific performance*

In this subsection it will be shown that property rights are regulated in English law in an indirect fashion accommodating the dualistic character of English private law. Under the rule discussed here, equitable ownership will arise when a contract becomes specifically enforceable. Lloyd LC wrote in *J. Sainsbury plc* v. *O'Connor (Inspector of Taxes)*, that '[b]y equitable owner is meant, inter alia, the purchaser under a specifically enforceable contract'.[58]

If a contract is specifically enforceable and if, as a result, a constructive trust arises, the seller becomes the trustee and the buyer becomes the beneficiary of that trust.[59] The trust is created by the application of the maxim that equity treats that as done which ought to be done. In

---

[57] A. J. Oakley, *Parker and Mellows: The Modern Law of Trusts*, 8th edn. (London: Sweet & Maxwell, 2003) 440–441.

[58] [1991] 1 WLR 963 (CA) at 972 (CA).

[59] Gareth Jones and William Goodhart, *Specific Performance*, 2nd edn. (London: Butterworth, 1996) 17.

other words, equity, through the lens of trust law, treats the buyer as if she has already acquired the interest contracted to be purchased. The contract is treated as giving the buyer an equitable interest in the property.[60]

To illustrate this point further, and in particular to highlight the embeddedness of the analysis in trust law, it is helpful to refer to a dictum by Lord Jenkins in *Oughtred* v. *Inland Revenue Commissioners*. He said there: 'The constructive trust in favour of a purchaser which arises on the conclusion of a contract for sale is founded upon the purchaser's right to enforce the contract in proceedings for specific performance. In other words, he is treated in equity as entitled by virtue of the contract to the property which the vendor is bound under the contract to convey to him. This interest under the contract is no doubt a proprietary interest of a sort, which arises, so to speak, in anticipation of the execution of the transfer for which the purchaser is entitled to call.'[61]

If the buyer can show that a contract is subject to specific performance, she will be considered the equitable owner from the moment the contract is concluded. In order to determine in which case the buyer of securities acquires equitable title as early as on conclusion of the contract, we need to proceed in a path-consistent fashion. We need to start by analysing the rules governing specific performance.

Specific performance is a remedy for the enforcement of contracts.[62] This is why our enquiry will take us briefly into English contract law.

Specific performance is a discretionary remedy, but the courts exercise their discretion according to settled principles.[63] The requirements for an order for specific performance are as follows.[64] First, there must be an enforceable contract between the parties. Second, the claimant must have furnished actual consideration in that she either has already performed or is now ready and able to perform. Third, the subject matter of the trust must be certain. Fourth, damages for breach of contract must be an inadequate remedy. These requirements will be discussed in turn in subsections 2.4.4.1–2.4.4.4. This discussion is not intended as a comprehensive study of specific performance of contracts, but rather as an illustration of the background of the

---

[60] Smith, *Property Law* 25.   [61] [1960] AC 206 at 240.
[62] Jones and Goodhart, *Specific Performance* 9.
[63] *Haywood* v. *Cope* (1858) 25 Beav 140 at 151, 53 ER 589 at 594 per Romilly MR.
[64] A. J. Oakley, *Constructive Trusts*, 3rd edn. (London, Sweet & Maxwell, 1997) 277.

rules governing the acquisition of property rights in securities under English law.

2.4.4.1 Enforceable contract

The courts will grant an order for specific performance of a contract only if there exists a valid subsisting contract between seller and buyer. The first requirement for an order for specific performance of a contract is that it be enforceable. This is, therefore, also the requirement for there to arise a constructive trust by operation of law and for the buyer to acquire equitable title to the securities. A contract is enforceable if it is valid, unconditional and possible. These requirements will be briefly analysed below.

The first requirement to be analysed is the requirement for a valid contract. Validity of contracts raises many questions which are general to the law of contracts and do not bear discussion here.[65] In the context of this book, we need only note that embedded in the analysis is contract law and briefly look at a few of the authorities relating to contracts for the purchase of shares.

The contract for the sale of securities does not have to be in writing. However, if a written transfer is executed the transfer is subject to stamp duty.[66] If one of the parties is a broker or an agent, she must send a written contract note to her principal,[67] but failure to send the contract note does not affect the validity of the contract.[68] Moreover, a buyer will not obtain equitable title under an otherwise valid contract if that would be inconsistent with its terms. This may be so where the parties intend that the transferor should retain the benefit of the shares.[69]

The second requirement to be satisfied for an order for specific performance is the existence of an unconditional contract of sale. Jenkins LJ said in *Parway Estates Ltd* v. *Commissioners of Inland Revenue* that there is a well-established principle 'that once a contract of sale is executed, the

---

[65] Treatment of these questions may be found in all of the standard text books: Treitel, *The Law of Contract*; Jack Beatson, *Anson's Law of Contract*, 27th edn. (Oxford: Oxford University Press, 2002).

[66] *Oughtred* v. *Inland Revenue Commissioners* [1960] AC 206.

[67] COB 8.1.3, FSA Handbook as of 26 May 2006, available from http://fsahandbook.info/ FSA/html/handbook/ (last visited 6 June 2006).

[68] A. Alcock [23.9], in Rt Hon. Lord Millet (ed.), *Gore-Browne on Companies*, 50th edn. (Bristol: Jordans, 2004).

[69] *Hood Barrs* v. *Commissioner of Inland Revenue (No. 3)* (1960) 39 T C 209.

subject-matter – the share in the present case – becomes in equity the property of the purchaser'.[70] Equitable ownership vests in the buyer at the date on which the unconditional contract of sale is signed. By the same token, equitable ownership is not transferred unless there is an unconditional contract.[71]

The requirement for an unconditional contract seems to be a difficult one to meet when securities are sold that have been issued subject to transfer restrictions. The London Stock Exchange will not list securities that are subject to transfer restrictions.[72] The impact of transfer restrictions on the sale of listed shares is therefore a question of no interest from the point of view of this book.

It is, nevertheless, worth noting that restrictions on transfers contained in the issuer's documentation do not as such prevent courts from ordering specific performance.[73] No order will normally be granted, however, if the directors of the issuing company have already exercised their authority to refuse to register a transfer. The cases then distinguish between contracts made on the stock exchange and contracts made privately outwith the stock exchange.[74] Contracts made outwith the stock exchange, which tend to involve shares in private companies, are not enforceable by an order for specific performance if the company refuses to register a transfer.[75]

Different rules apply to contracts made on the stock exchange. These rules go back to a time when transfer restrictions were no hinderance to a listing. There is no English case in which an order for specific performance of such a contract has been granted; there are, however, cases holding that the seller under a contract for the sale of shares at the stock exchange is not liable for breach of the contract if the company refuses to register the buyer.[76] There also two Scottish cases supporting

---

[70] (1958) 45 TC 135 at 148 (CA).
[71] *Hare* v. *Nicoll* [1966] 2 QB 130 (CA); *J. Sainsbury plc* v. *O'Connor (Inspector of Taxes)* [1991] 1 WLR 963 (CA).
[72] Rule 3.15, Stock Exchange Listing Rules as of June 2006, http://www.fsa.gov.uk/pubs/ukla/chapt03-3.pdf (last visited 4 July 2006).
[73] *Evans* v. *Wood* (1867) LR 5 Eq 9; *Paine* v. *Hutchinson* (1868) LR 3 Ch App 388.
[74] George Northcote, *Fry on Specific Performance*, 6th edn. (London: Sweet & Maxwell, 1985) 689–690.
[75] *Bermingham* v. *Sheridan* (1864) 33 Beav 660, 55 ER 525; *Wilkinson* v. *Lloyd* (1845) 7 QB 27, 115 ER 398.
[76] *Stray* v. *Russell* (1859) 1 El&El 888, 120 ER 1144; *London Founders Association, Limited* v. *Clarke* (1888) 20 QBD 576 (CA); *Hichens, Harrison, Woolston & Co* v. *Jackson & Sons* [1943] AC 266 at 279 per Thankerton LJ.

the idea that the seller becomes a trustee for the buyer if the company refuses to register a transfer made on the stock exchange.[77]

2.4.4.2 Claimant must be ready and willing to perform

Specific performance will only be granted, a constructive trust will only arise for the benefit of the buyer and the buyer will only acquire equitable title upon conclusion of the sales contract, if she has already performed, or is ready and willing to perform.[78] The principle formed the basis of the New South Wales Court of Appeal's decision in *Bonds & Securities (Trading) Pty Ltd* v. *Glomex Mines NL*.[79] The plaintiff sought a declaration that it was the equitable owner of certain shares as well as injunctive relief which would have had the effect of procuring its registration as legal owner. The remedy was not granted because the contract was not specifically enforceable. The purchase money had not been paid to the seller, but to the seller's broker, who had no authority to receive payments on the seller's behalf.

Specific performance may be granted in certain circumstances, even though the purchase price has not been paid and will not be paid in the near future. The purchase price in *Langen & Wind Ltd* v. *Bell* was dependent upon the average annual profit or loss over a period of the company whose shares were traded.[80] The seller, Bell, was the director of the company and was required to transfer the shares to Langen & Wind upon termination of his employment. Bell terminated his employment on 30 September 1970 and was immediately required to execute a transfer in favour of Langen & Wind. He was informed that the price could not be paid until the accounts for the year, which ended on 30 June 1972, had been approved and audited. Bell refused to execute the transfers until payment was made. The court directed him to perform his obligation, but the order granted him an unpaid vendor's lien to secure payment of the purchase price.

---

[77] *Stevenson* v. *Wilson* (1907) SC 445 (CS); *Lyle & Scott Ltd* v. *Scott's Trustees* [1959] AC 763 HL (Sc); these two cases are, generally, considered to be good authority in England (Alcock in *Gore-Browne on Companies* 23.12; Robert Pennington, *Company Law*, 8th edn. (London: Butterworths, 2001) 441 fn. 1 reaches the same conclusion but rejects *Stevenson* v. *Wilson* on other grounds).

[78] Jones and Goodhart, *Specific Performance* 68.   [79] [1971] 1 NSWLR 879.

[80] [1972] Ch 685.

2.4.4.3 Specific or ascertained assets

Specific performance will not be granted if the subject assets are not specific or ascertained.[81] This is related to the larger principle that the subject matter of a trust must be certain, a principle which applies to express trusts as well as to constructive trusts. The argument supporting the rule is that in the interest of certainty it must be possible to establish which assets are subject to the trust. This rule makes it difficult to establish a proprietary right in assets that are mixed with rather than physically separated from the trustee's own assets. It will therefore be analysed in more detail in the context of indirect holdings.[82]

2.4.4.4 Damages are an inadequate remedy

The next requirement for an order for specific performance reflects the historic origins of the remedy. Specific performance is an equitable remedy which was introduced because the common law had led to unjust results. The common law took, and still takes, the view that the award of monetary compensation can fully make good the loss suffered by breach of contract. This is true in most cases, but in certain circumstances the award of money does not entirely compensate the loss. In G. R. Northcote's words: 'for though one sovereign or one shilling is to all intents and purposes as good as any other sovereign or shilling, yet one landed estate, though of precisely the same market value as another, may be vastly different in every other circumstance that makes it an object of desire: so that it evidently follows that there would be a failure of justice, unless some other jurisdiction supplemented the Common Law, by compelling the defaulting party to do that which in conscience he is bound to do, namely, actually and specifically to perform his contract ... The defeat of justice which arose from ... the Common Law ... was met and remedied in certain cases by the ... Courts of Equity to compel specific performance.'[83]

Again, the argument is framed in a path-dependent way. The English courts do not reason that, if damages are an inadequate remedy, title to the securities passes to the buyer upon conclusion of the sales contract. The reasoning is more complicated than that: it involves the already

---

[81] Jones and Goodhart, *Specific Performance* 32.   [82] See subsection 7.3.
[83] *Fry on Specific Performance*, 6th edn. (London: Sweet & Maxwell/Ashford Press, 1985) 28–29.

familiar detour through the law of trusts, first establishing that, if damages would be an inadequate remedy, an order for specific performance will be granted. That then means that a trust arises and therefore, the buyer acquires equitable title.

The basic rule, then, is that specific performance will be granted where common law damages would inadequately compensate the plaintiff.[84] One test of whether damages are inadequate is to ask if specific performance will do more perfect and complete justice than an award of damages.[85] Another way of formulating a test was suggested by *Evans Marshall & Co. Ltd* v. *Bertola SA*: 'The standard question . . ., "Are damages an adequate remedy?", might perhaps, in the light of the authority in recent years, be rewritten: "Is it just, in all circumstances, that a plaintiff should be confined to his remedy in damages?" . . . '[86]

Specific performance is granted when property is sold that is unique or has a special value. Land is always thought to have this quality.[87] Land is unique in that one plot of land does not resemble another, even though they may have the same market value. A pecuniary remedy is thought to be inadequate protection of the buyer's rights, for she might not be able to purchase a satisfactory substitute. Conversely, the court will not order specific performance when the buyer can obtain a satisfactory equivalent to what she contracted for from some other source.[88] Whether the subject of a contract is unique depends on the terms of the contract; it depends on whether the parties contracted for a specific item, or for an item with particular specifications. If the contract is for a copy of a certain textbook, any textbook of that kind will satisfy the buyer and the contract will not be enforceable by specific performance; if the contract is for the copy of a textbook that used to belong to the author, an order for specific performance is more likely to be granted. The rule of thumb is that an order for specific performance is more likely the more rare the property is, and the more difficult it is to acquire a substitute on the market.

There are securities which are unique and for which a satisfactory substitute cannot be bought on the market, and there are securities for which a substitute is readily available. There is typically no market for shares in private companies, which is why a contract for the sale

---

[84] *Co-operative Insurance Society Ltd* v. *Argyll Stores (Holdings) Ltd* [1998] AC 1 per Lord Hoffmann at 11.

[85] Guenter Treitel, *The Law of Contract*, 11th edn. (London: Sweet & Maxwell, 2003) 1025–1026.

[86] [1973] 1 WLR 349 at 379 (CA).   [87] Jones and Goodhart, *Specific Performance* 128–132.

[88] Treitel, *The Law of Contract* 1020.

of shares in a private company is, ordinarily, enforceable by specific performance.[89]

For securities in public companies, a distinction lies according to whether they are readily available in the market. Shares in public companies are, ordinarily, available when they are listed on a stock exchange.[90] For this reason, it is generally true that a contract for the sale of listed shares is not enforceable by an order for specific performance.[91] In the seminal case *Cud* v. *Rutter*, shares in the South Sea Company were sold at a fixed price to be delivered three weeks after the contract had been entered into.[92] When that time came, the seller did not deliver the shares but offered to pay the difference between the purchase price and the value of the shares, which had risen in value in the meantime. The buyer sued for an order of specific performance which he was denied because the buyer could readily buy the quantity of shares he sought on the stock exchange; damages were considered to be an adequate remedy. Parker LC held that: 'a court of equity ought not to execute any of these contracts, but leave them to law, where the party is to recover damages, and with the money may if he pleases buy the quantity of stock agreed to be transferred to him; for there can be no difference between one man's stock and another's . . .'[93]

Similarly, in *Re Schwabacher*, the buyer of shares in the New Vaal Company sued for an order of specific performance.[94] The order was refused by Parker J, who said that:[95] 'although I have no doubt that it is within the power of a court of equity to decree specific performance of a contract for the sale and purchase of shares, yet when shares are dealt in largely on the market, and anyone can go and buy them as appears to be the fact in this case – there is no reason why they should not be in the same position as Government Stock is in the case of a contract for the sale and purchase of such stock.'

Exceptions to this rule exist because there may be circumstances in which listed shares cannot be obtained in the market. If the owner of

---

[89] *Jobson* v. *Johnson* [1989] 1 WLR 1026; *Grant* v. *Cigman* [1996] 2 BCLC 24; *Wood Preservations Ltd* v. *Prior* [1969] 1 WLR 1077 (CA); *Sahota* v. *Bains* [2006] EWHC 131 (Ch).
[90] Oakley, *Constructive Trusts* 277–278.
[91] *Michaels* v. *Harley House* [2000] Ch 104 at 113 per Robert Walker, LJ; Robert Pennington, *Company Law*, 8th edn. (London: Butterworths, 2001) 443; see also A. Neef, 'Recent Trends in the Specific Enforcement of Contracts to Sell Securities', (1953) 51 MichLR 408.
[92] (1719) 1 PWms 570, 24 ER 521.   [93] (1719) 1 PWms 570 at 571, 24 ER 521 at 522.
[94] (1908) 98 LT 127.   [95] (1908) 98 LT 127 at 128.

more than 50 per cent of the shares in a company agrees to sell her shareholding, the amount sold cannot be bought in the market and an order for specific performance will be granted.

An order for specific performance will also be given when shares in a public company are sold which are limited in number and which are not always to be had in the market. *Duncuft* v. *Albrecht* involved the sale of shares in the London and South-Western Railway Company.[96] Shadwell VC held that: 'it has been long since decided that you cannot have a bill for specific performance of an agreement to transfer a certain quantity of stock. But, in my opinion, there is not any sort of analogy between a quantity of 3 per cents or any other stock of that description ... and a certain number of railway shares of a particular description; which railway shares are limited in number, and which, as has been observed, are not always to be had in the market.'[97]

Specific performance of a contract for the sale of listed shares will also be granted where the shares are unique or otherwise unobtainable by virtue of the distribution of the shareholdings. The House of Lords enforced a contract for the sale of 12 per cent of the shares in a company by an order for specific performance in *Harvela Investments Ltd* v. *Royal Trust Company of Canada*.[98] There were in that case two families holding 43 per cent and 40 per cent of the shares, respectively, and a third shareholder holding 12 per cent. The third shareholder offered his shares for sale. Both families bid for the 12 per cent shareholding, in order to acquire control over the company. The case concerned a company whose shares were not listed, but the analysis would apply equally if the company had been listed. The reason for this is that the structure of the shareholding was such that the shares sold were not available elsewhere in the market and it was clear that the bidders wanted these particular shares to acquire control. An order for specific performance would have been granted even if the contract had been for listed shares.

Another situation justifying an order for specific performance of shares in public companies occurs when the contract concerns the particular shares held by the seller. For this to be true, the parties must have agreed that only the shares held by the seller, and not other shares of that kind, will satisfy the buyer. This possibility was first suggested by Shadwell VC in *Duncuft* v. *Albrecht* in his reference to

---

[96] (1841) 12 Sim 189, 59 ER 1104; see also *ANZ Executors and Trustees Ltd* v. *Humes Ltd* [1990] VR 615.

[97] (1841) 12 Sim 189 at 199, 59 ER 1104 at 1107–1108.   [98] [1986] AC 207.

'a certain number of railway shares of a particular description'.[99] The suggestion was taken up by Greene MR in *Re a Debtor*.[100] He held that a contract for the sale of listed shares was enforceable by an order for specific performance because it was, 'a contract for the sale and purchase of specific shares. It refers to "your preference shares", and that makes it not a contract to buy shares which the vendor is to buy on the market before that date of completion, but a contract for the sale and purchase of specific shares which at the date belonged to the vendor and which are still held by him.'[101]

Greene MR continued: 'certainly in the case of a contract for the sale and purchase of specific shares ... the Court of Equity has always exercised jurisdiction to order specific performance and moreover, the property in equity in the shares passes to the purchaser.'[102]

Irrespective of whether shares in private, public, or listed companies are sold, specific performance is also granted when the shares sold have not been fully paid.[103] In these cases, the company has a claim against the registered shareholder who is liable to pay the amount outstanding on the shares. If the buyer does not apply to have her name registered, the company will approach the seller when calls are made. The seller, in order to avoid liability, then sues for an order of specific performance instructing the buyer to apply for registration of her name.

In summary, the rule that an order for specific performance will be granted only if damages are an inadequate remedy helps to show the path-determined roots of English property law. The common law awards only damages. In circumstances in which this is considered to lead to unconscionable results, equity steps in to allow the buyer to claim delivery of the items purchased. Equity gives an order for specific performance in favour of the buyer. But equity's intervention does not stop here: whenever a contract is enforceable by an order for specific performance, a constructive trust arises. The seller is considered to hold the securities concerned as a trustee for the benefit of the buyer who, therefore, acquires equitable title to the securities.

The requirement for damages to be an inadequate remedy, however, significantly limits in scope the first heading under which equitable

---

[99] (1841) 12 Sim 199, 59 ER 1107–1108.   [100] [1943] 1 All ER 553 (CA).
[101] [1943] 1 All ER 553 (CA) at 554.   [102] [1943] 1 All ER 553 (CA) at 555.
[103] *Paine v. Hutchinson* (1868) LR 3 Ch App 388; *Cruse v. Paine* (1868) LR 6 Eq 641; *Coles v. Bristowe* (1868) LR 6 Eq 149; *London, Hamburgh, and Continental Exchange Bank, Ward and Henry's Case* (1867) 2 Ch App 431 at 438 per Crains LJ.

title arises. Damages are inadequate only when the buyer cannot buy substitute securities in the market. This is usually the case when securities in a private or public but unlisted company are sold, as there is no market where such securities are freely traded. When securities are sold, an order for specific performance is unlikely to be possible because the securities will be readily available in the market.

2.4.4.5 Conclusions

Subsection 2.4.4.4 analysed the rule that the buyer acquires equitable title to securities when the sales contract underlying the transaction becomes enforceable by an order for specific performance. This happens when the sales contract is enforceable, when the claimant is ready and willing to perform, when the securities which the contract relates to are ascertained and when damages are an inadequate remedy. The conclusion of this subsection is that the buyer of listed securities is not normally able to rely on the rules on specific performance to avail herself of equitable title to the securities.

In subsection 2.4.5, the question will be addressed as to whether equitable title arises out of a contract that is not specifically enforceable in circumstances where the securities have been appropriated to the contract and the purchase price has been paid.

2.4.5 Equitable title on appropriation of securities and payment of purchase price

Some academic commentators suggest that there is a rule that equitable title to securities passes to the purchaser independently of whether the contract is enforceable by an order for specific performance. There are two different schools of thought here. Some argue that a trust arises in favour of the buyer as soon as the subject matter of the sales contract can be identified. Others write that a trust arises only if the consideration has been paid by the buyer. There is also a prominent view that neither is correct and that a trust can arise only when specific performance is available.

These three positions will now be analysed. They all fit squarely into the path adopted by English law. Even if there is disagreement on which requirements need to be satisfied to give rise to a constructive trust, all commentators stand on the basis that a trust needs to be established and the general headings of English trust law need to be satisfied for an equitable interest to arise.

Robert Pennington writes that there is a distinction between sales of specific shares and sales of shares which are not identified in the contract.[104] In the first case, the equitable title to the shares passes to the buyer at once when the contract is made. The seller holds the shares as a bare trustee for the buyer subject to a lien in the seller's favour for any unpaid purchase price. If the contract is made for shares that are not identified in it, equitable title passes to the buyer only when the seller appropriates particular shares to the fulfilment of the contract. This usually happens when she executes and delivers the instrument of transfer to the buyer specifying the shares by number or quantity. Pennington does not qualify this proposition by pointing to a requirement for specific performance.

The authority cited by Pennington in support of this view is a dictum by Crains LJ in *London, Hamburgh, and Continental Exchange Bank*.[105] In the passage cited, Crains LJ states as the facts that, on a certain day, the transferor sold 30 shares to the transferee, and that on the following day executed a transfer to the transferee. Crains LJ then remarks that '[t]here is no doubt that this transaction constituted [the transferee] ... in equity the owner of the shares'. This dictum does not refer to a requirement for specific performance and insofar supports Pennington's thesis. The case, however, was about a seller enforcing a contract for the sale of partly paid shares where, as we have seen,[106] an order for specific performance would normally be given also in relation to listed shares.

Similar to Pennington, Alastair Alcock suggests that an effect of the shares being specified is that 'beneficial ownership passes to the purchaser'.[107] Alcock refers to a passage from *Re National Bank of Wales*,[108] which does not point to a requirement for specific performance. We need to note, nevertheless, that the case concerns the sale of partly paid shares, which again leads to the availability of an order for specific performance. Moreover, in that case the transferees' names had already been registered.[109] This normally results in legal title vesting in the transferee. *Wood Preservations Ltd* v. *Prior*[110] also advanced in support of Alcock's analysis, concerns the sale of 100 per cent of the shares in a company, a circumstance in which shares are not readily available in the market and in which specific performance will thus be granted. Again, the availability of specific performance was not referred to in the judgement as a decisive criterion.

---

[104] Pennington, Company Law 439.
[105] *Ward and Henry's Case* (1867) 2 Ch App 431 at 438.   [106] See p. 47.
[107] Alcock [23.12] in *Gore-Browne on Companies*. fn. 12.
[108] *Re National Bank of Wales, Taylor, Phillips and Richard's Case* [1897] 1 Ch 298 305–306.
[109] [1897] 1 Ch 298 at 304 per Lindley J.   [110] [1969] 1 WLR 1077 (CA).

Pennington's and Alcock's analysis receives support from the rules governing sales of goods. According to Sale of Goods Act 1979 (SGA 1979, s. 18, r. 1), property passes once a sales contract is complete if the contract is for the transfer of a particular good in a deliverable state. If the contract is for unascertained or for future goods, title to the goods passes when those goods are unconditionally appropriated to the contract.[111]

Other commentators put forward the thesis that a constructive trust arises irrespective of the availability of specific performance if the purchase price has been paid and if the subject matter of the contract has been specified. Meagher, Gummow and Lehane write, albeit without referring to transactions concerning registered securities, that the seller becomes a trustee for the buyer when the purchase price has been paid.[112] There is no mention of a requirement for the property to be identified; this requirement, however, can be inferred from the general rule requiring certainty of the subject matter of a trust.[113]

According to Meagher, Gammow and Lehane, prior to the payment of the purchase price a trust can arise only if the contract is enforceable by an order for specific performance. The authors, it seems, limit the availability of a constructive trust to circumstances where the purchase price has been paid because prior to payment of the purchase price the seller has an equitable lien over the property. The buyer's interest is considered to be too weak to be classified as proprietary.

The view that an equitable interest arises in relation to contracts that cannot be enforced by an order for specific performance has been contested by Sarah Worthington.[114] She refers to *Tailby* v. *Official Receiver*[115] and *Holroyd* v. *Marshall*,[116] which are the cases usually cited in support of the view that equitable ownership vests in the buyer irrespective of whether specific performance is available, and points out that both authorities concerned facts in which an order for specific

---

[111] SGA 1979, s. 18, r. 5.

[112] Meagher, Heydon and Leeming, *Meagher, Gummow, and Lehane's, Equity* para. 6–055; see also Craig Rotherham, *Proprietary Remedies in Context: A Study in the Judicial Redistribution of Property Rights* (Oxford: Hart, 2002) 169 referring to *Tailby* v. *Official Receiver* (1888) 13 App Cas 523.

[113] For this, see section 7.3.

[114] Sarah Worthington, 'Proprietary Remedies: The Nexus between Specific Performance and Constructive Trusts' (1996–7) 11 *Journal of Contract Law* 1.

[115] (1888) 13 App Cas 523.   [116] (1862) 10 HLC 191, 11 ER 99.

performance would normally be granted.[117] Sarah Worthington's view also can rely on the fact that the authorities cited by Pennington and Alcock, as has been pointed out above, concern cases where specific performance would normally be available.

Nevertheless we need to note that even though specific performance may have been available, none of the authorities reached their conclusions by relying on the fact that an order for specific performance was available. Moreover, Lord Macnaghten pointed out in *Tailby* v. *Official Receiver*[118] that: '[t]he truth is that cases of equitable assignment or specific lien, where the consideration has passed, depend on the real meaning of the agreement between the parties. The difficulty, generally speaking, is to ascertain the true scope and effect of the agreement. When that is ascertained you have only to apply the principle that equity considers that done which ought to be done if that principle is applicable under the circumstances of the case. The doctrines relating to specific performance do not, I think, afford a test or measure of the rights created.'

Policy considerations favour the proposition that the buyer is deemed to have a beneficial interest in the property once consideration has been paid. The buyer who has parted with the consideration has fulfilled her obligation: it seems only fair to have her acquire an interest in the object of the sales contract in turn.

If the effect of insolvency is taken into account, the policy reasons favouring the emergence of a constructive trust in favour of the buyer become even more forceful. In the seller's insolvency, a buyer who is left with a contractual claim will have her interest satisfied pari passu with the seller's unsecured creditors. In contrast, a buyer who has a proprietary interest will be able to have that proprietary interest satisfied in full. If, upon payment of the purchase price, the buyer was to receive a contractual right only, the seller's creditors would receive a windfall benefit to the buyer's detriment. The creditors would be able to take advantage of both the purchase price which upon payment becomes part of the seller's pool of assets, and the subject matter of the sale which would remain part of the seller's pool of assets available to the creditors. The better view prevents such a windfall from arising

---

[117] Sarah Worthington, *Proprietary Interests in Commercial Transactions* (Oxford: Oxford University Press, 1996) 197–201; Worthington, 'Proprietary Remedies 4–7.
[118] (1888) 13 App Cas 523 at 547–548.

and allows the buyer to acquire equitable title upon payment of the purchase price.

Prior to payment of the consideration, the buyer's interest is subject to a lien in favour of the seller. The existence of this lien causes some commentators not to classify the buyer's interest at this stage as proprietary. Admittedly, the seller continues to have a significant interest in the asset. The buyer's interest is only a conditional one: her interest is conditional upon payment of the purchase price. It is, however, within the buyer's discretion to pay the consideration and thereby to extinguish the seller's lien. The buyer can as of her own motion convert her conditional interest into an unconditional one. Given that it is in the buyer's hands to end the seller's lien, it seems that the better view is to classify the buyer's interest as proprietary even prior to payment of the purchase price.

A constructive trust, prior to and after payment of purchase price, can arise only if the subject matter of the trust is certain. All the views analysed above rightly stand on the basis that a trust interest arises only if the securities have been appropriated to the contract. Certainty of subject matter or appropriation has already been mentioned as a requirement for a trust to arise if an order for specific performance is available. A more detailed analysis will follow below.[119] For the time being, it suffices to note that a proprietary interest is conditional upon the securities to which that interest relates being appropriated to the contract.

Subsection 2.4.5 has been concerned with the rule that the buyer acquires equitable title to the securities if the securities have been appropriated to the contract. The conclusion was that the buyer acquires a proprietary interest in the securities irrespective of whether the purchase price has been paid. Prior to the payment of the purchase price, the buyer's interest is, however, subject to a lien in favour of the seller. In subsection 2.4.6 the rule that the buyer becomes the owner in equity when the seller has done everything in her power to divest herself of her interest will be examined.

2.4.6 Equitable title on delivery of transfer documents

Another rule of interest in this context lays down that a constructive trust arises and the transferee acquires equitable title when the transferor has done everything in her power to render the transfer effectual,

---

[119] See section 7.3.

even though something has yet to be done by a third party, such as registration of the transferee by the company. Equitable title is vested in the transferee as soon as the transfer documents are delivered to her.[120] Equity recognises the transfer and the buyer becomes the owner in equity when she receives the transfer form and the certificate.

Like the rules analysed in subsections 2.4.4 and 2.4.5, this rule also operates within the path-determined framework of English property law. The argument is expressed in terms of trust law; when the transferor has completely divested herself of the asset, a trust arises for the benefit of the transferee who, because she is a beneficiary of a trust, holds equitable title.

The case law on this point did not develop in relation to sales transactions; it is concerned with gifts. It is, nevertheless, of interest here because the rule can be applied to sales transactions by analogy. The argument is that if equitable title arises when a donor has done everything to effect the transfer, the same should apply to cases where a seller has acted in the same way. The concern about giving effect to unperfected gifts is that the donor is giving away assets without receiving a consideration in return. It requires unequivocal circumstances to have equity step in and give effect to a transfer that has yet to be perfected.[121] Equity will step in only if the donor has done everything required on her part to have title transferred to the donee.

When securities are transferred through a sale, the seller receives a consideration in return for her giving up the securities. In those circumstances there is less of a concern for protecting the transferor's interests than there is in cases of gifts. If the law accepts that a donor has completely given up her interests when she has done everything necessary to have title transferred to the donee, the law will have to accept that this is also true for a seller having equally completely disposed of her interest. Even though there is no authority on this point, the rule that a trust arises upon delivery of the transfer documents should apply, in principle, to sales transactions as well as to gifts.

The rule that the seller holds securities on constructive trust for the benefit of the buyer when she has delivered the transfer form

---

[120] *Pennington* v. *Waine* [2002] 2 BCLC 448; *Re Rose* [1949] 1 Ch 78; *Re Rose* [1952] 1 Ch 499 (CA); P. L. Davies, *Gower's Principles of Modern Company Law*, 7th edn. (London: Sweet & Maxwell, 2003) 693–694; Oakley, *Parker and Mellows: The Modern Law of Trusts*, 8th edn. (London: Sweet & Maxwell, 2003) 143–145.

[121] [2002] 2 BCLC 448 at para. 62 per Arden LJ.

together with the share certificates to her is referred to as the rule in *Re Rose*.[122]

There is debate on whether the rule in *Re Rose* is reconcilable with certain older cases, all of which are firmly rooted in the trust law analysis.[123] The transferor in *Milroy* v. *Lord*, a Court of Appeal decision from 1862, signed a deed purporting to assign shares and handed over a power to the transferee by means of which the latter might have transferred the shares into his own name.[124] The question arose whether the gift was perfected by handing over this power of attorney. It was held that the power of attorney did not perfect the transfer as between transferor and transferee because the transferee held the power of attorney as the agent of the settlor and because he could not, without express directions, be justified in converting an intended into an actual settlement.[125]

Using trust law language, Turner LJ wrote that:

in order to render a voluntary settlement valid and effectual, the settlor must have done everything which, according to the nature of property comprised in the settlement, was necessary to be done in order to transfer the property and render the settlement binding upon him. He may of course do this by actually transferring the property to the persons for whom he intends to provide and the provision will then be effectual, and it will be equally effectual if he ... declares that he himself holds it in trust for those purposes ...; but, in order to render the settlement binding, one or other of these modes must ... be resorted to, for there is no equity in this court to perfect an imperfect gift ... If it is intended to take effect by transfer, the court will not hold the intended transfer to operate as a declaration of trust, for then every imperfect instrument would be made effectual by being converted into a perfect trust.[126]

The result in *Milroy* v. *Lord* was that no trust arose for the benefit of the donee. The donee did not become the equitable owner even though the transferee was given a power by means of which he might have transferred the shares into his name.[127]

Re Fry[128] is a second case sometimes thought to be at odds with *Re Rose*. An intending settlor executed share transfers. The transfer was not

---

[122] [2002] 2 BCLC 448; *Re Rose* [1949] 1 Ch 78; *Re Rose* [1952] 1 Ch 499 (CA); Davies, *Gower's Principles of Modern Company Law* 693–694; Oakley, *Parker and Mellows* 143–145.

[123] Davies, *Gower's Principles of Modern Company Law* 693–694; Oakley, *Parker and Mellows* 143–145.

[124] (1862) 4 De GF & J 264 at 274, 45 ER 1185 (CA).

[125] (1862) 4 De GF & J 264 at 276, 45 ER 1185 (CA) at 1190 per Turner LJ.

[126] *Milroy* v. *Lord* (1862) 4 De GF & J 264 at 274, 45 ER 1185 (CA) at 1189–1190.

[127] (1862) 4 De GF & J 264 at 274, 45 ER 1185 (CA) at 1189–1190.   [128] [1946] Ch 312.

registered because the parties had not obtained the consent of the Treasury under a Defence Regulation. No constructive trust arose even though the transferor had delivered a transfer form and certificates to the transferee.

Milroy v. *Lord* and *Re Fry* seem to argue against the idea that the buyer becomes the beneficiary of a trust when the parties have complied with transfer formalities even though the transfer has not yet be registered. These cases were, however, explained on different grounds by the two cases called *Re Rose*. *Milroy* v. *Lord* was said to have been decided as it was because the parties did not use the proper form of transfer. The gift in that case could not have been perfected by executing the deed provided by the transferor.[129] Jenkins J said in *Re Rose* that if the parties in *Milroy* v. *Lord* had used the proper form, equitable title would have passed to the transferee on delivery of the transfer documents.[130] He also said that equitable title did not vest in the buyer in *Re Fry* because it was illegal under the Defence (Finance Regulations) Act 1939 to execute the transfers.[131]

The rule in *Re Rose* was articulated in two cases of the same name. By his will the testator in *Re Rose* gave shares to an Ernest Hook 'if such preference shares have not been transferred to him previously to my death'.[132] Before his death, the testator executed a voluntary transfer of the shares to Hook and delivered the certificates to him. This transfer was not registered until after the testator's death. The question arose whether the shares had been transferred before the testator's death or afterwards. It was held that the shares had been transferred before the testator's death because 'the testator had done everything in his power to divest himself of the shares in question to Mr Hook. He had executed a transfer. It is not suggested that the transfer was not in accordance with the company's regulations. He had handed that transfer together with the certificates to Mr Hook. There was nothing else the testator could do.'[133]

The point at which the donee acquired equitable title in the shares was brought into issue again in the second case called *Re Rose*, which was decided by the Court of Appeal.[134] The question fell to be decided in this

---

[129] *Re Rose* [1949] 1 Ch 78 at 89 per Jenkins J; *Re Rose* [1952] 1 Ch 499 at 509 (CA) per Evershed MR.
[130] [1949] 1 Ch 78 at 89.   [131] [1949] 1 Ch 78 at 89.   [132] [1949] 1 Ch 78.
[133] At 89.   [134] [1952] 1 Ch 499 (CA).

case for the purpose of the Revenue. The transaction would not be taxable provided that the disposition by the transferor had been made before 10 April 1943. The transfers had been executed on 30 March 1943 in the form required and handed to the transferees. The transferees were registered in the books of the company on 30 June 1943.

The Court of Appeal gave the same answer that had been given in the earlier Trial Court. Jenkins LJ wrote that 'these transfers were nothing more or less than transfers of the whole of the deceased's title, both legal and equitable, in the shares, and all the advantages attached to the shares, as from the date on which he executed and delivered the transfers – subject, of course, as regards the legal title, to the provisions of the articles of association of the company as to registration.'[135]

Jenkins LJ continued: 'In my view, a transfer under seal in the form appropriate under the company's regulations, coupled with delivery of the transfer and certificate to the transferee, does suffice, as between transferor and transferee, to constitute the transferee the beneficial owner of the shares.'[136]

However difficult it may be to reconcile *Re Rose* with *Milroy* v. *Lord* and *Re Fry*, the rule in *Re Rose* is now part of current English law. Lord Wilberforce said in passing in *Vandervell* v. *Inland Revenue Commissioners*: 'If the [taxpayer] had died before the college had obtained registration, it is clear on the principle of *In re Rose* ... that the gift would have been complete, on the basis that he had done everything in his power to transfer the legal interest with the intention to give, to the college.'[137] *Re Rose* was confirmed by the Court of Appeal in a case where the transfer documents were delivered to the issuer's auditor. This was, in the circumstances, held to be sufficient to give rise to a constructive trust for the benefit of the donee.[138]

It was moreover held in *Hawks* v. *McArthur* that, despite the failure of the parties to comply with pre-emption requirements set down in the articles, the transfers and the antecedent agreements operated as a sale by the seller to the buyer of the equitable interest in the shares.[139]

The rule that a constructive trust arises for the benefit of the transferee when the transferor has done everything in her power to divest herself of the securities applies to gifts. By way of analogy, it can also be

---

[135] [1952] 1 Ch 499 (CA) at 517.   [136] [1952] 1 Ch 499, at 518 (CA).
[137] [1967] 2 AC 291 at 330.   [138] *Pennington* v. *Waine* [2002] 2 BCLC 448.
[139] [1951] 1 All ER 22 at 27.

applied to sales transactions. When securities are transferred by means of paper documents, the constructive trust arises when the transfer form and the certificate are delivered to the buyer or his agent. The analysis is consistent with the path adopted by English law. A constructive trust arises, the seller becomes a trustee, the buyer becomes the beneficiary and in that capacity enjoys equitable ownership.

2.4.7 Express trusts

A trust also arises in English law as a result of an express declaration. Parties who wish to regulate the transfer of property rights in the context of a sale can do so by providing for the emergence of a trust for the benefit of the buyer at some point in time prior to registration of the transfer with the issuer. It will be shown in section 3.1 that the transfer systems set up by the stock exchange have taken advantage of this technique to give the buyer proprietary rights.

The express application of the English law of trusts in this context is, once again, evidence of the path-dependent development of English law. When documenting transactions, parties and their legal advisors prefer to adopt solutions that provide for certain results. This can be best achieved by applying legal techniques that are widely used and have been tested in the courts. Rather than, for example, attempting to bring the forward point in time at which the buyer acquires legal title by a provision to that effect in the sales contract, parties prefer to use trust law to achieve a similar result. As a result, English law continues to regulate property rights in securities through the mechanism of trust law.

2.4.8 Conclusions

The discussion in subsection 2.4.4 was concerned with the circumstances in which a constructive trust arises by virtue of the sales contract becoming enforceable by an order for specific performance. The conclusion was that for transactions concerning listed securities an order for specific performance will be available only in exceptional circumstances. In subsection 2.4.5 the question if equitable title can arise if specific performance is not available was analysed. Here it was concluded was that a conditional equitable interest arises as soon as the subject matter of the contract has become certain. The interest is conditional upon payment of the consideration. As soon as the consideration has been paid, the buyer acquires an unconditional equitable interest in the securities. In subsection 2.4.6 the case law that provides for the creation of a constructive trust when the seller has done every-thing in his power to divest herself of her interest was addressed. The conclusion was that the trust comes into existence when the seller has delivered the transfer form together with the securities certificate to the buyer. Subsection 2.4.7 concluded that express trusts are used in sales documentations set up by private parties and their legal advisors and also in the standard documentation underlying the securities settle-ment systems processing stock exchanges transactions with a view to regulating property rights between buyers and sellers.

2.5 Summary of the analysis

From the point of view of this book we need to observe that, in English law, the procedure whereby shares are transferred, the point in time when the buyer is considered to acquire property rights and the mech-anisms through which these property rights vest in the buyer developed in a path-dependent fashion. The current transfer procedure reflects the historic origin of English company law in trust law and in the law of partnerships. The very concept of registered securities and the transfer rules associated with them are shaped by the idea that a transfer of membership rights involves the admission by the issuer of a new member.

Even after securities have become freely transferable and have been so for a long time, transfer procedures do not operate around the docu-ment but rather operate around entering the transferee's name on a members' register kept by or on behalf of the issuer. The entry on the register is the act causing the transferee to acquire legal title to the securities, determining priorities as between competing transferees and causing the issuer to recognise the transferee as the new share-holder or as the new creditor.

The path-determined approach of English law is also illustrated by the fact that English law operates a dualistic model, distinguishing between legal and equitable ownership. A buyer acquires an equitable interest before she becomes the legal owner, and transfers of securities are embedded in this path-immanent model of property law.

Moreover, equitable ownership is created by a legal mechanism that is unique to the common law and does not exist in any civil law system. The method through which an equitable interest vests in the buyer requires the existence of a constructive or express trust. Equitable proprietary rights can arise only if a trust is created either by law or by an express declaration of the parties.

The rule analysed in subsection 2.4.4 does not straightforwardly make the buyer the equitable owner once the securities have been appropriated to the contract. The buyer first needs to establish that the sales contract is enforceable by an order for specific performance. For that, the contract must be valid, unconditional and enforceable. The buyer must have performed the consideration, or be willing and able to do so. An order for specific performance is not granted when damages are an adequate remedy. If all these requirements are satisfied, the sales contract will be enforceable by an order for specific performance. That also means that a constructive trust arises for the benefit of the buyer: the seller becomes the trustee, the buyer becomes the beneficiary. Because the buyer has become the beneficiary of a trust, she has acquired a property right in the securities called equitable title. The buyer's equitable title arises as soon as the specifically enforceable contract has been formed.[140]

Likewise, the rule in subsection 2.4.5 is not simply that a conditional proprietary interest arises upon appropriation of the securities to the contract or that an unconditional proprietary interest arises upon payment of the purchase price. The rule operates within the framework of trust law. The emergence of a proprietary interest is a consequence of the creation of a trust. A trust is created by law when the object of the sales contract is specified: the buyer becomes the beneficiary of that trust, the seller becomes the trustee. Until payment of the consideration, however, the buyer's interest is restricted by a lien that secures that payment for the benefit of the buyer.

The rule in Re Rose is not that the buyer becomes the owner when the necessary documents are delivered to her. The rule is also more complicated than that. It is, once again, expressed using the mechanisms and the language of trust law. The rule is that a trust arises when the transfer form and the certificates are delivered to the buyer. At this point, the seller becomes the trustee and the buyer become the beneficiary of a constructive trust. Because the buyer is a beneficiary of a trust, she has equitable title to the securities.

English law gives property rights in securities to the transferee in a path-determined way, through the lens of trust law. This makes

---

[140] *Lysaght* v. *Edwards* [1876] 2 ChD 499.

property law one of the most parochial areas of English law: it is difficult to think of a legal institution more indigenous to the common law than the trust. Trust law was, in turn, shaped by the historically determined division of jurisdiction between the law courts and the court of equity. This division is not replicated in the civil law world.

The German and Austrian law relating to transfers of paper securities will be analysed in chapter 10 and will show that German and Austrian law are doctrinally very different from English law. German and Austrian securities are predominantly issued in the form of bearer securities; few companies issue name shares. When securities are transferred the buyer becomes the owner after she has acquired possession of the certificates representing the securities. If a company issues name shares, the company needs to keep a shareholder register. The registration of the buyer's name in that register, however, does not determine the point at which the buyer becomes the owner. Similar to the rules applying to bearer shares, the buyer of German and Austrian name shares becomes the owner when the share certificated is endorsed in favour of the buyer and when she acquires possession of that endorsed certificate.[141]

Another difference between English law and German/Austrian law is that, in England, an equitable interest can arise prior to the delivery of the securities certificates to the buyer. In Germany and Austria, the buyer needs to acquire possession to the documents to acquire ownership in the securities. It will be shown that the requirement for possession is interpreted widely; nevertheless, the English rules are more favourable to the buyer in that an equitable interest can arise for the benefit of the buyer when a specifically enforceable contract has been concluded – or, at least according to some, when the securities have been appropriated to the contract. In those circumstances, ownership would not arise in German nor Austrian law.

Notwithstanding the differences in legal doctrine that exist between English law, on the one hand, and German and Austrian law, on the other, there also exists an important similarity between the two jurisdictions in terms of the outcomes produced by the respective legal doctrines. It is important to note that in both jurisdictions the delivery of securities documents (in England, together with a transfer form)

---

[141] See section 13.

operates to confer on the buyer in certain circumstances an interest in the underlying securities. In England, the interest is an equitable interest under the rule in *Re Rose* which does not exist in Germany or Austria. In Germany and Austria, the acquisition of possession to the securities certificates is a requirement that needs to be fulfilled for the buyer to become the owner of the securities.

3   Dematerialisation

The analysis contained in chapter 2 was concerned with securities transfers that are carried out by means of paper documents and applied to listed as well as unlisted securities. In this chapter, securities that are issued without paper certificates and their transfers will be examined, focusing exclusively on listed securities.

Paper documents were, traditionally, used in England to transfer both listed and unlisted securities. This changed when a transfer system was introduced through which transfers of listed securities could be effected by means of electronic instructions. The process whereby paper documents were replaced by electronic instructions is referred to as 'dematerialisation'.

It is important to stress from the outset that dematerialisation in England developed in a path-dependent manner. To illustrate this, we need first to determine how listed securities used to be transferred prior to dematerialisation (section 3.1). After that, the process which led to dematerialisation will be examined (section 3.2).

3.1 Talisman

Until 1996, securities sold the London Stock Exchange were transferred by means of paper certificates and transfer forms. Successive stock exchange rules implemented continuously refined logistical regimes through which the transfer documents where received from the seller, allocated to the buyers and lodged with the issuers.

One example is the system which was in place between 1979 and 1996.[1] This system was known under the acronym 'Talisman' which

---

[1] J. R. Bird [23.11], in Rt Hon. Lord Millet (ed.), *Gore-Browne on Companies*, 50th edn. Bristol: Jordans (2004); Robert Pennington, *Company Law*, 8th edn. London: Butterworths, (2001) 491–2.

stood for 'Transfer Accounting, Lodgement for Investors and Stock Management for Market Makers and Dealers'. Securities transfers were carried out every other week on what was called 'settlement' or 'account' days. Twice a year there was an interval of three weeks between the settlement days. Transfers were effected by means of Sepon (Stock exchange pool nominee), which acted as a nominee between account days on behalf of member firms and their clients who maintained Sepon accounts.

When a share transfer was agreed upon on the London Stock Exchange, both the buyer and the seller notified the stock exchange's settlement centre. This matched the buyer's and the seller's notifications and sent a 'sales docket' to them which evidenced the sales contract. The seller then handed the paper documents to the stock exchange and the shares were transferred into Sepon's name. Sepon became the securities' legal owner upon entry of its name on the register. Sepon, however, did not hold the securities for its own benefit. In a path-consistent manner, the underlying documentation made use of the principal mechanism available to English property law, the trust. When holding legal title to the securities between account days, Sepon acted as a trustee, thereby giving its clients the benefit of a proprietary equitable interest in the securities.

The securities continued to be held in Sepon's name until the next account day. Securities' transfers between account days were not recorded on the issuer's register, they were recorded only with Sepon. When securities were transferred, Sepon continued to hold the securities on trust. What changed, however, was the identity of the beneficiary. Between account days, equitable title was transferred from one transferee to another by book entry on Sepon's books.[2]

On account day, the securities were transferred into the name of the person who was the last buyer to acquire them before account day. This meant that a buyer who bought securities and sold them within the same account period did not acquire legal title to the securities.

The use of Sepon as a nominee reduced the number of transfers that had to be registered. However often securities were sold on the stock exchange between account days, only two transfers had to be registered: the transfer from the first seller to Sepon and the transfer from

[2] J. Benjamin and N. Jordan, 'Milking the Bull', [1993] *Butterworths Journal of International Banking and Finance Law* 211.

Sepon to the final buyer. The sales in between were recorded in Sepon's books only.

The role of the Talisman transfer system was to receive the transfer documents, to keep records of transfers between account days, to issue transfer forms at the end of an accounting period and to pass these transfer forms, together with the securities certificates, to the issuer to allow for registration of the name of the buyer who was the last to buy before account day. Talisman did not keep the issuer's register; it merely sorted documents and kept track of transfers between account days. Between account days, investors were protected through an arrangement providing for an express trust for the benefit of buyers of securities.

3.2 The need for reform

Paper-based transfer procedures, however sophisticated they may be, have limits as to the number of transfers they can process. In England it had become clear by 1987 that Talisman was unable to cope with the unprecedented trading volumes brought about by the privatisation programme of the 1980s. The need for reform became painfully apparent when the stock markets unexpectedly crashed on 19 October 1987.[3]

Sharp declines in securities values cause disturbance in any capital market. In England, however, the situation was exacerbated by the time-consuming paper-based settlement process. Because the market was falling rapidly, trading volumes increased and the stock exchange was unable to meet its standard settlement periods. The crux of the problem lay in the cumbersome process making physical delivery of large numbers of paper documents. Buyers who had entered into transactions before the crash took advantage of the delay in settlement to avoid completion of their transactions. This would not have been possible if the London market had had a settlement system that ensured prompt completion of transactions and, at the same time, was able to process large volumes. The obvious solution was to replace paper documents with computer entries. This replacement is often referred to as the 'dematerialisation of share transfers'.[4]

---

[3] Seligmann, *Michigan Yearbook of International Legal Studies*, vol. IX, 1988 1 (1).
[4] *Consultation Paper on Dematerialisation of Share Certificates and Share Transfers*, (London: Department of Trade and Industry) (DTI), 30 November 1988.

We have already seen that in English law certificates for registered instruments are documents of evidence only. When registered instruments are transferred a paper transfer form is completed to notify the issuer of the transfer. These two steps have historically evolved because the most reliable legal method through which registered securities could be transferred when securities started to appear first was by way of novation.

When paper documents were to be eliminated from the process of transferring and holding registered securities market participants did not first decide on the optimal operational solution and then create a new legal regime around it. Paper was rather eliminated by building on the existing legal framework: paper certificates and paper transfer forms were simply replaced by electronic instructions leaving the previous doctrinal analysis intact.

The Companies Act was amended in 1989 to allow for shares to be evidenced and transferred without a written instrument.[5] CA 1989, s. 207 enables 'The Secretary of State ... [to] ... make provision by regulations for enabling title to securities to be evidenced and transferred without a written instrument'. The regulations may make provision for procedures for recording and transferring title to securities, and for the regulation of those procedures and the persons responsible for or involved in their operation.[6] CA 1989, s. 207 gives power to the Secretary of State to reform only the transfer procedure, and does not contain a power to change substantive property law. This means that any change based on the statutory provision must not interfere with the common law governing transfers of registered instruments. This is the framework within which the market participants masterminding the reform had to operate.

The policy reasons justifying the limitation of the power given to the Secretary of State by the Companies Act 1989 are explained in a consultation document published in 1988.[7] The document reveals that the government had the following main matters in mind when considering the principles of the new regime:

---

[5] CA 1989 s. 207 (1989 c. 40) authorised the Secretary of State to adopt a respective regulation.
[6] CA 1989, s. 207 (2).
[7] *Consultation Paper on Dematerialisation of Share Certificates and Share Transfers*. (London: Department of Trade and Industry) (DTI), 30 November 1988.

- There should be no change to the detriment of the shareholder or of the company either in the relationship between them, or in the position of the company's register.
- The existing structure of rights and liabilities should be the basis for making corresponding provisions governing the obligations and liabilities of the operator of the system administering transfers of paperless securities which are referred to as uncertificated securities.[8]
- The government also aimed to avoid imposing on a new scheme advantages or disadvantages over the existing paper-based system.

The cautious approach adopted by the government at the time may have been a reaction to institutional pressure to protect vested interests. It is, however, also attributable to the fact that, as a matter of principle, radical change is seen as being undesirable: remaining as closely as possible within orthodox legal doctrine when creating new legislation is an end in itself. Governments aim at implementing policy objectives as effectively as possible; when drafting legislation government lawyers are instructed to achieve the highest possible degree of legal certainty.[9] This causes them to use well-established legal terms and legal concepts rather than creating a new statutory regime that does not fit with existing doctrine. This limits the range of choices available to law reformers and causes path-dependent legal development.

In addition to doctrinal constraints, market institutions also influence legal development. Their influence is, however, also shaped and constrained by the legal doctrine already in place. In England, the influence of financial market institutions on law reform became visible when the first attempt to create a dematerialised system was advanced under the acronym of TAURUS.[10] TAURUS was launched by the London Stock Exchange. The stock exchange and its participants were, however, unable to implement a transfer mechanism that would both be efficient and satisfy the desire of all parties involved to maintain as far as possible the role they had played in the process prior to dematerialisation.[11]

What we observe here is an example of the influence exercised by the institutions prevailing in the English capital market. Incumbent

---

[8] Securities for which a paper certificate is issued are referred to as 'certificated securities' (para. 3, Uncertificated Securities Regulation (USR) 2001, SI 3755/2001).
[9] This argument applies irrespective of whether a particular legal system uses rules or standards to regulate a certain matter (p. 226).
[10] TAURUS stands for 'Transfer and Automated Registration of Uncertificated Stock'.
[11] Brian Cheffins, *Company Law* (Oxford: Oxford University Press, 1997) 369.

institutions were able to delay reform. In particular, company registrars, to whom the maintaining of registers had traditionally been outsourced by issuers, were opposed to reform and lobbied to maintain a function in the new transfer process. The influence exercised by the registrars and other lobby groups caused the TAURUS project to become so complex and costly that it had to be abandoned in March 1993.[12]

3.3 CREST

3.3.1 Introduction

After the collapse of TAURUS, the Bank of England stepped in and created CREST, which is the current settlement system. CREST went live on 15 July 1996,[13] and it allows for dematerialised transfers.[14]

There would have been alternatives in drafting a new legal regime, all of which would have preserved the current institutional framework, but no attempt was made to draft, or even consult with market participants on, a new, perhaps more modern, legal framework. The Bank of England carried out the reform by modelling the new legal regime closely on the regime that had been in place before. At first, CREST did not maintain issuer registers; CREST was simply a system through which buyers and sellers communicated transfer instructions electronically. After having received matching instructions from both parties, CREST instructed the respective registrars to amend the register.[15] In the same way as the paper-based settlement systems that were in place prior to CREST were sorting systems for paper-based transfer instructions, CREST began its existence as a platform for the exchange of electronic transfer instructions between the transferor, the transferee and the issuer. The Bank of England simply transposed the paper-based procedure into an electronic environment; the doctrinal rules that had been in place before, the existence of which can be traced back to the rules that were in place when securities first appeared, also shaped the rules governing the paperless infrastructure when it was first implemented.

---

[12] Cheffins, *Company Law* 15, 407–409.

[13] CREST Domestic Legal Framework 1, http://www.crestco.co.uk and on the Company/ Timeline website last visited 20 July 2006.

[14] When it was first implemented, the operation of the system was governed by Uncertificated Securities Regulation (USR) 1995, SI 1995/3272. It is now subject to USR 2001, SI 2001/3755.

[15] Robert Pennington, *Company Law*, 8th ed. (London: Butterworths, 2001) 493–494.

Market infrastructure institutions are able to delay reform. However, when institutional pressure is overcome and reform is carried out, the form in which the law evolves to respond to change is determined by incumbent legal doctrine independently of institutional pressure.[16]

The records kept by CREST, originally, did not serve a legal function. This cautious start for the CREST system could be explained by a concern about the reliability of the computer system and its communication network. The fact that registration on decentralised registers kept by registrars remained of sole legal significance for determining ownership in securities would also have had significant appeal to registrars, whose function as keepers of the issuer register was preserved. In the same way as Talisman was a sorting system for paper-based transfer instructions, CREST began its existence as a platform for the communication of electronic transfer instructions between the issuer, the transferor and the transferee. This point will now be further explored.

Transfers of uncertificated securities within CREST are effected by instructions sent by or on behalf of holders to the CREST computer via a computer network which is established by network providers appointed by CREST.

In order to transfer securities in CREST, the issuer, the transferor and the transferee must all be members of the system. The issuer may resolve by resolution of its directors to become a member of CREST.[17] The transferor or the transferee may become members of CREST in two ways. They may either become users themselves, which means that they have to provide for the hardware and software necessary to establish a communications link to the system. If they do not wish to establish a link themselves, each of them may appoint a user (a sponsor) through which they issue instructions with respect to their securities. Whichever form of membership a securities holder chooses, she must appoint a bank to provide settlement bank facilities.

---

[16] As we saw in chapter 1, Lucian Bebchuk and Mark Roe use the term 'structure-driven path dependence' to describe the influence of the incumbent market infrastructure. When analysing the influence of pre-existing structures, however, the authors view incumbent institutions as being principally free to cause the adoption of any legal framework that suits their needs. They are able to shape the law, and are not viewed as being bound by legal constraints themselves. The view put forward in this chapter contests this. Structure-driven path dependence exists, but only in so far as institutions delay reform. The type of legal framework that is implemented is not a function of the influence of institutions, but is largely determined by legal doctrine.

[17] USR 1995, reg. 19; USR 2001, reg. 16.

CREST maintains two types of accounts for each member, a *member* account and a *cash memorandum* account. The member account shows how many and what kind of securities each member owns. The cash memorandum account shows how much credit the member has with her settlement bank.

The *CREST Manual 1996* provided for a detailed description of the administration of the electronic transfer process.[18] Once a sales contract was concluded, the seller and the buyer sent computer instructions to CREST. The seller instructed CREST to transfer her shares to the buyer and the buyer instructed CREST to transfer the purchase price to the seller. As soon as CREST received both instructions, it verified whether the input of the buyer and seller corresponded to each other. If the inputs matched and sufficient credit was available on the buyer's and the seller's respective accounts on settlement day, CREST processed the securities transfer.

The first step was that CREST amended its internal records. It debited the seller's account and credited the buyer's account with the securities, and debited the buyer's cash memorandum account and credited the seller's cash memorandum account with the purchase price. Simultaneously with these internal amendments, CREST sent instructions to the issuer to amend its register and to the settlement bank to transfer the purchase price to the seller. This process was called 'settlement'.[19]

For the first five years of CREST's operation, CREST records existed for internal purposes only. Most importantly, they did not constitute evidence of the holder's entitlement. CREST only received electronic instructions from both the buyer and the seller, matched those instructions and instructed the company or its registrar to amend the register. At that time, CREST operated only as a sophisticated electronic communication network; the difference between transfers effected through the CREST system and those effected through paper certificates was the method by which the transferee's entitlement would be evidenced to the issuer.

When certificated shares are transferred, the share certificate serves as a document of identification; the company issues a certificate to every shareholder. When a shareholder transfers her shares, she passes

---

[18] *CREST Manual* Version 1.0, issued 15 July 1996.
[19] The *CREST Manual* uses the term 'settlement' in the narrow sense described in the text. For a broader meaning of the term, see p. 1.

the certificate to the transferee and the transferee delivers the certificate to the company. The fact that she possesses the certificate provides the company with some evidence that she has obtained the transferor's authority to have the securities transferred into her name.

When CREST was first implemented, transfers occurred in a manner which closely mirrored the transfer procedure that had operated for paper-based securities. The rules originally governing CREST changed only the process whereby the issuer identified the transferee. The identification would take place by means of instructions sent through a centralised network; the CREST computer performed the identification process automatically and without the requirement for paper. A number of security measures ensured that the information sent through the network was as reliable as possible.[20]

Paper documents were replaced with electronic instructions but the actual transfer still required the involvement of the issuer; CREST simply assisted the issuer in identifying the transferee. Transfers still had to be recorded on decentralised securities registers. CREST maintained records of shareholdings, but those records reflected only the entries on the register kept on behalf of issuers. The CREST records, originally, did not constitute the securities register.

3.3.2 Legal title

When CREST first started, a transferee became the legal owner of securities when her name was entered on the securities register kept by or on behalf of the issuer, irrespective of whether the entry had been effected upon delivery of paper transfer documents or upon receipt of a CREST instruction. The legal significance of the issuer register remained unchanged. According to USR 1995, reg. 20, an entry on the register was 'evidence of such title to the units as would be evidenced if the entry on the register related to units of that security held in certificated form'. It is important to note that the register continued to be kept by the issuer, or on the issuer's behalf by a registrar.

3.3.3 Equitable title

In keeping with the path originally adopted by English law, the dualistic model of property law that distinguished between legal and equitable title continued to exist for transfer of both uncertificated and certificated

---

[20] CREST project team, *CREST Network and Security Requirements Specification* (release 2.3 January 1995) 24–30.

shares. Two observations support this conclusion. First, the legislature made no attempt in the regulations implementing CREST to modify the rules on equitable or beneficial ownership. Secondly, USR 1995 made explicit use of the rules on equitable title. Both of these observations will be examined further below.

The conclusion drawn in section 2.4 was that there are three possible rules which determine the acquisition of ownership in equity by the buyer. The first rule is that the buyer becomes the equitable owner of securities upon conclusion of the sales contract if that contract is enforceable by an order for specific performance.[21] The second rule is that the (unqualified) equitable title vests in the buyer when the securities have been appropriated to the contract and the purchase price has been paid.[22] The third rule is that the transferee acquires equitable ownership when the transferor has done everything in her power to divest herself of her interest.[23]

The first rule applies only if securities are transferred that are not readily available in the market and is therefore largely irrelevant for transactions carried out on the stock exchange. In this subsection only the second and third rule will therefore be examined, both of which developed at a point in time when paper documents were used to transfer securities. Paper documents have ceased to exist for uncertificated securities. There is no authority on how to apply these equitable rules to certificated transfers.

It is, nevertheless, possible for the courts to apply the rules that developed for paper transfers in relation to uncertificated transfers. When uncertificated securities are transferred there exists a point in time at which the securities have become appropriated to the contract and the purchase price has been paid. There also exists a point in time at which the seller has done everything in her power to divest herself of the securities. The courts could determine these points in time in the context of the respective current settlement system and apply the rules that developed for paper securities in relation to these points in time. Under the second rule, equitable title would pass to the buyer when the securities had become appropriated to the contract and when the purchase price had been paid through the uncertificated transfer system. Under the third rule, equitable title would pass to the buyer when she had done everything necessary in the context of the settlement system to transfer the securities to the buyer.

[21] See subsection 2.4.4.   [22] See subsection 2.4.5.   [23] See subsection 2.4.6.

Notwithstanding the fact that there appears to be scope for the application of the rules on equitable title to apply to uncertificated securities, one observation needs to be made. The introduction of an uncertificated transfer system in England has reduced the practical significance of equitable ownership: the time lag between the point in time at which securities are sold and the point in time at which transfers are completed has decreased. It used to be the case that there was a time lag of two, sometimes, three weeks between trade and settlement. If, for example, the seller became insolvent during that period, equity would make it possible for the buyer to assert a proprietary right to the securities notwithstanding that her name had not yet been entered on the issuer register. If securities are sold on the London Stock Exchange today, the transactions will normally settle within three working days after the sales contract has been entered into. It is possible for transactions to settle earlier than that: CRESTCo offers a service whereby transactions settle on the same day as the trade is made.[24] In those circumstances, the buyer is exposed to the risk of the seller's insolvency for a period of time that is shorter than it used to be when transfers were effected by means of paper documents, because the buyer will acquire legal title at an earlier point in time. Equitable title, if it arises at all in the circumstances, will only ever exist for a comparatively short time span.

The reforms that led to the creation of the current settlement system are the product of an effort of the British securities market to comply with what is perceived as best international practice. It is possible to view the fact that equitable title has lost some of its practical significance as a change that has caused the English transfer system to become like the German and Austrian systems. The argument supporting this conclusion would be that, in practical terms, England is reducing the significance of its dual-headed approach to property law by structuring securities transfers such that the buyer becomes the legal owner at an earlier point in time. This may be seen as an example of convergence; there exists no evidence, however, that convergence with other legal systems was one of the aims to be achieved by USR 1995.

The regulation implementing CREST did not only leave the law of equity intact, it also made explicit use of the concept of equitable ownership by adopting a rule concerning the acquisition of equitable title in

[24] http://www.crestco.co.uk/home/home.html#/products/dvp_intro.html (last visited 20 June 2006).

the course of a securities transfer. According to USR 1995, the buyer acquired equitable title at the time when the instruction which required the issuer to register a transfer was sent by CREST.[25] The transferee acquired title to the securities notwithstanding that the securities to which the instruction related might be unascertained.[26] The transferee acquired the equitable interest even if the transferor acquired her equitable interest at the same time as the transferee's equitable interest arose in the shares.[27] The equitable title of the transferee subsisted until the time when the transferee's name was entered on the issuer register.

The analysis presented here shows that ownership in equity continued to play a role after the implementation of the CREST transfer system. When switching over to an electronic transfer system, English law made use of the same legal techniques that had prevailed when paper documents were used to facilitate transfers. Notwithstanding the continued influence of incumbent legal doctrine, we can observe, however, that the introduction of an electronic transfer system reduced the time lag between the sales transaction and its completion. As a result, the buyer acquired legal title at an earlier point in time and the rules on ownership in equity began to lose some of their practical importance.

3.3.4 Conclusions

In England, the privatisation programme of the 1980s brought about the need for law reform. Paper documents were eliminated from the transfer process by way of dematerialisation. The process through which this was achieved shows the influence of incumbent providers of market infrastructure as well as that of incumbent legal doctrine.

Market infrastructure providers were able to delay reform and the first attempt to create a paperless transfer system (Talisman) had to be abandoned. When reform was successfully carried out, however, no attempt was made to create a legal infrastructure from scratch. The rules governing the paper-based system were transposed into the new one. The architecture of the CREST system mirrors the transfer procedure that had been in place previously and that originally developed as a reflection of the English law of novation.

England also continued to adhere to its dualistic approach to ownership; the distinction between ownership at law and ownership in equity remains. Ownership at law is transferred to the buyer when her name is entered into the securities register which, under USR 1995, was

---

[25] USR 1995, reg. 25.   [26] USR 1995, reg. 25 (6).   [27] USR 1995, reg. 25 (3).

maintained by the issuer rather than by CREST. The rules on ownership in equity also continue to apply although their practical significance has been noticeably reduced. An important effect of the 1995 reforms was to bring forward the point in time at which the buyer would normally acquire legal title to the securities. With the practical significance of ownership in equity decreasing, the English rules governing transfers of securities have become more in line with the rules prevailing in civil law countries. This development continued when the English law of uncertificated transfers was reformed in 2001.

3.4 The 2001 reforms

3.4.1 Introduction

The next step in the reform process was taken in 2001. The 2001 law reform project is an example of convergence: the Bank of England felt that the current system – in which there was a delay between the time when instructions were matched centrally with CREST and the transfer of legal title, which occurred only when the records were amended by the registrars – did not satisfy international best practice.[28]

There were a number of directions that law reform could have taken. The most direct way of bringing England in line with what was perceived to be best international practice would have been to pass a statute stating that legal ownership in uncertificated registered securities is transferred to the buyer when the records held by CRESTCo are amended. This, however, was not done; it would have required Parliament to intervene and that would have caused significant delay.

Moreover, and more importantly, the drafting of a statutory provision determining the point in time at which legal title is transferred to the transferee would have required a careful examination of the underlying common law. English common law does not enforce ownership rights by way of what is commonly known as the rei vindicatio in civil law jurisdictions. The common law does not provide for an action that results in an absolute declaration as to who holds legal title in a particular asset; the common law determines only the proprietary position as between the parties to the litigation.[29] It does not declare the successful claimant the absolute owner as against all third parties; it only

---

[28] Bank of England, *Securities Settlement Priorities Review* (March 1998); Bank of England, *Securities Settlement Priorities Review* (September 1998).

[29] Sarah Worthington, *Personal Property Law* (Oxford: Hart, 2000) 457–458.

resolves priority disputes between parties.[30] Because ownership rights are enforced only as between the parties participating in the respective dispute, there is no common law rule stating explicitly at which point in time ownership as against all third parties is vested in the transferee of registered securities. It is possible to distil from the common law the circumstances in which claims against third parties will be successful. Legal title normally vests in the buyer when her name is entered on the register of shareholders.[31] But the fact that the ownership rights are recognised in certain factual circumstances against certain claimants does not mean that title would not have vested in the transferee at an earlier point in time in different circumstances.[32]

A statutory provision attempting to determine a point in time at which absolute title is transferred to the buyer would have had to take into account the approach to the enforcement of English property law. Drafting such a provision would have required a significant amount of research on what the effect of such a provision would be on the mechanism through which English law enforces property rights. An inadequately drafted provision would not only not achieve the desired result; it could also have the effect of reducing the legal protection available to the transferee. Mistakes in drafting can cause the transferee to lose rights that would otherwise be available to her at common law. Drafting a provision determining the point in time at which title to securities vests in the transferee would have been a very difficult task, which England did not undertake.

England gave way to what was perceived as a pressure for convergence and changed its law to comply with best international practice. The way in which the change was effected is an example of how a legal system when carrying out law reform gravitates towards changing as little as possible of existing legal rules. England did not modify the common law; convergence was achieved without introducing a statutory rule regulating the point in time at which ownership vests in the transferee. England left the common law untouched and passed a rule stating that the CREST records relating to uncertificated securities constituted the register of holders of securities. USR 2001 changes only

---

[30] Michael Bridge, *Personal Property Law* (Oxford: Oxford University Press, 2002) 47, 162–164.

[31] CA 1985 s. 22; *J. Sainsbury plc* v. *O'Connor (Inspector of Taxes)* [1991] 1 WLR 963 at 977 (CA); *Re Rose, Rose* v. *Inland Revenue Commissioners* [1952] 1 Ch 499, at p 518–519 (CA); Pennington, *Company Law* 416.

[32] Pennington, *Company Law* 416–417.

the legal significance of the records kept by CREST, by transforming them into the register of uncertificated securities. This makes it possible for the English rules on priorities to continue to apply and it has the desired effect on the point in time at which the transferee acquires legal title to uncertificated securities. Because the legally significant records of uncertificated securities are now maintained by CREST, legal title to uncertificated securities normally vests in the transferee upon amendment of the CREST records. Working within the framework determined by the common law, the CREST records are classified as the shareholder register. This point will be further illustrated in subsection 3.4.2.

3.4.2 USR 2001

The electronic transfer procedure is still largely the same as it was when CREST was first implemented but CREST has in the meantime updated its Manual. The current CREST Manual was issued in December 2005; the principal structure underlying the technical detail governing transfers of uncertificated securities has, however, remained intact.

The buyer and the seller are still required to send electronic instructions through the CREST system, or to have these instructions sent on their behalf by a sponsoring user. One of the new features introduced since 1996 is that, as part of the central counterparty settlement service, instructions can now be created automatically on behalf of buyers and sellers. If a member opts to take advantage of that service, she does not have to input transfer instructions manually.

When the buyer's and the seller's instructions have entered the system, CREST still verifies if they correspond. If the instructions match, and if sufficient securities and cash are available on the buyer's and seller's respective accounts, CREST settles the transaction on settlement day. Settlement still involves an amendment of the CREST member and cash memorandum accounts together with instructions sent to the issuer and the settlement bank; USR 2001 has not interfered with the basic framework according to which CREST was originally set up.

USR 2001 has, however, had impact on the legal quality of the records maintained by the issuer and by CRESTCo, respectively.[33] When examining the changes brought about by USR 2001, we need to distinguish between two different types of securities – registered shares and other

---

[33] SI 2001/3755.

types of registered securities. The later category includes public sector securities and corporate securities other than shares. In subsections 3.4.2.1–3.4.2.2 the changes relating to both types will be examined. The new regime for registered shares will be discussed first.

3.4.2.1 Effect of entries on registers: shares

The USR 2001 abolished CA 1985, s. 361, which stated that the register of members is prima facie evidence of any matters which the Companies Act 1985 directed or authorised to be inserted in it.[34] This section gave special evidential quality only to the register maintained by or on behalf of the issuing company. The records kept by CREST, prior to USR 2001, contained the same information as the company register, but were not considered to be kept on behalf of the issuing company and were therefore not privileged by CA 1985, s. 361.

To change this, USR 2001 implemented a new regime. There are now two registers of shareholders – the Issuer register of members and the Operator (i.e. CREST) register of members. USR 2001, Sched. 4 determines the information which needs to be inserted into both registers.

The issuer register of members needs to contain the following particulars: the names and addresses of the members, the date on which each person was registered as a member and the date on which any person ceased to be a member.[35] With the names and addresses, there shall be entered a statement relating to the certificated shares held by each member.[36] The issuer register of members therefore contains records of all members irrespective of whether the shares are held in the certificated or in the uncertificated form. Certificated shares are to be identified by way of a statement.[37] There is no requirement for a special statement on uncertificated shares.

The CREST register of members needs to indicate the names and addresses of members who hold uncertificated shares in the company.[38] CREST is not required to keep records of certificated shares; it is also not required to record the dates of commencement and end of membership.

USR 2001, reg. 24 replaces the now-abolished CA 1985, s. 361 and states that a 'register of members' is prima facie evidence of any matter which is by USR 2001 directed or authorised to be inserted in it. The rule does not specify if it relates to the issuer or the Operator register of

---

[34] USR 2001, reg. 24 (4).   [35] USR 2001, Sched. 4, para. 2 (1).
[36] USR 2001, Sched. 4, para. 2 (2).   [37] USR 2001, Sched. 4, para. 2 (2).
[38] USR 2001, Sched. 4, para. 4 (1).

members. Since in USR 2001, reg. 24 and also in USR 2001, reg. 20 both registers are referred to as 'register of members', USR 2001 reg. 24 applies to both the issuer and the Operator register of members. Both the issuer and the CREST register of members constitute prima facie evidence of title to the shares and of other information contained in them by virtue of USR 2001.

USR 2001 has transformed the CREST records into the shareholder register. This upgrade is, however, subject to one important qualification. CREST is required only to maintain the register of uncertificated shares. Any records CREST may keep of certificated shares do not constitute prima facie evidence. The upgrade effected by USR 2001 privileges only CREST records of uncertificated securities.

USR 2001 has also downgraded the legal status of the register maintained by the company. The particulars entered on the issuer register of members are not considered prima facie evidence if they are inconsistent with the Operator register of members.[39] Since CREST is required by the USR 2001 to keep records only of uncertificated shares, this downgrade does not apply to certificated shares. As a result, a record on the issuer's register of members remains prima facie evidence of certificated shares, but has lost this quality in so far as the records of uncertificated shares are inconsistent with the CREST register. USR 2001 has reduced the evidential quality of the issuer records in that respect.

3.4.2.2 Effect of entries on registers: public sector securities, corporate securities other than shares

For public sector securities there now exists a CREST 'register of public sector securities' and 'records of uncertificated public sector securities' maintained by the Bank of England, the issuing local authority, or its registrar.[40] The latter records, however, do not enjoy special evidential status: only the CREST register constitutes prima facie evidence of any matters which are by USR 2001 directed or authorised to be inserted in it.[41]

For corporate securities other than shares, the issuer is no longer required to maintain a register of securities held in uncertificated form, but shall instead keep a record of entries made on the Operator register.[42] The issuer record of uncertificated securities does not

---

[39] USR 2001, reg. 24 (2).   [40] USR 2001, reg. 21 (1–3).
[41] USR 2001, reg. 24 (5).   [42] USR 2001, reg. 22 (2) b.

constitute prima facie evidence. Instead, the Operator keeps the register of uncertificated corporate securities. The Operator register provides for evidence in the same way as a register maintained by the issuer would provide for evidence.[43] USR 2001 did not interfere with any duty the issuer of corporate securities may be under to keep a register of certificated corporate securities; insofar as an issuer is under such a duty, this duty continues to exist.

3.4.2.3 Conclusions

USR 2001 upgraded the CREST records of uncertificated shares, of uncertificated public sector securities and of uncertificated corporate securities other than shares, to prima facie evidence. At the same time it downgraded the records maintained by the issuers in relation to uncertificated shares and, to an even greater extent, in relation to uncertificated corporate securities other than shares. USR 2001 has not interfered with the rules governing registers of certificated securities.

This revised transfer regime shows strong evidence of the original common law transfer procedures. The 2001 reforms serve as an example of how existing legal doctrine determines the content of the rules that will be implemented when a project of law reform is carried out: even when the aim of the law reform project is to cause a legal system to converge with what is perceived to be an international standard, national legal doctrine determines the content of the new legal rules.

This English law reform project also illustrates the nature of the influence exercised by incumbent market infrastructure providers. Keeping in line with existing legal doctrine, England decided to adopt a new rule whereby the CREST records would constitute the register of holders of securities. The proposal, however, did not carry this reform to its logical conclusion: it did not abolish the need for registers or records kept by or on behalf of issuers. USR 2001 preserves the decentralised registers for all certificated securities and also for uncertificated shares. Moreover, there continue to exist decentralised records of uncertificated securities other than shares. The reform proposal did not go so far as to abolish the need for issuer registers or records altogether.

In relation to shares, USR 2001 goes to pains to continue the decentralised shareholder register. To achieve this, the law is carefully drafted to accommodate a split register and to address issues arising out of

---

[43] USR 2001, reg. 24 (6).

possibly conflicting entries on the register. It would certainly have been easier to abolish company registers altogether and to have both certificated and uncertificated shares administered by CREST. CRESTCo should, it seems, be able to provide a service through which it converts uncertificated into certificated securities and issues paper certificates for those securities holders who prefer to hold their entitlements in a certificated form. CRESTCo should also be able to put in place the infrastructure necessary to have the shareholder register available for inspection.

It is possible to explain this continuation of decentralised registers by a desire not to interfere with the incumbent English market infrastructure. A transfer to CRESTCo of all the functions related to registered securities would have had considerable impact on the branch of the financial services industry which keeps registers on behalf of issuers and it seems likely that this delayed reform for the time being. There may, however, occur further steps of reform in the future that will increase the functions performed by CRESTCo and reduce the relevance of the services provided by registrars.

This leads to an important insight into the nature of the influence exercised by providers of market infrastructure. They are able to slow down the pace at which law reform is carried out but market infrastructure providers and the lawyers advising them are themselves limited by the legal doctrines in place in a particular legal system when law reform is carried out. They are not in a position to promote law reform that is not supported by the existing legal doctrine of a particular jurisdiction.

3.4.3 Legal title

The 2001 reform changed the rules governing the acquisition of legal title, a change which provides us with evidence of both convergence and path-dependence. The background of the 2001 reform, and the results achieved, show that convergence can occur even in an area of the law which is notoriously parochial. The way in which convergence was effected is, however, an example of path-dependent legal development. The background of the reform and its results will be discussed first.

USR 2001 goes back to a consultative paper published by the Bank of England in March 1998.[44] In the paper, the Bank sought the views of

---

[44] *Securities Settlement Priorities Review* (March 1998), available at http:\\www.bankofengland. co.uk.

market participants and other interested parties on the future of securities settlement systems in the UK. The responses to the paper were published in September of that year.[45]

One of the conclusions of the consultation process was that market participants felt that the London settlement system should comply with international settlement standards. The CREST system was criticised because it did not comply with the standards put forward by the Bank for International Settlements (BIS) and the European Central Bank (ECB). The BIS published a report in 1992 on securities settlement systems in which it identified settlement risks and analysed the functioning of the systems then operative.[46] The report emphasised that the payment of the purchase price and the delivery of securities should be as closely as possible linked to each other.[47] The report defined delivery of securities as the final transfer of securities:[48] in an ideal world, the buyer would become the owner of securities at the same time as the seller received the purchase money. In a report published in November 1997, the European Monetary Institute (EMI), the predecessor of the ECB, further developed the BIS principles. It identified nine criteria for assessing the quality of securities settlement systems that go beyond the BIS recommendations.[49]

CREST was designed to approach the BIS principles by means of a specific delivery versus payment mechanism. But the 1995 CREST mechanism did not fully achieve the delivery versus payment ideal; moreover, CREST did not fully comply with the upgraded standards issued by the EMI after CREST had been implemented. One of the deficiencies was that the final transfer (that is, the acquisition of legal title by the buyer) depended upon the issuer receiving the CREST instruction and registering the buyer's name. The conclusion of the consultation process carried out by the Bank of England was that this deficiency should be eliminated.[50]

---

[45] *Securities Settlement Priorities Review* (September 1998), available at http:\\www.bankofengland.co.uk.

[46] Committee on Payment and Settlement Systems (CPSS) of the Central Banks of the Group of Ten Countries, *Delivery Versus Payment in Securities Settlement Systems*, CPSS Publications 6 (Basle: Bank for International Settlements 1992).

[47] See the summary of the report at 1–9.   [48] At A2–3.

[49] *Standards for the Use of EU Securities Settlement Systems in ESCB Credit Operations* (Frankfurt am Main: Bank for International Settlements 1997); see also ECB, *Assessment of EU Securities Settlement Systems Against the Standards for their Use in ESCB Credit Operations* (Frankfurt am Main: Bank for International Settlements 1998).

[50] *Securities Settlement Priorities Review* (September 1998), para. 69.

The 2001 reforms are an example of convergence. The legislature intervened to make the English settlement system comply with international rules perceived by market participants to reflect best practice. English law was changed to converge with common international rules.

The method through which the reform was achieved is consistent with the path adopted by English law. The easiest way to bring forward the point in time at which the transferee acquires legal ownership would, of course, have been the adoption of a rule expressly stating that legal title vests in the transferee upon amendment of the Operator's records. This, however, did not happen. The reform process had to work around a notorious path-immanent obstacle. The English Parliament finds it very difficult to make time for legislation in the area of commercial law; it can be assumed that the forces driving the 2001 reform process felt that there was a fairly low chance that Parliament would be able to make time to adopt legislation legislation introducing a new rule on legal title on uncertificated securities. To be able to respond to market demands in a timely fashion, the authorities preferred to implement the reform through a statutory instrument (SI). This meant that the reform was effected in an indirect way.

The scope of an SI is, of course, determined by the provision enabling the relevant authority to act. The legal basis that was available for the 2001 reform was, unfortunately, limited. It did not seem to contain vires for interfering with the common law.

USR 2001 was adopted under CA 1989, s. 207. This provision gives authority to 'The Secretary of State ... [to] ... make provision by regulations for enabling title to securities to be evidenced and transferred without a written instrument'. The regulations may make provision for procedures for recording and transferring title to securities, and for the regulation of those procedures and the persons responsible for or involved in their operation.[51] CA 1989, s. 207 seems to give power to the Secretary of State only to reform transfer procedure and does not contain a power to change substantive property law.

USR 2001 does not directly interfere with the common law rules; the common law position continues to be that legal title vests in the transferee when her name is entered on the register of securities holders.[52] USR 2001 changes only the legal significance of the records kept by CREST, by transforming them into the register of uncertificated

---

[51] CA 1989, s. 207 (2).
[52] CA 1985, s. 22; J. Sainsbury plc v. O'Connor (Inspector of Taxes) [1991] 1 WLR 963 at 977 (CA); Re Rose, Rose v. Inland Revenue Commissioners [1952] 1 Ch 499, at 518–519 (CA).

securities. This has the desired effect on the point in time at which the transferee acquires legal title to uncertificated securities. Because the legally significant records of uncertificated securities are now maintained by CREST, legal title to uncertificated securities vests in the transferee upon amendment of the CREST records.

Working within the framework determined by the common law, the CREST records are classified as a shareholder register. The legal qualification of these records, but also the fact that, as already mentioned, the central CREST register is organised by issuer and not according to investors, is a function of the legal rules that were in place when the reform process was carried out. New law needs to fit with existing rules: even if the declared aim of new rules is to achieve convergence, this can be effected only by a reform that stays within the path adopted by the legal system concerned.[53]

3.4.4 Equitable title

Consistently with the legal doctrine prevailing in England, ownership in equity continues to play a role under USR 2001. Like USR 1995, USR 2001 does not abolish the equitable rules on ownership that developed in relation to paper transfers. USR 2001 also continues to have an explicit rule that refers to instances in which equitable ownership arises when uncertificated securities are transferred through CREST. Notwithstanding this, the practical role of equitable ownership has been further reduced under the new regime.

USR 2001 brought forward the point in time at which the buyer acquires legal ownership to uncertificated securities. The buyer of uncertificated shares, for example, now becomes the legal owner of those shares when the shares are credited to her CREST account. Under the rules implemented by USR 1995, equitable title would pass to the buyer at that point in time and legal title would not pass to the buyer until the register maintained by or on behalf of the issuer had been updated. To comply with international best practice, the rules were changed by USR 2001: the CREST records now constitute the shareholder register of uncertificated shares and the transferee acquires legal title when the CREST accounts are amended.

Equitable ownership now arises only as a result of the express provision in USR 2001 when securities are converted from the uncertificated to the certificated form. When uncertificated securities are transferred

---

[53] See also pp. 74–75.

to a transferee who prefers to hold them in certificated form, the transfer process incorporates a conversion of securities. This means that the relevant number of uncertificated securities is deleted from the Operator register of members. The Operator sends an instruction to the issuer for it to enter the relevant securities as certificated securities on the issuer register and at the same time to register the name of the transferee. There is a time lag between the deletion of the uncertificated securities and the entry of certificated securities on the issuer register. USR 2001, reg. 31 (2) states that the transferor shall retain legal title until the transferee's name is entered on the issuer register. It also provides for the transferee to acquire equitable title to the securities during that period.

It is worth noting here that the 2001 reform was undertaken even though the 1995 regime already complied with international practice. The transferee acquired a proprietary interest upon amendment of the records of the settlement system. This interest, however, was an equitable and not a legal interest. Civil lawyers are often puzzled by the concept of equitable ownership. The London market did not want to explain the difference between law and equity to Continental European investors;[54] it preferred to offer a system that was familiar to civil as well as common law investors. This is one of the reasons why the law was changed to allow for legal title to vest in the buyer when the securities were transferred on the books of the CREST settlement system and was a further example of convergence in this area of the law.

3.4.5 Conclusions

The law reform that was carried out in 2001 is an example of convergence. The aim of the reform was to adapt the English settlement system to best international practice. In order to achieve this, the point in time at which the buyer became the legal owner of securities was brought forward. This resulted in a further reduction of the practical significance of the English rules on ownership in equity. Nevertheless, the form in which the reform was carried out was determined by orthodox English legal doctrine. No attempt was made to create rules from scratch. Instead of putting in place new rules of property law, the reform was carried out consistently with the existing legal framework by classifying the CREST records as securities register. The reforms also show the persistent influence of market infrastructure

---

[54] CRESTCo, *International Securities in CREST* (London: CRESTCo 1998).

providers, who have benefited from the fact that the 2001 reform continued to provide for decentralised issuer registers.

3.5 Summary of the analysis

The analysis contained in this chapter showed that, until 1996, all English securities were transferred by means of paper documents. When the handling of paper certificates became too cumbersome, securities were dematerialised. English securities certificates constitute documents of evidence only: they do not, for example, like German or Austrian securities certificates, incorporate the entitlement to which the securities relate. This may have been one of the reasons why England found it easy to opt for dematerialisation. It will be shown in part II that, in contrast, Germany and Austria opted for immobilisation when their legal systems had reached a point when paper certificates became to cumbersome to handle.

The process whereby uncertificated securities were introduced in England was beset with difficulties. The first attempt to introduce an uncertificated transfer system (Talisman) had to be abandoned; it collapsed under the influence of diverging lobby groups. Market infrastructure providers succeeded in delaying reform and the Bank of England had to intervene to introduce the current CREST settlement system.

There would have been numerous ways in which a transfer system that looked after all interest groups concerned could have been devised. The individuals carrying out the law reform supporting the change to paperless transfers did not even attempt to explore alternative options available to them; dematerialisation was effected simply by modifying the legal doctrinal rules already in place.

The transfer process within CREST replicates the paper-based transfer process. When it was first introduced, CREST was only a service centre through which electronic instructions rather than paper documents were matched and forwarded to the issuer. The records maintained by CREST in relation to uncertificated securities have, in the meantime, been upgraded to constitute prima facie evidence of title to the securities, but the architecture of the system and the property law governing transfers has remained firmly rooted within English property law doctrine. There continues to be a distinction between legal and equitable title to the securities: ownership is not defined in absolute terms as it would be in a civil law system, but continues to exist as a relative entitlement.

Nevertheless, convergence can be observed. The reforms carried out in 2001 are examples of an attempt of the English securities market to adopt rules that are internationally competitive. This has, however, been achieved by bringing English law functionally into line with what seems to have emerged as an international standard of best practice. The form in which the change was implemented was determined by the legal doctrinal rules that already prevailed in England and that can be traced back to the time when securities first emerged on the English market.

4   Impact on the institutional framework

One of the conclusions of chapters 2 and 3 was that the legal doctrine that prevailed when securities first emerged impacted on the process through which paper documents were eliminated from the transfer process. The influence attributable to the legal doctrine that governs investment securities will be further explored in this chapter.

The first observation to be made in this context is that English legal doctrine had an impact on the type of service provider that emerged in England to support transfers of securities. Because the law of novation became the legal doctrine according to which securities were transferred when they first emerged in England, the issuers became involved in the administration of securities transfers. Over time, service providers came into existence that assisted issuers to maintain registers. These service providers are referred to as registrars; their business is to maintain registers on behalf of issuers. The emergence of this particular type of financial services industry can be explained by the legal doctrine that governs securities transfers.

Moreover, because English registered securities do not constitute negotiable instruments, but are documents of evidence only, English market participants do not have the same need as German or Austrian market participants to keep certificates safe.[1] If an English certificate is stolen or lost, the owner does not need to fear that a third party may acquire the securities in good faith.[2] This helps to explain why England

---

[1] For this, see chapter 11.

[2] The fact that the English registered securities do not constitute negotiable instruments does not mean that the purchasers of such securities are not protected against adverse claims. English law uses the rules on estoppel to protect buyers in certain circumstances in the case of unauthorised transfers. Other than in German and Austrian law, however, the buyer is compensated by the issuer and the original owner does not lose her title for

did not develop depositories for the purpose of handling registered securities; it also helps to explain why England may have found it easier to create dematerialised securities than Germany or Austria, where securities are considered to be tangibles.

It has already been mentioned that the law of novation is likely to have shaped the transfer rules that govern transfers carried out through paper documents.[3] The paper transfer process has in turn shaped the procedural rules that govern transfers of uncertificated securities within CREST.[4] Both observations go to show that legal doctrine has an influence on the type of infrastructure that emerges in a particular market.

Ever since the 2001 reforms, CREST has centrally maintained the registers of uncertificated securities other than shares. The register of uncertificated shares has also been centralised in the sense that the particulars contained on the CREST register have priority over the particulars contained in the issuer register. The way in which the central registers are organised also shows the influence of legal doctrine on market infrastructure.

There are two principal ways of organising a central register of securities. It is possible to structure such a register according to owners: if that is done, there will be an entry for every investor, against which the securities held by that person are recorded. The alternative is to organise a central securities register according to issuer: in that case, entries are made for every type of security issued by an individual issuer. Against those entries, the names of investors are recorded. Both methods achieve the same result: they provide for a means of identifying the individuals who hold title to securities.

Which of the two approaches is implemented in a particular legal system can nevertheless be explained as a function of the original path it adopted. In England, securities transfers are traditionally administered by issuers. It is no surprise, then, that USR 2001 requires the central register to be organised according to issuer. USR 2001, reg. 20 (1) explicitly states that 'in respect of every company . . . there shall be a register . . . maintained by the operator'. The structure of the current settlement system is shaped by the path originally adopted by English law.

---

the securities, Eva Micheler, 'Legal Title and the Transfer of Shares in a Paperless World – Farewell Quasi-Negotiability', *Journal of Business Law* 2002 358; Robert Pennington, *Company Law*, 8th edn. (London: Butterworths, 2001) 407–416.

[3] See section 2.3.   [4] See section 3.3.

The examples referred to in this chapter show that legal rules are more than a function of the balance of economic power prevailing between market participants. Market participants operate within a given legal framework; they are not restricted in innovating new ways of carrying out their business. The legal form which such innovations takes, however, is determined by existing legal doctrine. Once a new form has established itself, market participants innovate further and create service providers corresponding to this structure. The type of service provided by these new institutions – and, therefore, the setup of the new market infrastructure – continues to be subject to the doctrinal legal framework within which market participants have to operate.

5   Defective issues

5.1 Introduction

In chapters 2 and 3, the rules governing securities transfers were analysed. The aim of these chapters was to determine the procedural rules
according to which, and the point in time at which, the buyer became
the owner of the securities she purchased. The analysis was based on two
assumptions. The first was that the securities concerned had been
validly issued. The second was that the seller had authority to sell the
securities. In chapters 5 and 6, the rules that apply when these preconditions are not satisfied will be examined. Defective issues will be
analysed first and then in chapter 6 the rules governing unauthorised
transfers.

Securities are issued under a contractual arrangement between the
issuer and the person buying the securities from the issuer. It is possible
for this buyer to keep the securities throughout the issuer's existence or
until the securities have reached their maturity and are reimbursed.
This, however, will not happen in many cases. Securities are issued to
circulate in the market; investors buy them precisely because they want
to be able to sell them at any given point in time.

Because securities issues have a contractual basis, it is possible for
the contract underlying the issue to be defective. This can result in the
issuer having equities that it can raise against the buyer of the securities. If such equities exist, it is important to know if the issuer is able to
raise them not only against the original buyer, but also against anyone
who subsequently acquires the securities.

If the equities are good against subsequent purchasers, every purchaser would have to make enquiries as to the validity of the issue in
order to be certain that the right she had bought was not subject to
equities. This either delays transactions – or, more likely, affects the

price that issuers can achieve for the securities issued. If the risk of defective issues is to be borne by a subsequent buyer, subsequent buyers will price that risk and reduce the price they would otherwise be happy to pay for securities accordingly. This will also have a knock-on effect on the price the issuer achieves when securities are first issued. Because it is unknown to the market which securities are subject to equities, the market will discount all issues.

A rule allowing an issuer to enforce equities against subsequent buyers increases the cost of capital market-based finance. This should not be the case; in an ideal world the price of a security is entirely determined by an evaluation of the risk and the potential of the issuer's business. The rules governing transactions should not create a cost that negatively affects security prices. In order to avoid transaction cost, and to increase the efficiency of the securities transfers, legal systems have developed techniques that insulate buyers of securities against equities arising from defective issues.

English law has developed two mechanisms for protecting the market against equities arising out of a defective allotment. Both are shaped path-consistently by the legal techniques available to English private law. The first is *novation* and the second is estoppel. They will be examined in turn in sections 5.2–5.4.

5.2 Novation

The conclusion of section 2.1 was that the historic starting point seems to have been that securities were transferred by way of novation. Transfers originally involved an explicit admission by the issuer of the transferee; the transferee was, therefore, insulated against equities arising out of the contract between the issuer and the transferor. Her contract with the issuer was independent of the relationship that existed between the issuer, the transferor and any other investors who held securities before her.

We need to ask ourselves if we can continue to apply this analysis today how the transfer procedure has changed. The first change was brought about by the arrival of free transferability. When securities became freely transferable, the issuer became obliged to register transfers either by virtue of a provision to that effect in the issuing documentation or by a change in the default rules set up by the Companies Act. The existence of an obligation to register transfers does not in and of itself affect the transfer process; transfers of transferable securities may, in principle, still be analysed in terms of novation. Novation, however, requires the consent of the issuer to create a new and independent relationship with the transferee.[1] The novation analysis, therefore, can continue to apply only if the transfer process continues to involve a contractually binding statement on behalf of the issuer.

It is conceivable that companies which issued transferable securities at first continued to take securities transfers to the board of directors and to have board decisions resolving to admit transferees. It those circumstances there is no difficulty with classifying the board decision as the issuer's consent to creating a new and independent relationship with the transferee. It is also possible for issuers to organise the transfer process so that the board delegates the authority to admit transferees to the secretary or an employee. The person so authorised would then act as an agent for the issuer and in that capacity consent to the novation.

Over time, however, a distinct act of admission seems to have disappeared. Lord Halsbury observed at the beginning of the twentieth century that 'the corporation is simply ministerial in registering a valid transfer and issuing fresh certificates'.[2]

The problem of squaring the historically determined legal analysis with modern transfer procedure arises to an even greater extent when shares are issued and transferred in uncertificated form. With USR 2001, the issuer register has ceased to be of legal significance for transfers of uncertificated securities, as we saw in chapter 3. The Operator register now constitutes prima facie evidence of legal title to uncertificated securities. It would, of course, be possible to argue that the CREST maintains the register as an agent of the issuer and in that capacity admits transferees. CREST, however, does itself not explicitly admit transferees. Transfers of uncertificated securities are automated; the Operator register is amended in response to electronic instructions and it is difficult to see how this process could be analysed in terms of novation.

The registration of a transfer has been transformed into a simple administrative process. Current transfer practice has stopped containing an element of explicit consent aimed at creating a new and independent contract with the transferee. We need to ask ourselves, therefore, if we can continue to address securities transfers through the law of novation.

---

[1] Guenter Treitel, *The Law of Contract*, 11th edn. (London: Sweet & Maxwell, 2003) 673.
[2] *Sheffield Corporation* v. *Barclay* [1905] AC 392 at 396.

The courts are, unfortunately, silent on this point. There is no authority explicitly stating that the registration of the name of the transferee of transferable securities would amount to a novation of the issuing contract.

5.2.1 Novation by operation of law

One way of upholding the traditional analysis would be to conclude that the statutory rules requiring the company to register a share transfer provide for a novation by operation of law. Under CA 1985, s. 14, the memorandum and the articles bind the company and its members to the same extent as if they had, respectively, been signed and sealed by each member. This provision, however, does not indicate the process through which membership is transferred to a new member.

Another provision to consider in this context is CA 1985, s. 182, which states that shares are transferable in the manner provided by the company's articles but subject to the Stock Transfer Act 1963. Under CA 1985, s. 183 (1), it is not lawful for the company to register a transfer of shares unless an instrument of transfer has been delivered to it. CA 1985, s. 183 (5) requires a company which refuses to register a transfer to notify the transferee within two months after the date on which the transfer was lodged. It is difficult to see how the language used in these provisions could be construed as providing for a novation of the membership contract by operation of law. The rules, it seems, are concerned with the administration of share transfers rather than with the legal nature of the transfer process.

The last – and, perhaps, most promising – statutory rule is CA 1985, s. 22. That provision, as we have seen, states that 'a person who agrees to become a member of a company, and whose name is entered in its register of members, is a member of the company'. The wording of the rule suggests that there is some contractual element to the transfer of shares.

CA 1985, s. 22 (2), however, refers only to the agreement of the transferee to be a member of the company. It does not suggest that upon registration the company is deemed to have agreed to a new and independent relationship with the transferee. The provision altogether refrains from classifying the legal nature of transfers of shares; it certainly does not suggest that registration amounts to an extinction of the membership contract with the transferor and the creation of a new membership contract with the transferee.

There also exists an explicit provision in the Companies Act 1985 stating that the shareholders' register provides only for prima facie evidence of the shareholder's entitlement.[3] It seems that there is no alteration of existing rights, or creation of new rights based on entries in the register.[4]

There is, therefore, no obvious statutory basis supporting the proposition that a share transfer amounts to a novation by operation of law.

5.2.2 Novation by contract

Alternatively, it is possible to revert back to analysing transfers in terms of contract law, by propounding the argument that the company, when adopting its issuing documentation, has two alternatives in relation to securities transfers. The company can opt to have articles that restrict transfers, or it can decide to adopt the statutory default position whereby shares are freely transferable. If the company chooses to issue freely transferable shares it thereby agrees to all the transfers that will occur in the future.

Putting the argument in terms of contract law, the company would, upon incorporation, make an offer to all future transferees to accept them as shareholders provided that they are able to produce the documents necessary to have their name registered. The membership contract would then be novated when a transferee applied to the company to have her name registered and lodged the necessary documents with the company. This application would amount to an acceptance of the standing offer contained in the company's articles. The same analysis would apply if shares were issued in uncertificated form. In the case of uncertificated shares, the electronic application of the buyer to have the shares transferred into her name would be classified as the acceptance of the offer contained in the issuer's underlying documentation.

A similar scenario arises in the context of credit card transactions. There, the credit card company enters into two agreements. The first is concluded between the credit card company and the retailer: the credit card company agrees to pay all debt owed to the retailer arising out of card transactions. The second is concluded between the credit card company and the customer: the customer promises to pay to the credit card company all debt that arises out of her using the credit card. Whenever a customer and a retailer enter into a sales transaction and the customer pays by credit card, the debt arising out of the sales

---

[3] CA 1985, s. 361; CA 1985, s. 186.
[4] D. Frase, 'Dematerialisation and Taurus', [1991] *Butterworths Journal of International Banking and Finance Law* 73.

contract is extinguished and two new obligations arise. The first arises under the agreement between the credit card company and the retailer and obliges the credit card company to pay an amount equivalent to the purchase price but reduced by the transaction fee to the retailer. The second arises under the agreement between the credit card company and the customer and obliges the customer to pay an amount equivalent to the purchase price to the credit card company. This process whereby the debt under the sales contract is extinguished and replaced by other debt has been classified as novation.[5]

Credit card transactions are of interest here because when the sale transaction is carried out novation occurs without the retailer, the customer, or the credit card company explicitly agreeing to the extinction of one obligation and the creation of a new one. The respective agreement is contained in the underlying documentation which was signed by the parties when the credit card relationship was originally set up.

In the case of a securities transfer, a similar argument could be put forward. The argument would be that the issuer's agreement to the novation would not be given upon each transfer, but was contained in the company's articles or the contract underlying the bond issue. There is, however, one important difference. In the case of a credit card transaction there will be explicit terms in the agreement between the credit card company and both the retailer and the consumer. In the case of share transfers no such explicit terms exists.

Table A, reg. 23 to the Companies Act 1985 simply states that the instrument of transfer of a share may be in any usual form or in any form which the directors may approve, and shall be executed by or on behalf of the transferor. Table A, reg. 24 empowers directors to refuse to register transfers of unpaid shares or transfers of shares on which the company has a lien. There is no provision in Table A explicitly stating that upon registration the company terminates the relationship with the previous shareholder and enters a new contractual relationship with the transferee.

The consent to a novation of the membership contract would have to be inferred from the fact that the company issued transferable securities and carried out the registration procedure in relation to the

---

[5] Treitel, *The Law of Contract* 702; *Customs and Excise Commissioners* v. *Diners Club Ltd* [1989] 1 WLR 1196.

transferee. Under the standard terms, a contractually relevant state-ment would have to be read into a document which provides for an administrative procedure and is not concerned with committing the company to legally classifying the transfers. It is difficult to see how, in the circumstances, such an analysis could be adopted.

Moreover, whereas in the case of a credit card transaction there will be agreements between all parties concerned, in the case of a securities transfer there is no underlying agreement between the company and the transferee. When the company was first set up, the number of potential transferees was unlimited and would continue to be so throughout the company's existence. Credit card transactions will, in contrast, occur only between customers and retailers who have agreed to join a particular credit card scheme. Securities transfers occur between transferors who are currently members or creditors of the company and transferees who have no prior relationship with the issuer. It is therefore difficult to apply to share transfers the analysis adopted in relation to credit card transactions.

Finally, and perhaps most promisingly, the classification of the trans-fer process as novation could be upheld on the basis that the company is prominently involved in the verification of the transfer documents. Even if the issuer does not explicitly admit the transferee as a new member it nevertheless examines the transfer documents and com-pares the information contained in them with the data on the register. This involves a decision-making process on the part of the company which involves an act of will and has contractual elements.

5.2.3 Novation as a fiction

Notwithstanding these difficulties, the current orthodox view seems to be that transfers of transferable securities continue to involve a nova-tion of contractual rights.[6]

In the light of modern transfer practice, however, this analysis has become fictitious. The fiction is that the issuer accepts the offer of the transferee, agreeing to enter into a new membership or debt contract with her and, at the same time, terminates the contract with the transferor.

An unease with the continued application of the novation analysis seems to be reflected in academic writing by the ominous silence as to the classification of securities transfers under modern conditions. Both

---

[6] Robert Pennington, *Company Law*, 8th edn. (London: Butterworths, 2001) 398–399; Joanna Benjamin, *Interests in Securities* (Oxford: Oxford University Press, 2001) 3.05.

Robert Pennington in his seminal text on company law and Joanna Benjamin in her pathbreaking monograph on interests in securities trace the historical roots of registered share transfers and conclude that registered shares, historically, used to be transferred by way of novation. Both authors stop short of making a statement as to whether this analysis continues to be accurate in the current legal climate.[7]

It is telling that both books refrain from a definitive statement in this respect. It is possible that both authors see some difficulty in stating outright that modern share transfers are, in the same way as their historical counterparts, to be classified as novations. The authors, however, also refrain from adopting any new analysis that would classify share transfers in terms other than novation. They fail to explain how the traditional analysis is to be applied to modern transfer practice. It seems as if a new explanation is needed to do justice to share transfers in the face of modern transfer procedure. Before an attempt is made to advance such an explanation, the second mechanism through which English law protects buyers against defective issues will be examined.

5.3 Defective issues and estoppel

The second mechanism English law has used to protect buyers from equities arising out of the relationship between the seller (or any of her predecessors) and the issuer is perhaps even more than the first firmly embedded in English law. English law has achieved protection for the buyer by making use of its rules on evidence.

The purchaser of securities is, in certain circumstances, protected by the rules on estoppel. Securities certificates are prima facie evidence of the title of the member in whose name the certificate has been issued.[8] If the transferee acquires shares relying on certificates issued by the issuer in the transferor's name, the company is estopped from denying the transferor's title to the securities.[9] Likewise, if the company issues certificates representing that the shares have been fully paid by the transferor, it is estopped from proving the contrary against the transferee.[10] It has been suggested that similar rules apply to shares which have been defectively issued.[11]

---

[7] Pennington, *Company Law* 398–399; Benjamin, *Interests in Securities* 3.05.
[8] CA 1985, s. 186.   [9] See section 6.2.
[10] *Burkishaw* v. *Nicolls* (1878) 3 App Cas 1004; *Bloomenthal* v. *Ford* [1897] AC 156.
[11] Pennington, *Company Law* 405, referring to *Re General Estates Co.* (1868) LR 3 Ch 758; *Romford Canal Company* (1883) 24 ChD 85; *Webb* v. *Herne Bay Commissioners* (1870) LR 5 QB 642.

The rules on estoppel achieve a result comparable to the result achieved by the rules governing negotiable instruments. They transform shares into an asset that exists largely independently of the rules by which it was created. Relying on authority relating to debentures, it is possible to argue that the company, by issuing certificates and by registering transfers, represents that the shares have been validly issued and is therefore estopped from proving the contrary to a bona fide purchaser for value.[12]

These rules, however, were developed in an environment in which the company, or an agent on its behalf, issued certificates and registered transfers and thereby made representations to every individual transferee. The normal procedure was that the purchaser entered into an agreement with the seller upon having been presented with certificates issued by the company. The company was bound because of the representation it had made 'on the face' of the certificates.[13]

It is unclear, how, if at all, these rules protect the purchaser of uncertificated securities. When uncertificated shares are transferred, the contract is not entered into on the strength of a representation by the company; there are no certificates and the parties do not consult the register before they enter into a transaction. Securities are transferred through CREST and CREST does not make any representations to the buyer prior to her agreeing to buy securities.

5.4 Securities as negotiable rights

The final argument that may be advanced in order to insulate the transferee against equities is that securities are transferable under a statutory provision.[14] This provision does not provide that the transfer is subject to equities. Pennington writes that where a chose in action is assignable at law in this way, a purchaser for value takes it free of equities of which she is unaware.[15] Pennington supports this proposition by reference to

---

[12] Pennington, *Company Law* 405.

[13] *Webb* v. *Herne Bay Commissioners* (1870) LR 5 QB 642 at 651 per Cockburn J: 'The debentures on their face import a legal consideration', at 653 per Blackburn J: 'on the face of which it was expressly stated'; *Romford Canal Company* (1883) 24 ChD 85 at 92 per Kay J: 'represent on the face of them.'

[14] Companies Act 1985, s. 182 (1) b states, 'the shares or other interest of any member of a company . . . are transferable in a manner provided by the company's articles, but subject to the Stock Transfer Act 1963'.

[15] Pennington *Company Law* 405.

the authority on debentures. The cases he cites, however, appear to rely on estoppel or contract rather than the statutory rule governing their transferability.[16] Moreover, there is also a more general statutory provision providing for the assignment of choses in action.[17] This provision does not mention equities either, and there is no doubt that the assignee of an ordinary debt is subject to equities. For these reasons, the fact that the Companies Act is silent on the topic does not show that transfers take effect free of existing equities.

Nonetheless, Pennington's argument contains an important idea. This idea has also been voiced by J. S. Ewart, albeit in relation to estoppel and negotiable instruments.[18] Securities are rights of a certain kind; they are created to circulate in a liquid market. Ewart used the term 'ambulatory rights'. German scholars have also noticed this feature. Georg Opitz coined the term '*Wertrechte*' as referring to rights that enjoy negotiability notwithstanding the fact that they are not represented by paper documents.[19] H. Staub and O. Pisko classify securities as rights whose content is not determined by the act which created them but by their outward appearance in the market:[20] the nature of the asset justifies the disapplication of equities. This reason applies irrespective of whether there is an immediate representation by the issuing company or reliance by the transferee. The issuer is bound because it allowed securities, which are by their nature ambulatory, to be processed by CREST. This, of course, goes beyond orthodox notions of contract law as well as orthodox principles of estoppel, but may help us to understand the legal mechanics of modern transfer systems.

5.5 Summary of the analysis

The conclusion of this chapter is that English law uses two doctrinal tools to protect purchasers against equities arising out of defective issues. The first is the doctrine of novation, the second the law of estoppel. Both were developed in relation to certificated transfers but,

---

[16] *Re Romford Canal Company* (1883) 24 ChD 85 at 92–93 (estoppel); *Higgs* v. *Assam Tea Company* (1869) LR 4 Exch 387 at 394–396 (contract).

[17] LPA 1925, s. 136.

[18] J. S. Ewart, 'Negotiability and Estoppel', (1900) 16 *LQR* 135 at 142–144.

[19] Georg Opitz, *Fünfzig depotrechtliche Abhandlungen* (Berlin: Walter de Gruyter, 1954) 432–433, 721–723, 444–448.

[20] H. Staub and O. Pisko, *Kommentar zum Allgemeinen Deutschen Handelsgesetzbuch, Ausgabe für Österreich, Band II*, 2nd edn. (1910) Art. 307, para. 5.

in principle, continue to apply in relation to uncertificated transfers. England did not abolish the common law when it made it possible for companies to issue uncertificated securities; English legal doctrine will therefore continue along the path which it had previously adopted.

Notwithstanding this, it is currently difficult to see how the rules on novation and the law of estoppel apply to modern share transfers. Issuers no longer explicitly approve of securities transfers. The rules on estoppel were developed against a background of paper certificates and are therefore very difficult to apply when shares are transferred electronically. Nevertheless academic writers address securities transfers by referring to the historic starting point of the law and seem to suggest, without explicitly committing themselves, that the historic analysis still applies today. It is possible to explain the continuation of a rule protecting the buyer against equities arising out of the original issue by referring to the special nature of the rights concerned; this explanation, however, goes beyond the orthodox law of contract as well as the orthodox law of estoppel. The English courts have yet to analyse defective issues of uncertificated securities. When they do, they will apply the law in a manner that is predetermined by the path previously adopted by English legal doctrine.

From a comparative perspective it is important to note that English law has achieved a similar outcome as German and Austrian law. All the three legal systems have developed a mechanism protecting investors against defective issues. It will also become clear in chapter 10 that in addition to this functional similarity there even exists a doctrinal overlap between the three jurisdictions. It will also be shown that, similar to English law, German and Austrian law have yet to come to terms with applying their traditional analysis to modern securities transfers.[21] There is no evidence, however, that either of these systems will solve this difficulty by leaving the doctrinal path they have previously followed.

The focus of this chapter were the rules protecting buyers of securities against equities that exist because the securities concerned were issued under a defective contract. The focus of chapter 6 are the rules that apply when securities are transferred by a buyer who was not authorised to do so.

---

[21] For German and Austrian law see section 10.3.

6   Unauthorised transfers

6.1 Introduction

When an asset is sold under English law, the buyer acquires title to the asset only if the seller has authority to sell the asset concerned. The risk of an unauthorised transfer is thus carried by the buyer, who is left to sue the transferor, who may not be in a position to satisfy a claim. The same general rule also applies when securities are transferred.

The general rule is supported by the principle that no one can transfer an asset she does not herself have.[1] If the principle applied to transfers of securities without exception, all transfers of securities would necessarily involve the risk that the seller did not have authority to sell. The possibility that the risk materialises would be reflected in the purchase price a market buyer was willing to pay for already issued securities. The fact that the secondary market would apply a discount compensating for the risk of unauthorised transfers also reduces the price achievable by the issuer when securities are first issued.

Ideally, securities transfers do not involve legal risk of this type. The price of securities should not be deflated by transfer rules that create risk for market participants. England, like Germany and Austria,[2] has developed rules that contain the risk of unauthorised transfers for the benefit of the buyer. The rules adopted by England, on the one hand, and by Germany and Austria, on the other, stand on different doctrinal bases. They nevertheless achieve a similar level of protection. In this chapter the English approach will be analysed. The German and Austrian approaches will be analysed in chapter 10.

---

[1] The Latin proverb expressing this rule is '*nemo plus iuris transfere potest quam ipse habet*'.
[2] See section 10.2.

In England, the risk of unauthorised transfers is contained in the application of certain rules of evidence. The rules adopted by English law with a view to allocating the risk of an unauthorised transfer away from the buyer does not involve a change in the substantive entitlement to the securities. English law has opted not to interfere with the legal owner's title and applies the rules on estoppel to protect the buyer by allocating transfer risk to the issuer. Estoppel is a legal technique that restricts the issuer in proving that the buyer does not hold legal title to the securities; because the issuer is unable to prove that the buyer is not entitled to the securities it has to put the buyer in the financial position she would be in if she were the legal owner. The effect of the operation of the estoppel rules in this context has been described as 'negotiability by estoppel'.[3] The application of the rules of estoppel will be discussed in sections 6.2–6.3.

Section 6.2 contains an analysis of the rules that apply to certificated securities. The position of the legal owner of these securities will be examined first and then the issuer's liability and the liability of the person who instructed the issuer to amend the register will be discussed. In section 6.3 the law in relation to uncertificated securities will be examined. As with certificated securities the position of the legal owner will be analysed first; CRESTCo's and the issuer's liability will then be addressed.

6.2 Certificated securities and estoppel

6.2.1 Restoration of the legal owner's name on the register

Under English law, the legal owner of registered securities loses her entitlement only if she authorises a transfer,[4] waives her rights, or is otherwise estopped from proving her entitlement.[5] The legal owner does not carry the risk of unauthorised transfers.

If securities are transferred without the legal owner's authority she may sue the issuer to have the register rectified and to receive dividends and other benefits that have fallen due since the securities were transferred out of her name.[6] This rule applies notwithstanding the fact that

---

[3] W. Blair, 'Negotiability and Estoppel' [1988] *The Company Lawyer* 8 at 10; M Hapgood, *Paget's Law of Banking*, 12th edn., (London: Butterworths, 2003) 654.

[4] *Coles* v. *The Bank of England* (1839) 10 Ad & E 437, 113 ER 166; *Welch* v. *The Bank of England* [1955] 1 Ch 508; *Dixon* v. *Kennaway & Co.* [1900] 1 Ch 833.

[5] *Barton* v. *London and North Western Railway Co.* (1889) 24 QBD 77; see also *Davis* v. *The Bank of England* (1834) 2 Bing 39 , 130 ER 357.

[6] *Re Bahia and San Francisco Rly Co.* (1868) LR 3 QB 584; *Kai Yung* v. *Hong Kong and Shanghai Banking Corporation* [1981] AC 787; *Simm* v. *Anglo-American Telegraph Company* (1879) 5 QBD 188.

the buyer's name has been entered on the register. A change in the register does not interfere with the rights of the legal owner.[7]

The buyer acquires title only if her seller had authority to sell. Such authority can be express or implied. No authority will, however, be inferred from the fact that the owner entrusted a broker or an employee with transfer documents where that person used the documents to forge a transfer.[8] The legal owner is likewise not bound by a transaction effected by a co-trustee.[9] Moreover, she does not lose title if she fails to respond to notifications by the company warning her that a transfer has been lodged in relation to her shares.[10]

When an unauthorised transfer comes to light, the buyer's name will be removed from the register. The buyer cannot prevent the removal of her name from the register; in certain circumstances, however (analysed below) she will receive an indemnity from the issuer.

6.2.2 Liability of the issuer

The buyer whose name has been removed from the register may claim indemnity from the company if she had originally acquired the securities in reliance on certificates issued by it. English securities certificates are issued in the name of the legal owner and state her entire holding of a particular type of security. A certificate states, for example, that Jane Bloggs is the registered owner of 100 type A securities.

If Jane Bloggs is not the legal owner, the issuer will be liable to anyone who purchased the securities in reliance on the certificate showing her as the legal owner. The reason the issuer is liable in these circumstances is that share certificates are a declaration to 'all the world that the person in whose name the certificate is made out ... is a shareholder in the company'.[11] The statement that Bloggs is the legal owner was made by the issuer with the intention that it should be used as such a

---

[7] D. Frase, 'Dematerialisation and Taurus', [1991] *Butterworths Journal of International Banking and Finance Law* 73.

[8] *Welch* v. *The Bank of England* [1955] Ch 508 (broker); *Cottam* v. *Eastern Counties Railway Co.* (1860) 1 J & H 243, 70 ER 737 (broker); *Johnson* v. *Renton* (1879) Law Rep 9 Eq 181 (broker); *Simm* v. *Anglo-American Telegraph Company* (1879) 5 QBD 188 (employee).

[9] *Welch* v. *The Bank of England* [1955] 1 Ch 508; see also *Bank of Ireland* v. *Evans Trustees* (1855) 5 HCL 389, 10 ER 950; *Swan* v. *North British Australasian Co. Ltd* (1863) 2 H & C 175, 159 ER 73.

[10] *Re Bahia and San Francisco Rly Co.* (1868) LR 3 QB 584.

[11] *Re Bahia and San Francisco Rly Co.* (1868) LR 3 QB 584 at 595 per Cockburn J; *Shropshire Union Railways and Canal Co.* v. *R.* (1875) LR 7 HL 496; *Balkis Consolidated Company* v. *Tomkinson* [1893] AC 396.

declaration.[12] Any person who relies on the representation when purchasing securities can enforce the same rights against the company as can be enforced by a registered shareholder.[13] The issuer is liable to pay damages if it refuses to register her,[14] or if it strikes her name off the register.[15] The issuer is liable because, having represented to the buyer that the seller was the legal owner of the securities, it is estopped from proving that she was not.

An estoppel based on certificates protects only a claimant who can show that she has relied on the issuer's representation and thereby suffered some detriment. It does not protect a person who acquires forged transfer documents. This happens when the seller is, for example, not authorised to sell securities, but possesses a genuine share certificate (perhaps because she was entrusted with the certificate by the legal owner). To carry out the transfer in such a case the seller will have to forge the signature of the legal owner on the transfer form. It is also possible that an unauthorised seller will forge both the share certificate and the transfer form.

In both cases, the buyer suffered the loss not because of an inaccurate statement of the issuer, but because of forged documents. A person who acts on forged certificates does not rely on a representation made by the company, but on documents produced by someone else.[16] For this reason, the issuer is not estopped from proving that she has no title to the securities and does not need to indemnify the buyer. A person who acts on forged documents has to bear the misfortune arising from having accepted a forged transfer or having bought stolen securities.[17] Lord Halsbury supported this result by the pragmatic argument that the buyer is in a better position than the company to discover fraudulent or forged transfers. She is free to choose with whom to deal and is better

---

[12] *Re Bahia and San Francisco Rly Co.* (1868) LR 3 QB 584; *Webb* v. *Herne Bay Commissioners* (1870) LR 5 QB 642; *Balkis Consolidated Company* v. *Tomkinson* [1893] AC 396; *Dixon* v. *Kennaway & Co.* [1900] 1 Ch 833.

[13] *Simm* v. *Anglo-American Telegraph Company* (1879) 5 QBD 188 at 216 per Cotton LJ; *Re Otto Kopje Diamond Mines Ltd* [1893] 1 Ch 618 at 625–626 per Lindley LJ.

[14] *Balkis Consolidated Company* v. *Tomkinson* [1893] AC 396; *Re Otto Kopje Diamond Mines Ltd* [1893] 1 Ch 618.

[15] *Re Bahia and San Francisco Rly Co.* (1868) LR 3 QB 584.

[16] *Simm* v. *Anglo-American Telegraph Company* (1879) 5 QBD 188; *Cadbury Schweppes plc* v. *Halifax Share Dealing Ltd* [2006] EWHC 1184 (Ch).

[17] *Simm* v. *Anglo-American Telegraph Company* (1879) 5 QBD 188 at 205 per Bramwell LJ; *Royal Bank of Scotland* v. *Sandstone Properties Ltd* [1998] 2 BCLC 429.

able to judge from the circumstances under which the transaction is made whether the transfer documents are genuine.[18]

The conclusion of this subsection is that the common law protects certain buyers against unauthorised transfers. It does so by giving special evidential force to the securities certificate. This results in the buyer being able to sue the issuer for an indemnity. The risk of an unauthorised transfer thereby shifts from the buyer to the issuer.

The English method of protecting certain buyers against unauthorised transfers is firmly rooted within English market practice and English legal doctrine. Originally inspired by the law of novation, English practice causes issuers to make statements in certificates that identify the name and the holding of every individual owner. The law then protects the buyer by holding the issuer accountable for these statements by relying on the English rules of evidence which happen to have developed principles that are capable of protecting the buyer against adverse claims.

6.2.3 Liability of the person who instructed the issuer to amend the register

The conclusion of subsection 6.2.2 was that an English securities certificate can give rise to an estoppel and can trigger the liability of the issuer of the securities. The issuer is liable to indemnify a buyer who purchased securities in reliance on certificates that contained inaccurate information. The issuer does not, however, in all circumstances ultimately bear the risk of unauthorised transfers. The issuer is able to claim the cost of the indemnity from the person who acquired the securities from a seller who was not authorised to sell, but nevertheless produced a share certificate and a transfer form to that buyer. It goes without saying that, in such circumstances, the transfer form and sometimes also the certificates will be forgeries.

If the buyer of forged documents succeeds in having her name registered and in being issued with a certificate, that certificate will be inaccurate. It is, however, a genuine certificate made out by the issuer. In section 6.1 it was concluded that a third party who relies on this inaccurate certificate and buys the securities from the person who is named as the legal owner on them will be protected by estoppel. If it is later discovered that the securities were, originally, transferred without the legal owner's authority, the third party's name will be

---

[18] *Sheffield Corporation* v. *Barclay* [1905] AC 392 at 396.

removed from the register. The third party can then claim an indemnity from the issuer. The issuer can claim the cost she incurred to indemnify the third party from the buyer of the forged certificates or the person instructing the issuer to register a forged transfer. The buyer or her agent will be liable irrespective of whether she was aware of the forgery.

The basis of the liability is contract law. When an issuer is requested to exercise a statutory duty for the benefit of the person making the request, a contract for indemnity is implied.[19] The person requesting a transfer to be registered warrants that the transfer is genuine. The request includes a promise to indemnify the issuer if, by acting on the request, the issuer causes actionable injury or damage to a third party. The promise is accepted by the issuer when it acts on the request.

The leading authority on this point is a decision by the House of Lords in *Sheffield Corporation* v. *Barclay*.[20] In that case, Barclay presented forged transfer documents and instructed the issuer to put its name on the register. This caused a loss to the issuer and Barclay had to indemnify the issuer against that loss. Their Lordships reached this conclusion despite the fact that the bank had itself relied on the forged documents and had had no reason to believe they were forgeries. The rule in *Sheffield* was affirmed and extended by the Privy Council in *Kai Yung* v. *Hong Kong and Shanghai Banking Corporation*.[21] In that case, forged transfer documents were presented to the company not by the buyer himself but by a broker who acted on his behalf. The broker lodged the forged documents with the company requiring it to register the buyer. In the letter covering the documents, the broker referred to them as 'duly completed transfer deed(s)'. The broker, though he did not act on his own behalf, was held liable to indemnify the company against the loss it incurred by registering the forged transfer.

The conclusion of this subsection is that the person who instructs the company to register a transfer must indemnify it if the transfer documents are later discovered to be forgeries. This rule applies notwithstanding the fact that the person submitting the documents honestly and with good reason believed that they were genuine. The contributory

---

[19] *Sheffield Corporation* v. *Barclay* [1905] AC 392 at 399 per Lord Davey; *Welch* v. *The Bank of England* [1955] 1 Ch 508; *Kai Yung* v. *Hong Kong and Shanghai Banking Corporation* [1981] AC 787, PC; *Cadbury Schweppes plc* v. *Halifax Share Dealing Ltd* [2006] EWHC 1184 (Ch); see also *Bank of England* v. *Cutler* [1908] 2 KB 208 (CA).

[20] [1905] AC 392.   [21] [1981] AC 787, PC.

negligence of the company is no defence.[22] No liability arises, however, if the broker who instructed the issuer to amend the register did so in reliance on genuine but inaccurate share certificates issued by the issuer or its registrar.[23]

6.2.4 Conclusions

The English market chose to issue securities in the form of registered instruments. This means that market participants are not protected by the rules governing negotiable instruments and that the risk of unauthorised transfers is not carried by the legal owner. A legal owner of securities is not affected by amendments to the register without her authority and she is entitled to have her name restored to it. The legal owner loses her title to the securities only if she ratifies a transaction made without her authority or is otherwise estopped from proving title.

The risk of unauthorised transfers is managed by rules that reflect the path chosen by English market practice. The common law has developed a doctrinal technique to allocate the risk of unauthorised transfers away from the buyer. If the buyer acquires securities relying on forged transfer documents, she carries the risk of the forgery herself. This is supported by the policy consideration that she is in the best position to evaluate the circumstances of the transaction and to discover the forgery.

By contrast, if the buyer acquires securities relying on genuine certificates, which falsely name the seller as the legal owner, then she has a remedy against the issuer. The rationale of the remedy is, on the face of it, the nature of the paper document. That document is prima facie evidence of title created by the issuer to be relied on by the public. Underlying this, however, is the desire to satisfy the need of the market for certainty in securities transactions. Securities are issued to circulate freely in the market; this circulation would be significantly hindered by a rule requiring a buyer to verify whether her seller has obtained good title from her predecessors.

The issuer has a claim against any person presenting forged transfer documents and asking it to register a transfer. This claim is based on contract. A person who instructs a company to amend its register thereby warrants that the transfer is genuine and promises to

---

[22] *Royal Bank of Scotland* v. *Sandstone Properties Ltd* [1998] 2 BCLC 429, rejecting remarks by Lord Scarman in *Kai Yung* v. *Hong Kong and Shanghai Banking Corporation* [1981] AC 787, PC at 800.
[23] *Cadbury Schweppes plc* v. *Halifax Share Dealing Ltd* [2006] EWHC 1184 (Ch).

indemnify the indemnify if the documents are later found to have been forgeries.[24]

6.3 Uncertificated securities and estoppel

Section 6.2 examined the common law rules allocating the risk of unauthorised transfers inherent in securities transactions. Those rules were developed in relation to certificated transfers.

When securities are transferred by paper certificates and by paper transfer forms, the buyer's right is prima facie proven by the fact that she is in possession of the documents. The buyer is identified as transferee because she files a certificate and a transfer form with the issuer. The identification is carried out by the issuer or its registrar. When share transfers are carried out through CREST, the company is not involved in the process of identifying the buyer; in fact, no human eye is involved in the identification process. The authenticity of a transfer instruction is verified by the CREST computer system. This section will consider how the common law rules governing unauthorised transfers apply where shares are transferred in this way.

The rules through which the uncertificated transfer regime was implemented in England did not abolish the common law. USR 2001 only supplements the rules put in place by the English courts.[25] This is evidence of the path-dependent development of English legal doctrine. When England dematerialised securities it would have been possible to replace the common law with a completely new set of rules. This, however, was not done; the reform was carried out by adding new rules while at the same time leaving the previous rules untouched, leading to the conclusion that the common law, in principle, continues to apply to unauthorised transfers of uncertificated securities.

Nevertheless, the introduction of an uncertificated transfer system has an impact on the rules governing unauthorised transfers. The analysis contained in this section will show that, as in the paper-based environment, the law still protects the buyer against unauthorised transfers. The position of the buyer of uncertificated securities and also the position of the legal owner and of the issuer of such securities is, however, different from the position of these parties in relation to certificated securities, in three ways:

---

[24] But see *Cadbury Schweppes plc* v. *Halifax Share Dealing Ltd* [2006] EWHC 1184 (Ch).
[25] USR 2001, reg. 36 (10); USR 2001, reg. 46 (2).

- The first difference is that some of the risk of unauthorised transfers is now imposed on the legal owner.[26] This brings the solution adopted by English law closer to the solution adopted by German and Austrian law.
- The second difference is that the rules on estoppel appear to have lost their force.[27] The estoppel rules have the effect of shifting the risk of unauthorised transfers away from the buyer and on to the issuing company. It is very difficult to see how, if at all, they would operate in cases of unauthorised uncertificated transfers.
- USR 2001 compensates for this by imposing some of the risk of unauthorised transfers on the system operator, CRESTCo. CRESTCo is liable for damages arising out of forged transfers instructions. But, other than the issuer's liability, CRESTCo's liability is limited in two important ways. CRESTCo is liable only up to a statutory limit and ceases to be liable if it can identify the forger. In these circumstances, the risk of unauthorised transfers reverts back to the buyer, who is left with a claim that she will very likely be unable to enforce. This constitutes the third difference between certificated and uncertificated transfers.[28]

The application of the common law rules to uncertificated securities and the interaction of the common law with the statutory rules will be examined in more detail in subsections 6.3.1–6.3.4. The analysis will first focus on the rules governing the rights of the legal owner. After that, CRESTCo's and the issuer's liability will be examined.

6.3.1 Restoration of the legal owner's name on the register

At common law, the legal owner of registered securities does not lose title when her name is taken off the register without her authority. This rule has not been explicitly abolished by the rules governing the uncertificated transfer system.[29]

This book will proceed on the basis that a legal owner whose name is removed from the register without her authority is still, in principle entitled to have the register rectified.

Nevertheless, whereas the owner of certificated securities may confidently leave the certificates in the hands of someone else the owner of uncertificated shares needs to keep her system password secret. The legal owner is bound by instructions sent by anyone who has access to

---

[26] See section 6.3.1.   [27] See section 6.2.2.   [28] See section 6.3.2.
[29] For a wide interpretation of USR 1995, reg. 29 (now USR 2001, reg. 35) see R. Sykes, in *The Future of Money Market Instruments: A Consultation* (London: Bank of England, 1999) 31.

her computer: whenever an instruction is sent from her network computer, the instruction will be identified as a 'properly authenticated dematerialised instruction' and she will be bound by it.[30] The same rule applies to an investor who does not have a network connection but who has appointed a broker to operate the network on her behalf.[31] The broker acts as what is called a 'sponsoring user'.[32] The owner on whose behalf the broker has permission to access the network is not entitled to deny that an instruction was sent with her authority.[33] The system allows for restrictions on transactions made by brokers on behalf of clients,[34] but the fact remains that owners of uncertificated securities are protected to a lesser extent than the owners of certificated securities against fraudulent brokers.

This change is important because in many of the cases in this area the legal owner has left paper certificates with an employee or a broker. The owner was not bound by forged transactions effected by the person whom she entrusted with her certificates. Under the new regime, the legal owner is bound by an instruction that has been sent by any person who, with or without her authority, accesses the system from her computer. This rule shifts the risk of unauthorised instructions to the legal owner.

This new solution is more in keeping with that adopted by German and Austrian law, where the risk of unauthorised transfers is generally imposed on the owner of the securities.[35] This could be seen as an example of convergence as the outcomes produced by English, German and Austrian law, respectively, have become more similar to each other. It is important to note, however, that the three legal systems have become more like each other only at a functional level – that is, in terms of the outcomes produced by their respective legal doctrines. There is no convergence of legal doctrine. Moreover, the convergence that has occurred does not appear to have been a result intended by either the legislature or the market forces driving the reform process that led to USR 1995 and to USR 2001.

6.3.2 CRESTCo's liability for forged instructions

CRESTCo is liable under USR 2001 to any person who suffers a loss as a result of a forged instruction or an event causing an unauthorised

---

[30] USR 2001, reg. 35 (3).   [31] USR 2001, reg. 35 (2).   [32] URS 2001, reg. 3.
[33] URS 2001, reg. 35.   [34] USR 2001, Sched. 1, para. 15.
[35] For this, see section 10.2.

instruction to be sent.[36] Forged instructions are instructions that have been sent by someone who has accessed the system without having authority to do so. This occurs when a person accesses the system from a computer that is not part of the network; it also occurs if someone manipulates the network from within – when, for example, investor A sends an instruction from her network computer purporting to be investor B and induces the system to accept the instruction as the instruction of investor B. Causative events are anything other than forged instructions: a system failure that causes CRESTCo to amend an entry on the register without the owner's authority would be one example.

CRESTCo is responsible for loss incurred as a result of forged instructions or induced operator instructions; its liability is limited to £50,000. CRESTCo is strictly liable but ceases to be liable if it identifies the person responsible for a forged instruction or an induced Operator instruction.[37] To rely on this defence, CRESTCo must prove that a particular person caused the instruction or the causative event. It is not necessary that the person suffering the loss has a remedy against, or in fact succeeds in obtaining relief against, the person identified.[38] Under USR 2001, reg. 36, CRESTCo is not vicariously liable for the acts of its employees or agents as the generators of the instruction, and so it may avoid liability by naming the employee who caused the improper instruction.

USR 2001, reg. 36 imposes the risk of forged instructions on the operator of CREST. CRESTCo is liable if the security mechanisms of the system fail and allow instructions to be sent without them being authorised by the person entitled to do so. CRESTCo is strictly liable but its liability is limited to cases where the person interfering with the system cannot be identified. To put it in more general terms, CRESTCo is liable only if it cannot show who manipulated the computer network.

6.3.3 Liability of the issuer

The rule that an issuer is liable to any person who has acquired shares relying on certificates issued by the issuer does not apply in respect of uncertificated securities because the issuer does not issue certificates. Nonetheless the issuer still maintains a register which, at least to some extent, also constitutes prima facie evidence of title.[39] There is, however, no authority as to whether the register amounts to a representation by the issuer giving rise to an estoppel. Even if there were authority

---

[36] USR 2001, reg. 36 (1).   [37] USR 2001, reg. 36 (4).
[38] USR 2001, reg. 36 (4).   [39] USR 2001, reg. 24.

on this point, there are several reasons why the buyer's claim against the company would be difficult to assert.

The first and most significant is that the buyer of uncertificated securities is unlikely to consult the register before accepting a transfer. For this reason, when she buys securities, she does not rely on information contained in the register. The entries on the register do not induce her to enter into the transaction. It is only after the purchase has been made that the buyer takes notice of the data contained in the register. But, even then, she does not consult the register itself but inputs an instruction into CREST. If the seller inputs a matching instruction, the system will cause the register to be amended and the purchase price to be paid. This may put the buyer's mind at rest but in doing so she does not rely on the register itself, but on a mechanism provided by CREST. Admittedly, the company has appointed the system for the settlement of transactions in securities,[40] and the CREST mechanism itself relies on data which was originally taken from the issuer's register. It is doubtful, however, whether this fact is alone sufficient to show that the processing of the buyer's and the seller's instructions entails a representation by the issuer to the buyer.

Another problem is that the legal significance of the register of members maintained by the company has changed with USR 2001. As a result of the new regulation, the register of members consists of two parts: the issuer register that is kept by the company, and the operator register that is kept by CRESTCo. The issuer register still shows entries relating to both certificated and uncertificated securities and is, in principle, still prima facie evidence of title (USR 2001, reg. 24 (1)). This rule is, however, subject to a qualification. The qualification, which applies to entries relating to uncertificated shares only, is that where an entry on the company's issuer register is inconsistent with an entry on its operator register, the data on the issuer register ceases to be prima facie evidence of title.[41] There is no provision stating that the operator register is prima facie evidence of title to uncertificated shares.[42] An

---

[40] USR 2001, regs. 14–17.

[41] USR 2001, reg. 24 (2); there is a further rule stating that a person whose name is on the issuer register is not to be deemed a member of the company unless her name is shown as the owner of certificated shares on that register or as the owner of uncertificated shares on the operator register (USR 2001, reg. 24 (3)).

[42] The operator register is prima facie evidence in relation to public sector securities (USR 2001, reg. 24 (5)) and, subject to certain qualifications, also in relation to corporate securities other than shares (USR 2001, reg. 24 (6)). There is no corresponding rule

inconsistency between the issuer and the operator register will not frequently occur. In that event, however, there is no record available providing for prima facie evidence of title. This makes it more difficult for the buyer to rely on the estoppel rules.

The last reason that a buyer's claim is going to be difficult to enforce is that a company which is permitted to rely on a properly authenticated dematerialised instruction (padi) is protected by the rules on such instructions.[43] USR 2001, reg. 35 (8) states that a person who is permitted to accept a matter 'shall not be liable in damages or otherwise to any person by reason of his having relied on the matter that he was permitted to accept'. If a padi causes the company to amend the register and thereby to make a representation which triggers the rules of estoppel, the basis of the company's liability is not that it relied on the padi in amending the register. The investor suing the company will base her claim on the company's having breached its duty to register her as a member – or, having so registered her, to continue to treat her as a member. The company will be liable because the representation deprives it of the right to prove that the seller from whom the investor acquired the shares was not the owner of them. However, the padi was causally responsible for the company's liability: the company would, but for the instruction, not have amended the register and would not have been caught by the estoppel rules. As a result, it would have been in the position to defend the investor's claim. This type of liability arises, albeit indirectly, 'by reason of [the company's] having relied' on the padi. USR 2001, reg. 35 (8) is drafted in wide terms; it states that the company shall not be 'liable in damages *or otherwise* to any person'.[44] Although there is no authority on point, it is arguable that USR 2001, reg. 35 (8) abolishes the company's liability which would otherwise arise as a result of the estoppel rules.

All this means that it is unlikely that a buyer of uncertificated shares has a claim against the company if she relied on data provided by the CREST system that is later discovered to have been incorrect. If the error is due to a forged instruction, the person who suffered a loss has a claim against CRESTCo under USR 2001, reg. 36. CRESTCo's liability is, however, limited to £50,000 and can be avoided by CREST identifying the person who has interfered with the system.

---

providing for prima facie evidence in cases where an entry on the issuer register in relation to uncertificated shares is inconsistent with an entry on the operator register.
[43] USR 2001, reg. 35 (8).   [44] Author's emphasis.

Under USR 2001,[45] the company is liable for a breach of statutory duty to any person who suffers a loss if it amends the register other than in accordance with an operator instruction, a court order, or an enactment.[46] This liability does not exclude liability on any other basis.[47] This rule echoes the rules in *Dixon* v. *Kennaway & Co.* and *Hart* v. *Frontino*.[48] In both cases, the company was liable in circumstances where its secretary had improperly amended the register.

The result of this analysis is that a company's liability for incorrect representations as to a person's shareholding has been replaced by a liability of the legal owner, on the one hand, and by a liability of the system operator for damages that arise due to forged instructions, on the other. The risk of an unauthorised transfer has thereby been shifted away from the company to CRESTCo. This change, however, leaves the buyer without any protection in cases where damages exceed the statutory limit – and, most importantly, where CRESTCo can identify the forger. It leaves the buyer with a very likely unenforceable claim and thereby pushes the forgery risk back to the buyer and onto the market.

6.3.4 Securities as negotiable rights

One possible way of preserving the issuer's liability in cases of unauthorised transfers is to look at the policy reasons justifying the operation of the rules of estoppel in the case of unauthorised transfers of certificated securities. The issuer's liability was never based on technical legal points alone. It was supported by the idea that securities have created to circulate in a fluid market. The law recognised this purpose and enhanced the transferability of securities by protecting the buyer. In *Davis* v. *The Bank of England*, Best CJ justified the liability of the issuer to the buyer for forged transfers in the following words:

If this not be the law, who will purchase stock, or who can be certain that the stock which he holds belongs to him? It has ever been an object of the legislature to give facility to the transfer of shares in the public funds. This facility of transfer is one of the advantages belonging to this species of property and this advantage would be entirely destroyed if a purchaser should be required to look

---

[45] USR 2001, reg. 46 (1).   [46] USR 2001, reg. 28 (6).
[47] USR 2001, reg. 46 (2).   [48] [1900] 1 Ch 833; (1870) LR 5 Exch 111.

to the regularity of the transfers to all the various persons through whom such stock has passed.[49]

The risk of an unauthorised transfer was accordingly imposed on the company not only because it issued shares but also because it had the most to gain from the transferability of the shares. In speaking of the liability of the company, Cockburn J said in *Re Bahia and San Francisco Rly Co.*:

The company are bound to keep a register of shareholders, and have power to issue certificates certifying that each individual shareholder named therein is a registered shareholder of the particular shares specified. This power of granting certificates is to give the shareholders the opportunity of more easily dealing with their shares in the market, and to afford facilities to them of selling their shares by at once showing a marketable title, and the effect of this facility is to make the shares of greater value. The power of giving certificates is, therefore for the benefit of the company in general.[50]

The company as the ultimate beneficiary also has the greatest incentive to improve and monitor the reliability of the transfer mechanism. It is possible to argue that the new transfer rules have taken the handling of transfers out of the companies' hands and have entrusted CRESTCo with it. It seems fair that CRESTCo should also be saddled with some of the risk of unauthorised transfers. What seems less reasonable, however, is that this should result in a shift of some of the transfer risk back to the buyer who, of all the parties involved, is in the worst position to control it. The computer-based transfer system was introduced to speed up transfers; it was not intended to change the legal nature of securities, and enhanced transferability is part of that legal nature. The ideas justifying the effect of the estoppel rules in relation to certificated transfers support the proposition that the risk of unauthorised transfers of uncertificated securities should not be carried by the buyer. Admittedly, issuers have no influence over the verification of unauthorised transfers. But the same can be said of the liability for forged paper transfers; issuers are liable in those cases even if they take all precautions in effecting the transfer. It remains to be seen if these

---

[49] (1824) 2 Bing 39 at 409, 130 ER 357 at 363; the decision was later reversed on different grounds, (1826) 5 B & C 185, 108 ER 69. The principle on which the case was decided was later confirmed by *Coles* v. *The Bank of England* (1839) 10 Ad & E 437 at 449, 113 ER 166 at 171 and *Sloman* v. *The Bank of England* (1845) 14 Sim 475 at 486, 60 ER 442 at 447; see also *Welch* v. *The Bank of England* [1955] Ch 508 at 530 per Harman J.

[50] (1868) LR 3 QB 584 at 594–595.

considerations will persuade the courts to operate the estoppel rules in relation to the buyer.

6.3.5 Conclusions

The risk of unauthorised transfers of uncertificated securities is allocated in a different way to the risk of unauthorised transfers of certificated securities. There are three differences.

The first is that the legal owner of certificated securities is not bound by transfers that have been forged by an employee or a broker whom she has entrusted with her securities certificates. Under the new regime the legal owner is bound by an instruction sent by an employee or her broker albeit without her authority. This shifts the risk of unauthorised transfers away from the buyer and onto the legal owner. This movement is to be welcomed because risk is most efficiently carried by the person who is in the best position to control it. The legal owner of uncertificated securities is in the best position of all the parties involved to restrict access to her network connection point. Likewise, the sponsored CREST member is free to choose her sponsor and can thereby reduce the risk of her shares being transferred without her authority.

The second difference is that CRESTCo is liable for damages arising out of forged transfer instructions. This insulates the buyer to some extent against the risk of unauthorised transfers, but the protection given by the statutory rule is weaker than the effect created by estoppel. CRESTCo is liable only up to £50,000 per incident, and it ceases to be liable if it identifies the forger.

The third difference is that although the estoppel rules may not have been abolished, it is not easy to see how they will operate against the issuing company. It is doubtful whether they will still provide a tool helping the buyer to claim an indemnity from the issuer in cases of unauthorised transfers.

6.4 Summary of the analysis

Inspired by the legal regime that was in place when securities first emerged in England, English issuers to this date predominantly issue registered securities. Certificates that are made out for registered securities are not considered to be negotiable instruments. The buyer of such securities is therefore subject to the general rule that she will acquire legal title to the securities only if the seller has authority to sell them. The effect of this general rule is, however, mitigated by the English law of estoppel.

The law of estoppel is part of the English law of evidence. It prevents the issuer from proving that the buyer purchased securities from a seller who was not authorised to sell and as a consequence requires the issuer to treat the unauthorised buyer in the same way as it treats a legal owner. It is important to note that the rules on estoppel operate only indirectly in that they do not transfer ownership to the buyer; they only require the issuer to treat the buyer as if she were the legal owner. The issuer will very likely satisfy the claim of the buyer by purchasing securities in the market and transferring them to her. As a result the buyer will also become the legal owner of the securities. As a matter of legal doctrine, however, that result is achieved only indirectly.

The issuer's liability, moreover, arises only if the buyer bought the securities relying on certificates that were genuine, but inaccurate. This occurs where the issuer – induced, for example, by a fraudster – produces a share certificate which refers to a person as the owner who does in reality not hold legal title to the securities and where the buyer purchases these securities in reliance on that certificate.

The rules on estoppel were developed in relation to certificated securities. They are difficult to apply when uncertificated securities are transferred without the owner's authority because, as a result of the implementation of the uncertificated transfer system, the buyer has ceased to rely on a representation made by the issuer prior to purchasing securities.

English law has yet to come to terms with unauthorised transfers of uncertificated securities. From the point of view of this book it is important to note that England did not abolish the case law that developed in relation to unauthorised transfers when it dematerialised securities transfers. English legal doctrine continues its path-dependent development: USR 2001 only supplements the common law by adding a rule on the issuer's liability.

Moreover, the law of unauthorised transfers, as it appears to stand after dematerialisation, allocates some of the risk arising out of unauthorised transfers away from the issuer and imposes it on the legal owner of uncertificated securities. This brings the outcomes produced by English law closer to the outcomes achieved by German and Austrian law. It does not bring English legal doctrine closer to German and Austrian legal doctrine, but nevertheless is an example of functional convergence. Interestingly, there is no evidence that convergence of legal rules in relation to unauthorised transfers would have been an outcome which was intended by those who masterminded and implemented the reform that led to USR 1995 and USR 2001.

Chapters 2–6 were concerned with instances in which investors held securities directly. It was assumed throughout these chapters that the name of the investor was entered on the securities register. In chapter 7, the property rights of investors who hold securities indirectly will be examined.

7   Indirect holdings

7.1 Introduction

In England, an investor can hold securities in one of three principal ways. Firstly, she can hold the securities in her name in certificated form. In that case, her name is on the securities register; she receives a paper certificate and is considered to hold legal title to the securities.

Secondly, an investor can hold securities in her own name, but in uncertificated form. To be able to hold securities directly in uncertificated form, an investor needs to become a participant of CREST. There are two ways of participating in CREST – by becoming a user or by appointing a sponsor who is a user. The difference between the two is that users have a computer link with CREST. A user needs to acquire the hardware and software necessary to connect to the network. Participants who are not users do not have such a computer link, but access the system through a sponsor who has network access and acts in the name of the participant.[1] The later form of participating in CREST is also referred to as 'personal membership'.[2] In both cases the investor's name appears on the securities register and the investor holds legal ownership to the securities.

Thirdly, an investor can opt to have the securities held by an intermediary on her behalf; in that case, the securities are held indirectly. The investor does not hold legal title to the securities and the name of the intermediary or a nominee company appears on the securities register. There are two standard ways in which intermediaries hold securities for clients. The first is for the intermediary to hold the

---

[1] *CREST Manual* (07.12.2004) 1–2–3–1–2–5.
[2] CRESTCo, *Personal Membership in CREST* (February 2000), http://www.crestco.co.uk/publications/fact_sheets/pm_facts.pdf (last visited 14 November 2006).

securities in a manner which makes it possible for specific securities to be attributed to individual clients. This method of holding client securities requires a higher level of administration on the part of the intermediary and is therefore frequently associated with a higher level of service charges. The second way of holding securities indirectly is for the intermediary to hold securities on behalf of several clients and without allocating specific securities to individual clients. If securities are held on an unallocated basis, they are sometimes referred to as being held in a 'pooled account' or in an 'omnibus account'. Holding client securities on an omnibus basis is frequently cheaper than holding them on an allocated basis.

The legal position of an investor holding securities directly either in certificated or in uncertificated form was analysed in chapters 2–6. In this chapter, the legal position of investors holding securities indirectly through an intermediary will be examined.

Irrespective of whether securities are held through an intermediary on an allocated or on an unallocated basis, it is important to determine the circumstances in which clients hold a proprietary interest in the securities held on their behalf. In order to determine if an investor enjoys property rights in indirectly held securities, we need to embark on a path-dependent enquiry and examine the English rules on equitable ownership. The conclusion of section 2.4 was that equitable ownership arises when a trust has been created. A trust comes into existence by operation of the law (constructive trust) or as a result of an express declaration (express trust). Trusts that arise by operation of law have been analysed in section 2.4 and in subsections 3.3.3, and 3.4.4. The purpose of this chapter is to focus on express trusts that are established for the benefit of clients who wish to hold securities indirectly.

Before the circumstances in which an express trust arises are analysed it is helpful to remind ourselves of the some of the characteristics of trusts. It has already been noted that English property law has adopted two concepts of ownership, ownership at law and ownership in equity.[3] When a particular asset is held on trust, the trustee holds legal title to the asset and the beneficiary holds equitable title to the asset. The analysis is slightly modified when securities are held indirectly through a chain of intermediaries. In those circumstances the intermediary with whom the ultimate investor has its immediate relationship does not hold legal title to the securities. Instead, that

---

[3] See section 2.4.2.

intermediary holds equitable title to securities held on its behalf by another intermediary. The ultimate investor holds equitable title to the entitlement created in favour of its immediate intermediary.

When securities are held indirectly, the intermediary acts as a trustee and the investor acts as the beneficiary. As a result in English law, unlike in German or Austrian law, intermediaries have a property interest in the securities that they hold on behalf of clients. This property interest is, however, subject to the client's equitable property interest. The equitable interest continues to exist even if the securities are sold by the intermediary without the client's authority. It is extinguished only if a third party acquires the securities in good faith and for value. The investor's equitable interest also has priority in the intermediary's insolvency and prevails over claims raised by the intermediary's general creditors. It will be shown below that, using different legal doctrine, German and Austrian law achieve a similar level of protection for investors holding securities indirectly as in English law.[4]

For an express trust to arise under English law, three requirements need to be satisfied. These requirements are also referred to as the 'three certainties'. The first one is certainty of intention. The second one is certainty of beneficiary. The third one is certainty of subject matter. Certainty of beneficiary does not usually cause a problem in the context of securities markets[5] and will not be discussed further in this book. The following sections will focus on certainty of intention and certainty of subject matter, respectively.

7.2 Certainty of intention

Consistently with the path adopted by English law, the requirement for certainty of intention focuses on the intention of the intermediary holding the securities. The intention can be inferred from an express provision to that effect in the documentation underlying the relationship between the intermediary and the client; it can also be inferred from the fact that the parties clearly intended that the client's assets should form a separate fund in the hands of the intermediary.[6] There is no requirement for the client to consent to the creation of a trust. Even if the client will in most cases have requested, or at least consented to,

---

[4] See section 12.3.
[5] Joanna Benjamin, *Interests in Securities* (Oxford: Oxford University Press, 2001) 2.42.
[6] Benjamin, *Interests in Securities* 2.41.

her assets being held on trust, as a general rule of trust law a trust will arise by virtue of the intermediary's intention only.

The requirement for certainty of intention needs to be satisfied irrespective of whether securities are held on an allocated basis or in a pooled account.

Concerning the requirement for certainty of intention, there exists a parallel between English and German law. The issue of certainty of intention also arose in German law, albeit at an earlier stage. Prior to the implementation of the current statutory regime the relationship between clients and intermediaries was analysed purely in terms of the law of contract. In order for a proprietary interest to arise, the client and the intermediary needed to provide for a special type of bailment contract in their documentation. There are two types of bailment contracts in German law, regular deposits and irregular deposits.[7] A proprietary interests of the bailee existed only in cases of regular deposits. In order to determine if the client had a proprietary interest it was necessary for the court to determine which of the two types of contract was intended by the parties. This also involved an examination as to whether there was an intention to create a property right. In German law, however, the necessary intention needs to be contained in an agreement to which both parties gave their consent. In England, it is sufficient if the intermediary has formed the intention to hold the securities on trust for the investor.

7.3 Certainty of subject matter

A property right creates a relationship between the owner and an asset and for a property interest to arise we need to be able to determine the asset to which the interest relates. Any legal system that has rules on property law needs to have rules governing the identification of assets. In English law, the identification problem is analysed path-consistently within the law of trusts: a trust can arise only if the subject matter of the trust is certain.

In England, the requirement for certainty is easily met when the trust concerns individual items of particular specification – for example, a plot of land or a certain piece of antique furniture. It is also easy to satisfy when a fluctuating class of assets is held on trust for one particular beneficiary.[8] Difficulties arise, however, when the trust concerns

---

[7] See section 12.1.1.
[8] For an analysis of property rights in a fund, see R. C. Nolan, 'Property in a Fund', 120 (2004) *LQR* 108–136.

fungible assets held on behalf of multiple clients. The problem is that English law has traditionally adopted an onerous requirement for certainty. In the following subsection, the requirement for certainty in the context of fungibles will be examined; tangible goods will be analysed first followed by an analysis of intangibles.

7.3.1 Tangible goods

The rule that the subject matter of a trust must be certain was first established in cases involving tangible assets. The courts held,[9] prior to the Sale of Goods Act 1979, that if goods were sold that were not physically separated but were part of a larger stock a trust would not arise and the buyer would not acquire equitable title in part of the stock.

The rule that, special arrangements aside, a trust does not exist for the benefit of the buyer of a part of an identifiable bulk goes back to the decision in Re Wait.[10] The parties, in that case, agreed to buy and sell 500 tons of wheat out of a bulk of 1,000 tons of a designated cargo whereby the seller was not entitled to supply the wheat from another source. The Court of Appeal held that the 500 tons were not specific or ascertained goods. This was because there was no appropriation or identification as to effect an equitable assignment giving the purchaser an equitable interest in the 500 tons or a lien in respect thereof. Atkin LJ wrote that a 'seller or a purchaser may, of course, create any equity he pleases by way of charge, equitable assignment or any other dealing with or disposition of goods . . . But the mere sale or agreement to sell or the acts in pursuance of such a contract . . . will only produce legal effects which the Code states.'[11]

Sargant LJ gave a dissenting opinion. He said that the agreement for the sale of specific goods amounted to an equitable assignment enforceable against the particular parcel of goods in the vendor's hands. The purchaser of the 500 tons, having paid part of the purchase money, was entitled, according to Sargant LJ, to have the 500 tons made over to him on payment of the remainder of the purchase price. He could not see 'any real difference in the equitable position of the respondents, because they agreed to buy not the whole 1,000 tons parcel but 500 tons'.[12]

---

[9] Re Goldcorp Exchange Ltd [1995] 1 AC 74 at 90 (PC).
[10] [1927] 1 Ch 606 (CA).
[11] [1927] 1 Ch 606 (CA) at 636 per Atkin LJ; the reference to 'Code' is a reference to the Sale of Goods Act 1893 (56 & 67 Vict c 71).
[12] [1927] 1 Ch 606 (CA) at 645 per Sargant LJ.

The decision in *Re Wait* was considered by the Privy Council in *Re Goldcorp Exchange Ltd.*[13] Goldcorp, in that case, undertook to hold gold bullion on trust for customers. Goldcorp stored the gold it its vault but did not keep the gold of individual customers separately. In the company's insolvency the customers tried to establish a proprietary claim over the gold. Their claims competed with the claim of a bank, whose interests were secured by a floating charge. The customers failed to establish a proprietary claim because Goldcorp had not allocated gold bullion specifically to individual customers; they essentially failed because there was no customer name tag on the gold bullion.

The Privy Council took the view that the dissenting opinion in *Re Wait* was prompted by the fact that the purchaser could point out the bulk and say that her goods were definitely there although she could not tell which part they were. The Board agreed with the majority in *Re Wait* in rejecting this view. The Board advised that under a simple contract for the sale of unascertained goods no equitable title could pass merely by virtue of the sale.[14]

A similar claim had been rejected some years earlier in *Re London Wine Company, (Shippers) Ltd.*[15] A wine importing company sold wine to individuals who left the wine in possession of the company's warehouse agent. There was no segregation of any wine cases in favour of any particular individual. In the vendor's insolvency, the individual purchasers tried to assert a proprietary interest in the wine. Oliver J held that the purchasers did not have a proprietary interests because there had been no allocation and, accordingly, the certainty of the subject matter necessary to create an equitable interest was not present.[16] He compared that case to that of a farmer who declares himself to be a trustee of two sheep out of his flock without identifying them. The farmer, according to Oliver J, cannot be said to have created a perfect and complete trust whatever right he might confer by such declaration as a matter of contract.

Oliver J continued:[17] 'And it would seem to me to be immaterial that at the time he had a flock of sheep out of which he could satisfy the

---

[13] [1995] 1 AC 74 (PC) at 90–91.
[14] *Re Goldcorp Exchange Ltd* [1995] 1 AC 74 (PC) at 91; *Re Goldcorp* is a New Zealand case. In England, the law in *Re Wait* was changed by SGA 1995, s. 20A by which on payment of the purchase price the purchaser acquires property in an undivided share of the bulk, thereby becoming an owner in common of the bulk.
[15] [1986] PCC 121.
[16] *Re London Wine Company, (Shippers) Ltd* [1986] PCC 121 at 137 per Oliver J.
[17] At 137 (italics in the original).

interest. Of course, he could by appropriate words, declare himself to be a trustee of a specified proportion of his whole flock and thus create an equitable tenancy in common between himself and the named beneficiary, so that a proprietary interest would arise in the beneficiary in an undivided share of the flock and its produce. But the mere declaration that a given number of animals would be held on trust could not, I should have thought, without very clear words pointing to such intention, result in the creation of an interest in common in the proportion which that number bears to the number of the whole at the time of the declaration.'

A trust arises and equitable ownership passes, however, when the seller, after having signed the contract, purchases goods answering the contractual description and puts them into his own stock. The seller in *Holroyd v. Marshall* purchased the machinery he had promised to deliver to the buyer from a third party after he had entered into the sales contract with the buyer.[18] The buyer acquired equitable title in the machinery on acquisition of the machinery by the seller because the machinery could be unequivocally attributed to the sales contract. In *Holroyd v. Marshall* the court held that at:

law property, non-existing, but to be acquired at a future time, is not assignable; in equity it is so. At law . . . although a power is given in the deed of assignment to take possession of after-acquired property, no interest is transferred, even as between the parties themselves, unless possession is actually taken; in equity it is not disputed that the moment property comes into existence the agreement operates upon it.'[19]

The court continued:

if it should still be thought that the deed, together with the act of bringing the machinery on the premises, were not sufficient to complete the mortgagee's title, it may be asked what more could have been done for this purpose. The trustee could not take possession of the new machinery, for that would have been contrary to the provision of the deed under which Taylor was to remain in possession until default in payment of the mortgage money after a demand in writing, . . . And if the intervenient act to perfect the title in trust be one proceeding from the mortgagor, what stronger one could be done by him than fixing and placing the new machinery in the mill, by which it came, to his knowledge immediately subject to the operation of the deed?[20]

---

[18] (1862) 10 HLCas 191, 11 ER 999.
[19] (1862) 10 HLCas 191 at 220, 11 ER 999 at 1010 per Lord Wensleydale.
[20] *Holroyd v. Marshall* (1862) 10 HLCas 191 at 225, 11 ER 999 at 1112 per Lord Wensleydale.

Lord Mustil agreed with this result in *Re Goldcorp*, writing that 'there is no difficulty with a transaction whereby B promises A that if in the future goods belonging to A come within the physical control of B he will hold them as a bailee for A on terms fixed in advance by the agreement'.[21]

It follows from what was said above that putting the Sale of Goods Act 1979 aside a trust arises only for the benefit of the buyer and equitable ownership vests in the buyer only when the tangible goods sold can be identified and are physically separated from other assets of the same type owned by the seller. Where the parties agree to buy and sell goods that are part of an identified or unidentified bulk, no trust exists and the buyer does not acquire equitable title unless the seller has declared herself a trustee of a fraction of a certain pool of assets.[22]

Moreover, a declaration to hold certain assets on trust does not suffice to create a trust in relation to a fraction of a pool of assets of that type. The courts will not read the intention to hold a percentage of a bulk on trust into a trust declaration relating to certain assets. This means that in relation to tangible fungibles a trust declaration regarding 50 units of the tangible concerned will create a trust only if 50 units have been physically separated from other units held by the trustee. No trust will arise as long as the units concerned are mixed with other units of the same tangible asset belonging to the trustee.

7.3.2 Registered securities

We have seen above that the requirement for certainty of the subject matter of a trust is relatively onerous when the assets the trust concerns are tangibles. The law seems less strict in relation to intangibles and in this subsection the rules governing trusts of intangible assets will be addressed.

In *Hunter* v. *Moss*,[23] the Court of Appeal determined whether the subject matter of a trust of shares was sufficiently certain. The case concerned an express declaration of a trust of registered shares. The declaration concerned 5 per cent of the shares of the settlor's total shareholding. Dillon LJ observed that all the shares belonged to one class, that 5 per cent of the total shareholding amounted to 50 shares, and the defendant held

---

[21] [1995] 1 AC 74 at 97 (PC) per Lord Mustil.
[22] R. Goode, 'Ownership and Obligation in Commercial Transactions', [1997] *LQR* 433 at 449; Sarah Worthington, *Proprietary Interests in Commercial Transactions* (Oxford: Oxford University Press, 1996) 28.
[23] [1994] 1 WLR 452 (CA).

personally more than 50 shares. He continued: 'it would not be good enough for the settlor to say, "I declare that I hold 50 of my shares on trust for B", without indicating the company he had in mind of the various companies in which he held shares. There would be no sufficient certainty as to the subject matter of the trust. But here the discussion is solely about the shares of one class in the one company.'[24]

Dillon LJ added that a bequest by the defendant to the plaintiff of 50 of his ordinary shares in M.E.L. would be a valid bequest on the defendant's death which his executors or administrators would be bound to carry into effect, and came to the conclusion that the subject matter was sufficiently certain and that a trust was validly created in favour of the beneficiary. The trust was established over 50 shares out of the 950 held by the defendant. The beneficiary therefore had the right to ask that 50 shares be delivered to him.

Hunter v. *Moss* was followed by Neuberger J in *Re Harvard Securities Ltd*.[25] The firm in that case, which had been licensed as 'dealer in securities and investment adviser', went into liquidation because it was unable to acquire authorisation under the Financial Services Act 1988. The liquidator applied for a determination of the question whether the company or its clients had a proprietary interest in shares held by a nominee company. Harvard Securities had purchased shares with a view to selling them on to its clients in smaller parcels. The clients were not registered in order to avoid registration fees. Harvard kept records in which there were entries against the names of each client, showing the name of shares; the date of sale to the client; where any bonus or rights had been issued; the date on which any or all of the shares were sold back to Harvard; and the balance (if any) of the client's holding. Neuberger J found that the fact that *Hunter* v. *Moss* concerned an express trust was no basis for distinguishing the case from *Re Wait*, *Re London Wine* and *Re Goldcorp*. The only difference he could find between *Hunter* v. *Moss* and these other cases was that *Hunter* v. *Moss* involved shares and the others involved tangible goods. He wrote, that in 'all the circumstances . . . it seems to me that the correct way for me, at first instance, to explain the difference between the result in *Hunter*, and that in *Wait*, *London Wine* and *Goldcorp*, is on the ground that Hunter was concerned with shares, as opposed to chattels'. But while Neuberger J felt bound to follow *Hunter* v. *Moss*, he was not convinced by the distinction.

[24] *Hunter* v. *Moss* [1994] 1 WLR 452 (CA) at 457 per Dillon LJ.
[25] [1997] 2 BCLC 369.

7.3.3 Analysis

The requirement for certainty deserves attention from the point of view of indirectly held securities. A proprietary interest for the benefit of an investor who holds securities indirectly arises only if the requirement for certainty is met. If securities are held on an allocated basis, they are appropriated to a particular beneficiary; the requirement for certainty is fulfilled and the beneficiary enjoys equitable ownership. If securities are held in omnibus accounts, the position is different; there is no appropriation of particular securities to individual clients. This does not seem to matter much because the current position in English law appears to be that there exists an onerous requirement in relation to tangibles and a less onerous requirement for certainty in relation to intangibles. Securities are intangibles in English law; for equitable ownership to arise for the benefit of an investor holding securities indirectly it seems to suffice that there exists a bulk of securities of which the securities belonging to the investor form part.

It would therefore be possible to rely on the authority relating to intangibles without carrying out any further analysis. This is, however, not a prudent approach to take. The reason is that the leading case concerning tangibles was decided by the Privy Council. The leading authority regarding intangibles is a decision by the Court of Appeal and the position in relation to intangibles still needs to be decided by the House of Lords. Moreover, there exist eminent academic contributions discussing how (if at all) the decisions in *Re Goldcorp* and in *Hunter* v. *Moss* can be reconciled with each other. The views put forward in the debate will be analysed in subsection 7.3.3.1. US authority supporting the decision in *Hunter* v. *Moss* will be examined and it will then be argued that policy reasons favour the approach taken in *Hunter* v. *Moss* over the approach adopted in *Re Goldcorp*. Finally it will be shown that in the context of a law reform project advanced by the Law Commission, the rule in *Hunter* v. *Moss* was referred to as stating good law.

7.3.3.1 Academic commentators

Some scholars have been no more convinced by the distinction between shares and tangible goods than Neuberger J was in *Re Harvard Securities Ltd*.[26] David Hayton criticises *Hunter* v. *Moss* by pointing out that a problem arises when a part of the bulk is defective. Even if shares of

---

[26] [1997] 2 BCLC 369; see, e.g., Sarah Worthington, 'Sorting Out Ownership Interests in a Bulk', [1999] *JBL* 1.

one class of a particular company are identical, a defect can arise insofar as some of them could have been acquired by a forged gratuitous transfer.[27] To whom does the defective part of the bulk belong? Another problem David Hayton mentions is that of shortfalls.[28] A shortfall occurs where a broker has acquired identical shares for several customers without allocating specific shares to individual customers, and his total shareholding is not sufficient to satisfy the claims of all his customers. The problem is how to divide up the insufficient shareholding between the individual customers.

Joanna Benjamin agrees with the proposition that at least listed shares are identical and indistinguishable, but she does not agree that these shares are incapable of being allocated. She draws a comparison between shares and cash. According to Benjamin, cash may be allocated even though it is identical; she explains that equity has developed rules for tracing or allocation of trust money in circumstances where allocation by identifying cash is impossible. These rules do not permit allocation of commingled property within a mixed account or fund; rather, they permit the allocation of property that has passed through a mixed account. The subject matter of allocation is the property that enters or leaves the pool, as it enters or leaves. The debits and credits, or payments into and out of the pool are allocated to particular persons, but the bulk remains a 'black box' within which the individual entitlements of particular persons are unallocated.[29]

Benjamin's conclusion is that 'it is currently unsafe to rely on the suggestion in *Hunter* v. *Moss* that property rights can arise under a trust without attaching to any particular asset'.[30] She points out, however, that the parties could, by providing for a clear express provision, declare a custodian to be a trustee of a specified proportion of a bulk of securities. But special contractual provisions of this sort aside, '[c]ase law indicates that such arrangements will not arise by operation of law'.[31]

Roy Goode offers a way of distinguishing *Hunter* v. *Moss* from the authorities relating to tangible assets. His view is that shares and other securities are not fungibles. They are not individual assets, but a co-ownership right of one large asset. Shares are a co-ownership interest in the share capital of the issuing company. Debt securities are a

---

[27] David Hayton, 'Uncertainty of Subject Matter of Trusts', [1994] *LQR* 335.
[28] Hayton, 'Uncertainty of Subject Matter' 340.
[29] Joanna Benjamin, 'Custody – An English Law Analysis', [1994] *Butterworths Journal of International Banking and Finance Law* 189.
[30] Joanna Benjamin, *Interests in Securities* 48.   [31] Benjamin, *Interests in Securities* 192.

co-ownership interest in the sum of money outstanding under the particular debt issue. An issue of securities is a single asset which is incapable of being split off into separately owned units. A transfer of a part simply gives rise to co-ownership of what constitutes in law a single indivisible asset.[32] Shares of the same issue are no more than fractions of a single asset, namely the share capital of the issuing company. This is how Roy Goode explains the decision in *Hunter* v. *Moss*. There is no requirement for physical separation because it is impossible to segregate part of the issue from the remainder.

The problem with this view is that it does not sit squarely with current company law principles. Shareholders do not own the share capital. The share capital does not exist as an asset, it is rather a figure on the company's balance sheet reflecting the contributions made or owed by the shareholders to the company and serving as a tool to determine distribution of dividends and of other benefits. The shareholder's contributions are used by the company in the company's business. That business is owned by the company. Shareholders do not have a proprietary co-ownership right to the business or the assets representing it. A share is an 'interest of a shareholder in the company measured by a sum of money, for the purpose of liability in the first place, and of interest in the second, but also consisting of a series of mutual covenants entered into by all the shareholders'.[33]

Moreover, a share and any other unit of a security including debt securities is capable of separation from other units of the same issue. Seperation can be effected by means of keeping separate entries on the shareholders' register. These entries can all show a particular intermediary as legal owner but are still separate holdings identified by an individual account designation. This does not amount to physical separation, but is nevertheless a technique allocating specific units to certain investors.

If the intermediary holds legal title for clients without such a separation, issues of appropriation arise if one of the transfers to the pool was ineffective because the seller did not have authority to sell. In such a case, the buyer does not acquire legal title. If the securities have been transferred into the name of the custodian, the custodian's books will show a larger number of securities than are actually available to the trust. In the case of such a shortfall, the law needs to work out to which

---

[32] Roy Goode, 'Are Intangibles Assets Fungible?', [2003] *LMCLQ* 379 at 382.
[33] *Borland's Trustee* v. *Steel Bros & Co.* [1901] 1 Ch 279.

of the investors holding the securities of that type with the intermediary the shortfall is to be allocated. This involves an exercise of identification, securities units need to be appropriated to beneficial owners.

Notwithstanding the difficulties involved in reconciling the case law on registered securities with the case law on tangibles, the last word on the requirement for certainty in cases of trusts of registered securities is the decision in *Hunter* v. *Moss*.[34] The result achieved by that case is wholeheartedly to be welcomed. It is supported by American case law, policy considerations and by the Law Commission. All three points will be discussed below.

7.3.3.2 US authority

The ruling in *Hunter* v. *Moss* fits squarely with prominent American case law.[35] The US federal courts were faced with the same problem as the English Court of Appeal and allowed for property rights in fungibles even though physical separation had not yet taken place. Moreover, they have found rules addressing shortfalls. The American authority will be discussed in the following paragraphs.

In *Re AO Brown & Co.*,[36] the District Court, S.D. New York, had to consider whether or not equitable ownership was vested in the buyer of shares even though the shares had not been appropriated to the buyer. The buyer had purchased shares through a broker. The broker used the buyer's money to purchase the shares but did not deliver the certificates to the client; instead, he sold the shares to someone else. The broker became insolvent and the receiver found shares of the same kind the broker had originally purchased for the buyer among the broker's assets. Those shares had not been bought with the buyer's money nor had they been appropriated to the buyer. Learned Hand J decided, however, that the buyer had a proprietary interest in the shares that were found in the broker's insolvency. He said in his speech that there is no earmark on shares and referred to *Richardson* v. *Shaw*,[37] a decision of the United States Supreme Court. There the court gave the example of an elevator man who had depleted the elevator below the amount due to all grain depositors. The court stated that when the elevator man subsequently puts back into the elevator enough, or part of enough, wheat to answer his obligation to all of the depositors, they become co-owners of it. The elevator man's general creditors were not entitled

---

[34] [1994] 1 WLR 452 (CA).   [35] [1994] 1 WLR 452 (CA).
[36] 171 F 254 (SDNY 1909).   [37] 209 US 365 (1908).

to the subsequent accretions because there was no doubt that the subsequent filling must be assumed to be an appropriation by him of as
much of his property to make good the conversion. This reasoning was
applied to shares in *Re AO Brown & Co.*,[38] and it was held that brokers do
usually mean their stocks on hand to belong in the first instance to their
customers until they have enough to answer their obligations.

The leading United States Supreme Court case is *Gorman v. Littlefield*.[39]
The broker kept shares of the kind he had bought for the client in a tin
box along with shares in other companies and for other clients. It was
customary to take certificates from that box in order to make delivery to
clients. The broker became insolvent and his client asserted a proprietary claim over some shares in the box. The court held that the client
had a proprietary interest in the shares notwithstanding that they had
not been allocated to the client. It was held that where shares of the
same kind are in the hands of a broker and those shares were held for a
particular client, the client does not need to put her finger upon particular certificates purchased for her in order to claim a proprietary
interest. It is enough that the broker has shares of the same kind. It
was the right and duty of the broker, if he sold the certificates, to use his
own funds to keep the amount good, and this he could do without
depleting his estate to the detriment of other creditors who had no
property rights in the certificates held for particular customers. No
creditor could justly demand that the broker's estate be augmented by
a wrongful conversion of the property of another in this manner, or ask
that property be applied for the general purpose of the estate which
never rightfully belonged to the bankrupt.

Gorman v. *Littlefield* was applied by the same court some years later in
Duell v. *Hollins*.[40] The facts in *Duell* v. *Hollins* were materially the same
as the early cases, with one important exception. Where as in *Gorman* v.
Littlefield the bankrupt broker's tin box contained more than enough
shares to satisfy the proprietary claims of all of its clients, in *Duell* v.
Hollins there was a shortfall. The Supreme Court held that the shares
should be allotted to the customers on a pro rata basis, although they
were not the identical shares purchased for any of the customers. The
fact that the broker had kept insufficient shares fully to satisfy all his
clients was held not to be enough to prevent the application of the rule

[38] 171 F 254 (SDNY 1909).   [39] 229 US 19 (1913).
[40] 241 US 513 (1916); for the English rules on shortfalls, see *Clayton's Case* (1816) 1 Mer 572
and *Barlow Clowes* v. *Vaughan* [1992] 4 All ER 22.

in *Gorman* v. *Littlefield* in so far as the circumstances permitted. *Duell* v. *Hollins* and *Barlow Clowes* v. *Vaughan* show that the problem of shortfalls can be dealt with in a sensible and fair way.

The rules established by the United States Supreme Court in *Gorman* v. *Littlefield* and *Duell* v. *Hollins* have since been affirmed and refined by federal legislation. The Securities and Investor Protection Act of 1970 (SIPA)[41] gives clients of financial intermediaries a proprietary interest in all the shares held by the intermediary on client accounts irrespective of whether the shares have been appropriated to particular clients or not.

American case law not only supports the position taken by the Court of Appeal in *Hunter* v. *Moss*, it protects investors to a greater extent than the English case. In *Hunter* v. *Moss* the trust related to a part of an identified bulk. In American case law there is no requirement for there to exist an identified bulk.

7.3.3.3 Policy considerations

The result in *Hunter* v. *Moss* is also supported by policy considerations. Investors entrust brokers and custodians with their assets. They have two options. They can decide that they are not concerned about the solvency of their chosen service provider and that they are content with a contractual claim to have securities delivered to them. On the other hand, they may feel that they prefer to have property rights in the securities held on their behalf by the broker or custodian to be able to claim their assets in the intermediary's insolvency.

The law should facilitate both of these arrangements. Parties should be able to use straightforward language in their documentation without having to work their way around irreconcilable case law.

Moreover, an onerous requirement for appropriation disadvantages retail investors. If a retail investor wishes to be protected by a property interest, the law should not make compliance with this request difficult by imposing onerous requirements. The more cumbersome the requirement for appropriation, the less likely it will be that intermediaries feel able to offer property-based arrangements.

Strict requirements for appropriation also have the disadvantage of increasing the likelihood that parties will not comply with them because they are unaware of them or because they intentionally neglect to observe them. Clients, in particular retail clients, for whose protection property rights will have been put in place by the parties

---

[41] PubL 91-598 December 30, 1970, 84 Stat. 1636.

concerned, have no practical means of ensuring that their assets are in fact kept in accordance with the formalities imposed by the law. This may lead to undesirable results.

There are also, as the Law Commission pointed out, strong economic reasons favouring a proprietary claim of investors holding indirect securities. Such investors take the risk associated with the securities they hold. The intermediary does not share this risk, and is not liable to the investor if the issuer defaults or if the securities fall in value. The intermediary merely acts as a conduit for the capital, income and other economic benefits that flow from the underlying securities. The intermediary's financial interest lies in the fees and service charges associated with the services provided. Giving the intermediary's creditors a claim over client assets would result in a windfall; it would give those creditors access to funds to which the intermediary made no contribution.[42]

Moreover, creditors are likely to be aware of the fact that securities held on behalf of clients do not belong to the intermediary and therefore do not rely on their availability when entering into a credit relationship with the intermediary. In *Re Goldcorp*,[43] for example, the allocation requirement operated in favour of a bank whose claim was secured by a floating charge. When granting the secured loan the bank must have known that Goldcorp had guaranteed to all of its customers that it would store gold allocated to them so that each customer would have a proprietary interest in the gold stored. The bank must have assumed that Goldcorp actually stored the assets accordingly. When the bank granted the loan, it had no reason to believe that it would later acquire an interest in customer gold. Nevertheless, the bank was able to take advantage of assets that in economic terms belonged to Goldcorp clients and received a windfall benefit.

The rule in *Re Goldcorp* makes it difficult to set up property-based arrangements. Documentation will have to be carefully drafted to protect clients whose assets are kept on an unallocated basis. This exposes investors to the insolvency risk of their intermediary.[44] Retail investors who are less able than professional investors to protect themselves by

---

[42] Law Commission, *Project on Intermediated Investment Securities, Second Seminar: Issues affecting Account Holders and Intermediaries* (June 2006), available from http://www.lawcom.gov.uk/docs/investment_securities_seminar_paper_2.pdf 11

[43] [1995] 1 AC 74 (PC).

[44] Roy Goode, 'Ownership and Obligation in Commercial Transactions', [1997] *LQR* 433 at 453.

seeking legal advice and using appropriate documentation are most likely to be affected by this risk. *Hunter* v. *Moss* goes some way towards remedying this disadvantage for registered securities. The American authority discussed in this book makes it possible for English law, by relying on common law authority, to develop further towards achieving a regime that protects the interests of retail as well as professional investors.

The approach adopted in *Hunter* v. *Moss* helps to create a balance between the legal protection available to professional and retail investors. Statutory reforms have set out to reduce the risk involved in securities transfers. These reforms have benefited professional investors and have fallen short of assisting retail investors. To give two examples:

- CREST was implemented to reduce the risk involved in transactions effected on the stock exchange. CREST provides for a delivery versus payment mechanism which allows for title in the securities to pass to the buyer only if she can at the same time pay the purchase price. This mechanism reduces the time period during which one party is exposed to the other party's insolvency risk. But the mechanism is available only to CREST members who are predominantly professional market participants.
- CREST also enhances the legal position of professional investors by reducing settlement periods. Under Talisman, the last of the paper-based settlement systems, system members first acquired an equitable interest and then had to wait until the end of the settlement period to receive legal title. CREST, at first, shortened the time period between payment and transfer of legal title and, in 2001, made legal title available simultaneously with payment of the purchase price. Again, this improvement has increased the safety of CREST members and not of retail investors who hold securities through an intermediary.

The rule in *Hunter* v. *Moss* and the US authorities supplementing it remedies this imbalance by establishing a legal regime that makes it very easy for clients to assert a proprietary interest in property held by an intermediary.

Hunter v. *Moss* is the leading authority on the point of property rights in registered securities kept in an unallocated bulk of securities of the same kind. The case was decided by the Court of Appeal and so provides clients wishing to rely on it with some certainty. Because of the Privy Council's advice in *Re Goldcorp*, however, the position in English law is also burdened with some uncertainty. It is no surprise that the Financial

Markets Law Committee (FMLC) put forward a proposal for reform. Based on the FMLC proposal, the Law Commission has launched a law reform project relating to indirectly held securities. Both initiatives support the approach taken by *Hunter* v. *Moss*. The FMLC proposal and the Law Commission project will be analysed in subsection 7.3.3.4.

7.3.3.4 Law reform

The rules governing property rights in indirectly held securities have been the subject of a proposal for law reform. FMLC, which is located in the Bank of England, has put forward a proposal for the implementation of a statutory regime. The FMLC was established to identify issues of legal uncertainty or misunderstanding in the framework of the whole-sale financial markets which might give rise to material risks, and to consider how such issues should be addressed. It published a report in 2004 on the need for legislation on indirectly held securities.[45]

The authors of the report concluded that the position as stated in *Hunter* v. *Moss* is good law.[46] They also recommended that, in order to avoid any lingering doubt, a statutory regime be introduced which makes it clear that, unless otherwise agreed, investors in a particular issue of securities held by an intermediary in a common pool have co-proprietary interests in the pool.[47] The report does not contain a proposal giving the account holder a new form property right hitherto unknown to English law. It continues to rest on the protection afforded to beneficiaries under English trust law.[48]

The Law Commission took up the proposal put forward by the FMLC and announced a law reform project on intermediated securities in March 2005.[49] In March and in June 2006, two seminars were held where members of the public in general and representatives of the London financial market in particular were invited to give their views and comments on the proposed law reform. In order to facilitate the

---

[45] http://www.fmlc.org/papers/fmlc1_3_july04.pdf (last visited 27 June 2006).
[46] FMLC, *Issue 3: Property Interests in Securities* (London: Bank of England, 2004), available from http://www.fmlc.org/papers/fmlc1_3_july04.pdf 14.
[47] FMLC, *Issue 3: Property Interests in Securities* 15.
[48] Law Commission, *Project on Intermediated Investment Securities, Second Seminar: Issues affecting Account Holders and Intermediaries* (London: Law Commission, June 2006), available from http://www.lawcom.gov.uk/docs/investment_securities_seminar_ paper_2.pdf 23.
[49] Law Commission, *Ninth Programme of Law Reform*, Law Com 293 (London: Law Commission, March 2005), available from http://www.lawcom.gov.uk/docs/ 9th_Prog_Final.pdf.

discussion at these seminars, the Law Commission published two seminar papers.

In the first, the Law Commission stressed that securities held by an intermediary for an account holder should be protected from the intermediary's liquidator and creditors.[50] In the second, the Law Commission confirmed the view that the position as stated in *Hunter v. Moss* is good law.[51] The Law Commission concluded that this makes it possible in most circumstances for parties to create an express trust in favour of investors holding securities indirectly.

Nevertheless, the Law Commission expressed the view that the financial markets would benefit from clarifying the position, both generally as regards commingled securities and specifically in the case of accounts that mix customer and intermediary assets. The Law Commission proposed that the securities credited to an account holder's account should be considered outside of the intermediary's estate without the need to consider further whether or not they can be allocated for trust purposes.[52] There is no mention, however, that this is to be achieved by way of abandoning the traditional approach adopted by English law. On the contrary, the analysis presented by the Law Commission in both of its seminar papers was firmly rooted within the trust law analysis prevailing in England. Moreover, the Law Commission stressed, with a view to commenting on the possibility of adopting a harmonised European regime, that different legal systems have developed various means of ensuring that commingling of customer securities in a pooled account does not affect their protection against claims by creditors of the intermediary. The protection afforded by any European legal framework should be without prejudice to the protection given earlier and additional rights that an account holder may have under domestic law to the extent that such rights do not conflict with the legal framework rules.[53]

---

[50] Law Commission, *Project on Intermediated Investment Securities, First Seminar: Objectives for a Common Legal Framework* (London: Law Commission, March 2006), available from http://www.lawcom.gov.uk/docs/seminar1.doc#_Toc129072694 14–5, 26.

[51] Law Commission, *Project on Intermediated Investment Securities, Second Seminar: Issues Affecting Account Holders and Intermediaries* (London: Law Commission, June 2006), available from http://www.lawcom.gov.uk/docs/investment_securities_seminar_paper_2.pdf 17.

[52] Law Commission, *Project on Intermediated Investment Securities, Second Seminar* 19.

[53] Law Commission, *Project on Intermediated Investment Securities, Second Seminar* 26.

7.3.4 Conclusions

English law relies on trust law as a mechanism enabling market participants to create a proprietary interest in favour of investors wishing
to hold securities through intermediaries. For a trust to arise for
the benefit of an investor, three requirements need to be satisfied,
also referred to as the 'three certainties'. There must exist certainty of
intention, certainty of beneficiary and certainty of the subject matter
of the trust. The first two requirements were briefly examined in
sections 7.1 and 7.2, respectively. The conclusion of these sections was
that they are unlikely to cause problems when securities are held
indirectly by intermediaries. The requirement for certainty of the subject matter required more analysis.

In English law, there exist two approaches regarding the certainty
requirement. The first has been adopted by the courts in relation to
tangibles. It is not possible, under English law, to create a trust over
tangible assets which are commingled with assets held by the trustee
for her own benefit. If a trust declaration provides for a trust to arise
over a certain number of tangible fungibles, the trust will arise only
once the respective number of fungibles have been physically separated
and appropriated to the trust. As long as the fungibles are still mixed
with fungibles held by the intermediary in its own name, the beneficiary does not acquire an equitable interest.

The second approach has been adopted by the courts in relation to
securities. The leading authority on point is the Court of Appeal decision in *Hunter* v. *Moss*. The court in that case upheld a trust declaration
relating to 50 shares out of a total of 950 shares held by the trustee.
There was no further requirement for appropriation; it was sufficient
that the securities formed part of a bulk of securities held by the trustee.
The requirement for certainty of the subject matter in relation to securities appears to be less burdensome in English law than the requirement
for certainty in relation to tangibles: a trust arises for the benefit of a
beneficiary even if an intermediary holds client securities commingled
with own securities.

The analysis carried out in this section showed that the position
adopted in *Hunter* v. *Moss* is supported by American case law as well as
by policy considerations. The fact the *Hunter* v. *Moss* is good law has also
been confirmed in a paper published by the Law Commission.

The conclusion of this section is that an investor acquires an equitable
interest in indirectly held securities when a trust is established in her

favour. For that to occur the securities to which the trust relates need to be identified. When securities are held in pooled accounts, an investor will acquire equitable ownership in the securities when the bulk of which the securities form part has been identified; it is not necessary for the intermediary to segregate specific securities out of that bulk and to appropriate them to the investor.

7.4 Summary of the analysis

The purpose of this chapter was to determine the circumstances in which investors who do not wish to hold securities directly have property rights in the securities that they hold through intermediaries.

In England, the law of trust operates as the tool through which investors are able to avail themselves of proprietary rights in indirectly held securities. An investor holds a proprietary interest in securities held on her behalf by an intermediary if a trust has been established in her favour by the intermediary. This proprietary interest is enforceable in the intermediary's insolvency and prevails over charging orders issued by general creditors of the intermediary. It subsides only if legal title to the securities is transferred to a purchaser in good faith and for value.

Under the trust law analysis, the intermediary holds legal title and the investor holds equitable title to the securities. If securities are held through a chain of multiple intermediaries, the ultimate investor's immediate intermediary does not hold legal title because its name is not entered in the securities register. Instead the investor's immediate intermediary holds equitable title securities held by another intermediary on its behalf. In these circumstances, the ultimate intermediary holds an equitable title to the entitlement held by its immediate intermediary.

England is in the process of introducing law reform clarifying property rights in relation to securities held by intermediaries. The proposals put forward in this context are based upon the analysis currently adopted by English law. No attempt has been made to create a system for indirect holdings of securities that would operate according to rules that are independent of the current legal analysis; this is evidence that English law is likely to continue its path-dependent development.

It will be shown in part II that both German and Austrian law enable investors who hold securities indirectly through intermediaries to enjoy property rights in these securities. German and Austrian law use a different legal doctrine to achieve this result.[54] Nevertheless, in terms of outcomes, the level of protection in the three jurisdictions is similar. Under both approaches investors hold property rights to securities that have preferred status in the intermediary's insolvency and that take priority over claims raised by the intermediaries' unsecured creditors. One difference between English law, on the one hand, and German and Austrian law, on the other, is the point in time at which the respective property rights arise. In English law, assuming that the underlying documentation does not regulate the matter differently, the buyer acquires equitable title to securities when the requirements imposed by the three certainties have been satisfied. This frequently occurs before the securities have been credited to the buyer's account.[55] In Germany and in Austria, co-ownership to securities usually passes to the buyer when the securities are credited to her account.

---

[54] See section 12.3.
[55] Law Commission, *Project on Intermediated Investment Securities, Second Seminar* 25.

8 Conclusions on English law

Part I of the book analysed the English law of securities. English securities are issued predominantly in the form of registered securities. They do not constitute negotiable instruments. Securities certificates are documents of evidence only. When securities first appeared in England they were transferred by way of novation. This doctrinal mechanism has sent English law down a path on which it has remained since then. The transfer procedure that was in place when securities first emerged reflects the law of novation and has shaped transfer procedures that have been adopted ever since, all the way down to the rules that govern uncertificated securities.

In England, property rights in securities are deeply imbedded in the path adopted by English private law. England approaches property rights in securities from the perspective of its historically determined dual-headed jurisdiction at law and in equity. An investor becomes the owner at law when her name is entered on the securities register. It is possible for an investor to acquire equitable title to the securities prior to that; equitable title, however, vests in the buyer only if a trust is created in her favour either by operation of law or by an express declaration. Neither ownership at law nor ownership in equity are enforceable through an action that would establish that the claimant has absolute title to the securities. Property rights in England are established only as between the parties who participate in the respective litigation.

When paper certificates became too cumbersome to handle, the English securities market opted for dematerialisation of securities. The form in which this dematerialisation was carried out shows the influence of the legal doctrinal tools that had been in place prior to dematerialisation. Nevertheless, dematerialisation has caused English law to become more like German and Austrian law, albeit at a functional rather than a doctrinal level.

English legal doctrine has also had an impact on the type of service provider that has emerged in the English securities market. The procedural steps that need to be taken to transfer securities and that have been shaped by the law of novation have faciliated the emergence of registrars who maintain securities on behalf of issuers in the English market.

Investors are traditionally protected against defective issues in English law through the doctrine of novation and the doctrine of estoppel. It is difficult to see how both doctrines operate in the context of modern uncertificated transfers. That is, however, a matter for the courts to resolve and they will do so consistently with the path adopted by English law.

English legal doctrine protects investors against unauthorised transfers through the law of estoppel. Similar to the situation in relation to defective issues, it is not clear how, if at all, the traditional rules apply to uncertificated transfers. Nevertheless it is fair to conclude that the courts will develop the law consistently with the principles put in place by incumbent English legal doctrine. In addition to the rules on estoppel, the regulation governing uncertificated securities put in place rules on unauthorised transfers that supplemented the common law. The changes that appear to have occurred as a result of the implementation of the new transfer regime have caused English law to become more like German and Austrian law. These similarities, however, have also occurred at a functional rather than a doctrinal level.

England uses trust as the doctrinal tool to protect investors who hold securities indirectly through intermediaries. Investors who hold securities indirectly under English law acquire property rights in these securities if a trust is established for their benefit. The current position is that investors hold proprietary rights even if securities are held on a commingled basis in pooled or omnibus accounts. A law reform confirming this position has been proposed, and again, the protection afforded by English law is functionally but not doctrinally similar to the protection available under German or Austrian law.

After this analysis of English law, the German and Austrian law of securities will be examined in part II of the book. As with the analysis of English law, the discussion on German and Austrian law will at first focus on the historical background of the law of securities in both jurisdictions. After that, the current theory underlying securities and their transfers in German and Austrian law will be examined, including defective issues and unauthorised transfers. Paper transfers will be addressed first. Transfers that are effected without the need to move paper documents will then be analysed.

PART II

German and Austrian law

In German and Austrian law most securities are issued in the form of bearer instruments[1] and these instruments are considered to be tangibles. The underlying theory in modern German law is that securities certificates are paper documents of a very special type. The right to which the paper document relates materialises in the document and can therefore be transferred according to the rules governing tangibles. If the paper document is transferred, the buyer not only acquires title to the paper, but also becomes entitled to the right to which the paper relates. The German-language term for German securities is '*Wertpapier*' and is used in both German and Austrian usage. The word '*Wertpapier*' literally means 'paper of value' and the term refers to the fact that the document relating to the security embodies a valuable right. The term is also designed to reflect the theory underlying German and Austrian securities, that the rights to which the securities certificate relates and the certificate merge and become one tangible asset. As a result, securities, their transfers and indirect holdings of securities are all subject to the rules governing tangible assets.

The analysis adopted by modern German and Austrian law, however, emerged only some time after securities were first issued. In chapter 9, the historic starting point and the development that led to the modern German theory will be examined. First, the rules governing securities when they emerged will be analysed (section 9.1). It will be shown that securities were at the time classified as debt and that transfers of securities were analysed in terms of assignment. The law of assignment, however, had significant disadvantages, examined in section 9.2. To overcome them, legal scholars propounded several theories during the

---

[1] Some companies have now replaced bearer shares with name shares (see chapter 13).

first half of the nineteenth century, analysed in section 9.3. The theory that developed into the modern German orthodox view was originally put forward by Friedrich Carl von Savingy, who advanced the view that securities were to be classified as tangibles (section 9.4). Savigny's theory, however, became generally accepted only after the German and Austrian law of tangibles had adopted certain doctrinal rules. The conclusion of chapter 9 will be that Savigny's view became generally accepted only after the doctrinal framework of all the states of Germany and also Austria had implemented a rule that protected the purchaser of tangibles against adverse claims. The modern German approach did not develop as a theory that would be independent of the legal rules that were in place in other areas of the law and it rests firmly on certain rules governing the law of tangibles.

In chapter 10, the rules governing securities in modern German and Austrian law will be analysed. It will be shown how the law of tangibles is applied to securities and their transfers in both German and Austrian law and the analysis will focus on securities which are not held with intermediaries. The German and Austrian rules will also be compared to the English rules, followed in section 10.1, by those governing the transfer of ownership. After that the rules governing unauthorised transfers and defective issues will be examined (section 10.2 and section 10.3, respectively).

Chapter 11 deals with the impact of the legal analysis of securities and the doctrinal rules governing their transfers on the institutional setup of German and Austrian market infrastructure. It will be shown that in both Germany and Austria securities depositories have emerged as the prevailing type of service provider assisting clients who wish to hold securities indirectly. The analysis contained in chapter 11 will lead to two conclusions. The first is that the rules governing securities and their transfer – in particular the rule protecting the purchaser against adverse claims – facilitated the development of this particular type of service provider in the German and the Austrian market (section 11.1). The second is that the fact that securities are governed by the rules on tangibles has inspired Germany and Austria to eliminate paper from the transfer process by way of immobilisation rather than by way of dematerialisiation (section 11.2).

In chapter 12 the legal position of investors holding securities indirectly through intermediaries will be analysed. It will be shown that in German and Austrian law the law of bailment is applied in order to enable investors to create property rights in indirectly held securities. In order to facilitate indirect holdings, German and Austrian law have also developed a sophisticated doctrine of co-ownership and co-possession. This particular form of doctrinal analysis has emerged in both Germany and Austria because securities have become classified as tangible movables. This legal analysis provides the normative framework within which the securities market, and the legal rules supporting it, have developed. The analysis impacted on the way in which paper was eliminated from the transfer process, notwithstanding the fact that Germany had implemented an alternative transfer system for Government bonds which could have served a model for creating a paperless transfer system.

Chapter 13 offers an analysis of the emergence of name shares in the securities market practice and it will be concluded that this is an example of functional rather than doctrinal convergence.

9 The historic starting point

Securities seem to have first appeared in Germany and Austria during the Napoleonic wars,[1] issued by the state to raise finance to cover the cost of the wars. The instruments were actively traded in a liquid market.[2] Securities were also used in Germany and Austria to raise finance for the construction of railways and for other large-scale projects.[3]

Before we embark on a consideration of how Austrian and German law analysed securities when they first appeared, we need to remind ourselves that Germany did not exist as a unified nation throughout most of the nineteenth century. It consisted of a collection of smaller states, each of which constituted a jurisdiction of its own.[4] This book will not provide an analysis of the law of all the states that now form

---

[1] Heinrich von Poschinger, *Beitrag zur Geschichte der Inhaberpapiere in Deutschland* (Erlangen: Deichert, 1875) 31; Ulf Siebel, *Rechtsfragen internationaler Anleihen* (Berlin: Duncker und Humblott, 1997) 97–99; N. Th. Gönner, *Von Staatsschulden, deren Tilgungsanstalten und vom Handel mit Staatspapieren* (München: Fleischmannsche Buchhandlung, 1826) 49–54.

[2] Klaus Hopt, 'Ideelle und wirtschaftliche Grundlagen der Aktien-, Bank- und Börsenentwicklung im 19. Jahrhundert', in Helmut Coing and Walter Wilhelm (eds.), *Wissenschaft und Kodifikation im 19. Jahrhundert Band V* (Frankfurt am Main: Vittorio Klostermann, 1980) 156–157; Gönner, *Von Staatsschulden*, 182; C. Schumm, *Die Amortisation verlorener oder sonst abhanden gekommener Schuldurkunden nach gemeiner deutscher Praxis mit Berücksichtigung deutscher Partikulargesetze, besonders im Betreff der auf Inhaber (au porteur) gestellten Staats- und öffentlichen Kreditpapiere* (Heidelberg: Mohr, 1830) 39–40; H. Trumpler, 'Zur Geschichte der Frankfurter Börse', *Bankarchiv* 9 (1909/1910) 100–101; Anton Niebauer, 'Die Begebungspraxis bei Österreichischen Staatsanleihen', *Bankarchiv* 6 (1906/1907) 35.

[3] Helmut Coing, *Europäisches Privatrecht, 19. Jahrhundert*, vol. II (München: Beck, 1989) 95–96; Georg Bruns, *Entwicklungsprobleme des Effektenwesens* (Frankfurt am Main: Fritz Knapp Verlag, 1966) 12–15.

[4] For this, see Reinhard Zimmerman, 'Savigny's Legacy: Legal History, Comparative Law, and the Emergence of a European Legal Science', (1996) 112 *LQR* 575.

part of the German state; it will focus on the law of the state of Prussia as well as analysing Austrian law.

Prussia adopted a Civil Code in 1794, referred to in English translation as the 'Prussian Civil Code'.[5] The German title is '*Allgemeines Landrecht*', abbreviated to 'ALR'. The Prussian ALR was replaced by the German Civil Code (BGB) in 1900. In 1811, Austria adopted a Civil Code which was influenced by the ALR, enacted under the name of 'General Civil Code' (*Allgemeines Bürgerliches Gesetzbuch*), abbreviated to 'ABGB'. The Austrian ABGB is still in force.

It has already been pointed out that modern German and Austrian law classifies securities as tangibles. This analysis, however, started to appear only during the mid-nineteenth century. Before then, securities were also issued with the help of paper documents, but were nevertheless classified as intangibles. This earlier classification, the shortcomings attached to it and the way in which these shortcomings were overcome to create the modern theory will be examined in the following sections.

9.1 Securities as intangibles

There exists evidence that supports the conclusion that, until the late nineteenth century, securities were considered to be intangibles rather than tangibles. The first piece of evidence is the legal terminology used in legislation and legal writing. The term '*Wertpapier*', which is shaped by the theoretical framework underlying securities in modern German and Austrian law, was not used in legislation or in legal writing until the mid-nineteenth century. The instruments that are now referred to as '*Wertpapiere*' were, when securities started to become popular, referred to in different legal language, consisting of a somewhat cumbersome reference to the paper documents used for transfer purposes.

The first part of the ALR, for example, defines certain legal terms. One of these is what could be translated into English as 'capital investments':[6] 'Papers issued to the bearer, e.g. banknotes, mortgage debentures, shares, etc., irrespective of whether they carry interest, are like

---

[5] Eric Weitz, *Prussian Civil Code, Excerpts Translated from Allgemeines Landrecht für die Preussischen Staaten* (Berlin: 1821).

[6] The German term is '*Kapitalvermögen*'.

other debt instruments considered to be capital investments.'[7] 'Papers issued to the bearer' would in modern writing be termed a 'Wertpapier',[8] but not only does the definition in the ALR not contain the modern German term it also appears from the provision that mortgage debentures and shares were considered similar in their legal nature to debt, which is classified as an intangible rather than as a tangible.

Language similar to that appearing in the ALR can be found in the ABGB, which contains rules governing 'debt notes that are issued to the bearer'.[9] There is another rule on 'letters of debt issued to the bearer'.[10] Both provisions refer to what would now be called bearer securities.[11] Like the ALR, the ABGB does not contain the modern term 'Wertpapier' or a provision implementing the modern theory.

The hypothesis that in the late eighteenth and early nineteenth century securities were not yet considered to be tangibles is also supported by an analysis of the writings of academic commentators of the time. The analysis of some of these leads to two observations. The first is that securities appear to have been classified as 'debt' or as 'obligations'

---

[7] ALR part 1, title 2, s. 12, which reads in German: 'Die auf jeden Inhaber lautenden Papiere, zB Banknoten, Pfandbriefe, Aktien u.s.w., sie mögen Zinsen tragen oder nicht, werden gleich anderen Schuldinstrumenten zum Kaptialvermögen gerechnet'; see also ALR part 1, title 15, s. 47 which refers to 'papers and documents issued to the bearer' ('auf den Inhaber lautende Papiere[n] und Urkunden').

[8] This conclusion is confirmed by a monograph published in 1900 which compares the then newly enacted German BGB with the Prussian ALR which had come into force over 100 years earlier. The book was written with a view to assisting members of the German legal community to familiarise themselves with the new Civil Code. The BGB of 1900 contains a set of rules on certain bearer securities. These provisions are informed by the modern German theory that the rights the document relates to materialises in the paper document and therefore receive the same treatment as a tangible. In the chapter comparing the then newly enacted modern German law with the previous regime contained in the Prussian ALR, the author observes that the ALR did not contain a designated section on bearer securities, but nevertheless incorporated rules governing these instruments, albeit dispersed through the code. He points to the provision analysed in this book as examples of how the ALR took securities into account (Franz Leske, Vergleichende Darstellung des Bürgerlichen Gesetzbuches für das Deutsche Reich und der Landesrechte, Band III, Das Bürgerliche Gesetzbuch und das Preußische Allgemeine Landrecht, Berlin: Liebmann, 1900 319).

[9] ABGB, s. 1393: 'Schuldscheine, die auf den Überbringer lauten' ('debt notes that are issued to the bearer').

[10] ABGB, s. 371: 'auf den Überbringer lautende Schuldbriefe.'

[11] This proposition takes authority from the explanatory notes to the Austrian ABGB (Julius Ofner (ed.), Der Urentwurf und die Beratungsprotokolle des Österreichischen Allgemeinen Bürgerlichen Gesetzbuches, vol. 2, Wien: Alfred Hölder, 1889 237); explanatory notes are regarded as authority for interpreting statutory provision in the Austrian and German legal tradition.

rather than as tangibles by a significant number of eminent legal scholars. The second is that transfers of securities were considered to be
primarily governed by the law of assignment. A selection of these contributions will be analysed in the following paragraphs.

In a book published in 1821, the author discussed the validity of
forward sales contracts relating to Government bonds; he classified
such transactions as the buying and selling of debt owed by the
government. By using the term 'debt', the author adopted a classification that puts Government bonds in the category of intangibles
rather than in that of tangibles.[12] In another monograph published
in 1826, the author analysed the legal nature of those Government
bonds which as a consequence of the Napoleonic wars had become
a widespread instrument to facilitate state finance. He explicitly
rejected the view that Government bonds were tangibles, insisting
that a distinction needed to be made between the paper documents
evidencing the debt issued by the government and the debt itself.
The document was a tangible: the debt, however, was an intangible.[13]

A commentary on the ALR published in 1804 contained the view that
bearer instruments were in some respect similar to other debt in that
they could be bought and assigned. In other respects they were similar
to money because, in some German states, there existed a rule protecting the bona fide purchaser against adverse claims. In any event, they
were not considered to be movables or even immovables.[14] This contrasts sharply with the position in modern law, where securities are
considered to be tangible movables.

Likewise, the author of a leading commentary wrote in 1854 that
bearer instruments were a 'special type of obligation'.[15] They were not
transferred by way of assignment, but rather like tangibles by way of
delivery of the paper document.[16] The author, however, stopped short
of classifying bearer instruments as tangibles.

---

[12] Josef von Wayna, *Antwort auf die Stock-Jobbery, und der Handel mit Staatspapieren nach dem jetzigen Zustande, politisch und juristisch betrachtet* (Wien: Gerold, 1821) 27–33.
[13] Gönner, *Von Staatsschulden* 172–177.
[14] *Commentar zum allgemeinen Landrecht für die preußischen Staaten*, vols. 1, 2 (Breslau: Hamberger, 1804) (no author mentioned) 14.
[15] Johann Caspar Bluntschli, *Deutsches Privatrecht*, vol. 2 (München: Literarisch-artistische Anstalt, 1854) 22. The author refers to bearer instruments as '*Schuldscheine auf den Inhaber*', which are classified as '*eine besondere Gattung von Obligationen*', for which this book offers the translation 'special type of obligations'.
[16] Bluntschli, *Deutsches Privatrecht* 23.

Bills of exchange, which are traditionally grouped into the same category as securities by Austrian and German law,[17] were also, until the mid-nineteenth century, considered to be intangibles. In a leading commentary published in 1823, the author discussed bills of exchange in the chapter on the 'law of obligations', and not in the chapter on the 'law of things'.[18] The same analysis was adopted in a book published in 1797.[19]

These examples lead to the first observation made in this section. They show that a significant number of legal scholars considered securities to constitute 'debt' or 'obligations'.

The second observation following from an analysis of mid-nineteenth century legal writing is that there exists a significant number of contributors who analyse the transfer of securities in terms of *assignment*. Assignment is the legal method through which intangibles are transferred; the law of assignment does not apply to tangibles.[20]

In the mid-nineteenth century, a distinguished German scholar published a treatise of several volumes containing a systematic analysis of the Prussian civil law. Volume 3 of the treatise referred to an 'obligation for which there exists a written document . . . [that] . . . is issued to the bearer'.[21] The text also uses the French term '*lettres au porteur*' which in English means something like 'letters [issued] to the bearer'. As in the earlier literature, the author does not classify these obligations or the letters issued in connection with them as 'tangibles'. Their transfer is rather discussed together with the transfer of other obligations in the chapter dedicated to the assignment of rights.[22]

---

[17] See Friedrich Wilhelm Ludwig Bornemann, *Systematische Darstellung des Preußischen Civilrechts mit Benutzung der Materialien des Allgemeinen Landrechts*, vol. 1, 2nd edn. (Berlin: Jonas, 1842) 106. The author refers to a bill of exchange as a debt instrument, which for that reason is part of what ALR part 1, title 2, s. 12 defines as 'capital investment' (*Kapitalsvermögen*).

[18] Carl Friedrich Eichhorn, *Einleitung in das deutsche Privatrecht mit Einschluss des Lehensrechts* (Göttingen: Vandenhoeck und Ruprecht, 1823); in the book, the law of obligations is referred to as '*Recht der Forderungen*'. The law of things is referred to as '*Rechte an Sachen*'.

[19] Wilhelm August Friedrich Danz, *Handbuch des heutigen deutschen Privatrechts* (Stuttgart: Löflund, 1797).

[20] Christoph Christian von Dabelow, *System des gesammten heutigen Civil-Rechts*, vol. I, 2nd edn. (Halle: 1796) 317.

[21] Friedrich Wilhelm Ludwig Bornemann, *Darstellung des Preußischen Civilrechts mit Benutzung der Materialien des Allgemeinen Landrechts*, vol. 3, 2nd edn. (Berlin: Jonas, 1843) 76.

[22] Bornemann, *Darstellung des Preußischen Civilrechts*, vol. 3 65–103.

Likewise, the ABGB regulates the transfer of what it refers to as 'debt notes that are issued to the bearer' in the section on assignment.[23] The rule suggests that the transfer of bearer debt notes would, in principle, be governed by the general law of assignment. It states in somewhat cumbersome language that 'debt notes that are issued to the bearer are assigned by means of delivery and, apart from physical possession, do not require any further evidence of the assignment'.[24] The fact that the transfer of such debt notes was inserted into the section on the law of assignment shows that the ABGB, historically, did not consider securities to be tangibles.

There is, therefore, evidence that the starting point of Prussian and Austrian law was to classify securities as intangibles rather than as tangibles. The legal classification of the ancestors of modern German and modern Austrian securities was therefore very similar to the classification used in early – and, indeed, in modern – English law.

From a similar starting point, English law maintained the original classification and went on, as we have seen, to adopt a novation-based analysis, whereas German and Austrian law began to qualify securities as tangibles and went on to apply the law relating to tangibles to transfers of securities. England adopted a preference for registered, Germany and Austria adopted a preference for bearer, securities.

What we observe here is divergence rather than convergence, and there may be more than one reason for this development. One factor, however, that has influenced the path along which the two legal systems have progressed is the legal environment that existed at time when securities first appeared.

Like English practice, German and Austrian practice began to create the financial instruments that are now known as securities at a time in their history when an unprecedented need for large amounts of capital appeared in the economy. In England, this first happened in the early-to-mid-eighteenth century, during the period leading to the South Sea Bubble.[25] In Germany and in Austria, securities were first utilised by governments as a method to cover the cost the states incurred when fighting the Napoleonic wars in the late eighteenth century.

---

[23] ABGB, s. 1393: '*Schuldscheine, die auf den Überbringer lauten.*'

[24] ABGB, s. 1393: '*Schuldscheine, die auf den Überbringer lauten, werden schon durch die Übergabe abgetreten, und bedürfen nebst dem Besitze keines andern Beweises der Abtretung.*'

[25] Gönner, *Von Staatsschulden*, 13.

What is more important than the timing as such is the fact that when the instruments appeared in England, assignment of debt was not yet generally possible other than by way of novation. The conclusion of part I of this book was that the fact that novation was the most robust technique available to transfer obligations when securities first appeared caused England to shape securities around the law of novation and to rely predominantly on registered securities.

In German and Austrian law, on the other hand, assignment was generally possible when securities first appeared. There was, therefore no need to apply the law of novation to facilitate transfers of securities. The rules on assignment, however, had significant disadvantages, which had to be overcome by German and Austrian legal doctrine. The shortcomings of the law of assignment, and the theories put forward in order to overcome them, will be analysed in the following sections.

9.2 Shortcomings of the law of assignment

The conclusion of section 9.1 was that, when securities first appeared in Germany and Austria, they were classified as intangibles and that their transfers were considered to be governed by the law of assignment.

The assignment of debt was, at the time, possible under the German ALR as well as the Austrian ABGB. Debt and equity securities could therefore be placed on the market by issuers with a view to being transferred by taking advantage of the general law of assignment contained in the civil codes of the time. There was no need in German and Austrian law for the issuer to consent to a transfer.[26] This may explain why German and Austrian law never relied on the law of novation to analyse securities or their transfers, and why registered securities never took root in German or Austrian law.

The fact that German and Austrian law originally classified securities as intangibles and considered their transfers to be governed by the law

---

[26] It is also worth noting in this context that in German law at an earlier stage obligations were considered to constitute personal debt that could not be transferred without the debtor's consent. In particular, Roman law – but also, it seems, the German common law – took this position (Heinrich von Poschinger, *Die Lehre von der Befugniß zur Ausstellung von Inhaber-Papieren*, München: Lindauer, 1870 12). Practice developed techniques making the transfer of obligations possible. Interestingly, some sources report that one of the techniques used was novation (Arthur Engelmann, *Das Preußische Privatrecht in Anknüpfung an das gemeine Recht*, Breslau: Koebner, 1883 203). The transfer would be effected by means of extinguishing the obligation towards the transferee and creating a new, but identical, obligation with the transferor.

of assignment had the advantage of providing a legal basis permitting their transferability, but the analysis also had disadvantages. The first of these consisted in the fact that under German common law it was impossible to have a contractual relationship with an unidentified creditor.[27] German common law would enforce a contract only if the obligee was identified. If securities are issued to the bearer, this rule is, on the face of it, infringed. The issuer of a bearer instruments does not undertake to perform an obligation towards an identified individual: the obligation is to be performed in favour of the person who presents the certificate to the issuer at the time when the obligation becomes due.

The ABGB takes the same position: a debt note is valid only if it contains the name of the creditor (ABGB, s. 1001). Debt notes issued to the bearer, of course, do not refer to the creditor's name.

This rule did not cause problems when securities first appeared because they were originally issued in the name of the respective investors. The issuer would also make out a certificate. The certificate was considered to be a document evidencing the entitlement of the holder, whose name was stated in the certificate. The rights issued were transferred without the involvement of the issuer, the assignment being carried out by way of a written note on the certificate.

Over time, however, the requirement for there to be evidence of each transfer was considered to be too burdensome. Market practice gradually shifted towards replacing name certificates with bearer certificates. At the request of investors, issuers also began to issue certificates to the bearer,[28] a practice difficult to square with the existing law.

Another problematic issue was that the law of assignment subjects the buyers to adverse claims arising out of unauthorised transfers. If an investor buys debt from a seller who was not entitled to sell the debt, she does not acquire title to the debt. The law of assignment does not protect the bona fide purchaser against adverse claims. Market participants would either have to enquire into the material entitlement of the seller – or, alternatively and more likely – would price the risk of unauthorised transfers into every transfer. The latter would reduce the price that could be achieved on the secondary market – and, in turn, also the price for which securities could be first issued.

---

[27] Friedrich Carl von Savingy, *Das Obligationenrecht als Theil des heutigen römischen Rechts*, vol. II (Berlin: Bei Veit und Comp, 1853) 94; Poschinger, *Beitrag zur Geschichte* 34.

[28] Gönner, *Von Staatsschulden*, p. 182.

This problem did not arise in the two jurisdictions analysed in this book. The ABGB and the ALR both had a provision protecting the bona fide buyer of securities.

The ALR contained a provision on money and 'papers or documents issued to the bearer'.[29] The rule restricted the right of the legal owner to reclaim these instruments from a bona fide holder: the owner could ask to have the instruments delivered back to her only if they were, with certainty, identifiable from other securities and if the current holder had acquired them without consideration.

The ABGB states in s. 371 that the owner is able to claim 'letters of debt issued to the bearer' from a third party holder only if she is able to identify the securities her entitlement relates to and if the third-party holder ought to have known that she is not entitled to the securities.

There were, however, other German states that did not have special rules protecting the purchaser of securities against adverse claims. This caused academic commentators to try to suggest ways in which the purchaser could be protected in those jurisdictions which did not have explicit rules against adverse claims. Academic scholars also tried to provide an explanation justifying the rules that under Prussian and Austrian law the purchaser of securities was protected against adverse claims whereas the purchaser of other debt was not.

In order to achieve both tasks, they suggested ways in which they could justify that the law of assignment did not apply to the transfer of securities. Three theories put forward at the time warrant special mention. The proponents of the first theory claimed that securities were assets of a special kind that fell into a category different from tangibles and intangibles. The second theory was based on the view that contract law could explain the special rules that governed securities. According to the third theory, securities were governed by a special type of contract which had its origins in Roman law. These three theories will be analysed in turn in subsections 9.3.1–9.3.3 below.

9.3 Theories overcoming the law of assignment

9.3.1 Nature of the instrument

Some of the legal writing published in the early nineteenth century suggests that the fact that securities could be issued to an unidentified

---

[29] 'Auf jeden Inhaber lautende Papiere und Urkunden' (ALR, part 1, title 15, s. 47).

creditor and that there existed legal rules protecting the bona fide purchaser against adverse claims could be explained by the unique nature of the instruments. Nikolaus Theodore Gönner, at the time a leading German scholar in the field, wrote that securities were a legal institution of their own. They were created with a view to allowing a certain kind of debt to circulate freely between market participants. Because of their unique legal nature, the name of the creditor did not appear on the paper document evidencing securities. According to Gönner, the unique nature of the instruments also explained why there existed special rules protecting the good faith purchaser against adverse claims. He wrote that a purchaser was protected against adverse claims irrespective of whether there existed an explicit statutory rule to that effect.[30]

Gönner did not classify securities as tangibles. He explained that securities were not subject to the rules on assignment by classifying them as a new and independent legal category which was subject to special rules. These special rules were designed for these instruments and had as their objective to facilitate their circulation.[31]

Gönner's view had significant influence on the legal writing of his time and his work was cited with approval by a number of important scholars.[32] Among the scholars following Gönner's approach, the writings of C. Schumm are of particular interest, since he specifically rejected the view that securities were tangibles. Schumm pointed out that the fact that paper documents were used to transfer securities did not serve as an explanation justifying the special rules governing their transfer.[33]

---

[30] Gönner, *Von Staatsschulden* 193, 236.   [31] Gönner, *Von Staatsschulden* 194.

[32] Johann Adam Seuffert, *Praktisches Pandektenrecht*, 2nd edn. (Würzburg: Verlag der Stahel'schen Buchhandlung, 1848) 128–129; Christian Friedrich Glück, *Ausführliche Erläuterung der Pandekten*, vol. XVI, 2nd edn. (Erlangen: Palmsche Verlagsbuchhandlung, 1844) 441–442; C. F. Mühlenbruch, *Die Lehre von der Zession der Forderungsrechte*, 3rd edn. (Greifswald: Ernst Mauritius 1836) 457–459; C. J. A. Mittermaier, *Grundsätze des gemeinen deutschen Privatrechts*, vol. II, 7th edn. (Regensburg: Manz, 1847) 7–9; Heinrich Gottlieb Philipp Gengler, *Lehrbuch des deutschen Privatrechts*, vol. I (Erlangen: Verlag von Theodor Bläsnig, 1854) 170–172; Josef Unger, *Die rechtliche Natur der Inhaberpapiere* (Leipzig: Breitkopf und Härtel, 1857) 24–25.

[33] C. Schumm, *Die Amortisation verlorener oder sonst abhanden gekommener Schuldurkunden nach gemeiner deutscher Praxis mit Berücksichtigung deutscher Partikulargesetze, besonders im Betreff der auf Inhaber (au porteur) gestellten Staats- und öffentlichen Kreditpapiere* (Heidelberg: Mohr, 1830) 49.

9.3.2 Contract

Later in the nineteenth century, some scholars propounded the view that the law of contract explained the special rules that govern securities. The theory claimed that securities were issued under special contractual terms, the aim being to contract out of those rules on assignment that were perceived to be a hindrance to the circulation of securities among market participants. As a result of these terms, the creditor did not have to be named on the security, and it was therefore possible to issue securities for the benefit of the bearer. The terms also provided protection against adverse claim by contracting out of the nemo dat rule: a good faith buyer of securities acquired title upon delivery of the documents to her even if the seller was not entitled to transfer the securities.[34]

The major disadvantage of the theory was that it could not claim that the special terms which were said to govern securities were explicitly agreed upon by the parties; there was no written documentation to that effect. The proponents of the theory therefore claimed that the terms were contained in an implicit agreement between the issuer and the first buyer of a particular security. Buyers who purchased securities from another investor rather than from the issuer were deemed to have, by purchasing the instruments, agreed to these implied special terms.

9.3.3 Transfer by novation

Another popular mid-nineteenth-century theory was based on the hypothesis that securities were a modern equivalent of a type of contract that had existed in Roman law.[35] This type of contract was not explicitly referred to in the civil codes of the time but existed nevertheless because the modern law never abolished it and thus made it possible for an obligation to be owed to an unidentified creditor such as the bearer of the paper document.

Transfers of obligations arising out of this special type of contract were said not to be effected by way of assignment, but rather by way of

---

[34] Heinrich Thöl, *Das Handelsrecht in Verbindung mit dem allgemeinen deutschen Handelsgesetzbuch*, vol. I, 4th edn. (Göttingen: Verlag der Dieterichschen Buchhandlung, 1862) 321–337; J. Binding, 'Der Vertrag als alleinige Grundlage der Inhaberpapiere', *Zeitschrift für das gesamte Handelsrecht und Wirtschaftsrecht* 10 (1866) 400.

[35] Carl Einert, *Über das Wesen und die Form des Literalcontracts wie dieser zur Zeit der Justinianischen Gesetzgebung ausgebildet gewesen und Vergleichung desselben mit dem Wechsel* (Leipzig: Tauchnitz, 1852) 77–87.

what was termed 'delegation'.[36] The issuer, when first issuing securities, took upon himself two sets of obligations. He promised to pay
the bearer a sum of money specified in the document; he also gave the
first bearer and any subsequent bearer an irrevocable power of attorney
to agree on his behalf to pay the sum of money promised to any subsequent buyer. As a result, a transfer of securities did not involve an
assignment of an obligation and transfers were rather carried out
by way of novation. When securities were transferred the seller was
deemed to act in two capacities. He would on his own behalf agree to
give up his entitlement and to transfer it to the buyer. The seller would
also exercise the power of attorney and agree on the issuer's behalf to
pay the buyer the amount for which the security was issued.

The theory identified a way of avoiding the rules on assignment. It
suffered, however, from the same flaw as the theory discussed in the
subsection 9.3.2. Like the previous theory, it had the disadvantage that it
could not rely on documentation containing explicit terms providing for a
power of attorney for the benefit of the bearer or containing an agreement
between the issuer, the seller and the buyer upon transfer of the securities.

9.3.4 Conclusions

The three theories analysed in subsections 9.3.1–9.3.3 are evidence
that the law of assignment was, in principle, considered to apply to
securities transfers and that that was considered to have significant
shortcomings. The rules on assignment were perceived by the legal
community as a hindrance to market practice. Several prominent scholars suggested ways in which these deficiencies could be overcome but
none of the theories proved to be influential in the long term. What
became the modern theory appeared in the mid-nineteenth century and
will be examined in section 9.4.

9.4 Securities as tangibles

The solution that developed into the modern orthodox view was
put forward by Friedrich Carl von Savigny.[37] He began by analysing

---

[36] Unger, *Die rechtliche Natur der Inhaberpapiere* 87–120, 149.

[37] Savigny is widely considered to have developed the theory that later came to be known
as 'Verkörperungstheorie': Heinrich Brunner, in Wilhelm Endemann (ed.), *Handbuch des
deutschen Handelsrechts*, vol. II (Leipzig: Fues's Verlag, 1882) 143; L. Goldschmidt, *System
des Handelsrechts*, 4th edn. (Stuttgart: Verlag von Ferdinand Enke, 1892) 165; Dorothee
Einsele, *Wertpapierrecht als Schuldrecht* (Tübingen: J. C. B. Mohr (Paul Siebeck), 1995) 5.

securities in terms of the German common law – that is, the legal rules that applied in the German territories before the civil codes were implemented. He concluded that German common law could not enforce contracts giving rights to an unascertained creditor such as the bearer of the document evidencing the entitlement.

Savigny also thought that classifying the process whereby securities were transferred as an assignment would have the disadvantage that the buyer would not be protected against adverse claims. He expressed the view that the widespread use of the instruments and the practical need for transferability led the law to recognise that the instruments and their transfer were governed by special rules that did not involve the application of the law of assignment.

Savigny proposed that the rules on assignment could be avoided by accepting that custom had created new law: commercial practice had caused the law to recognise a new legal method for the transfer of obligations. This method used paper certificates issued to the bearer for the transfer of certain obligations. The form so developed made it possible for the law to apply the rules governing the transfer of tangibles to the transfer of obligations and thereby to avoid the disadvantages of assignment.[38]

Savigny's approach was motivated by the insight that securities required special transfer rules. It is important to note that the theory provides a satisfying explanation of the special rules governing securities only in the context of a particular doctrinal framework. It does not provide an explanation that could be applied in a jurisdiction that does not have rules protecting the bona fide purchaser of tangibles against adverse claims.

When Savigny's theory was first formulated Austria and Prussia had a general rule on the good faith acquisition of tangibles and one on the good faith acquisition of bearer securities. In both jurisdictions, the theory helped explain why obligations evidenced in bearer securities received the same preferential treatment as tangibles. The theory also worked in German states which had no rules protecting the bona fide buyer of securities, but did have rules protecting the bona fide buyer of tangibles. Applying the theory made it possible to justify the application of the rules on tangibles to securities but it did not work for those jurisdictions which had no such rule.

---

[38] Savigny, *Das Obligationenrecht als Theil des heutigen römischen Rechts*, vol. II (Berlin: Bei Veit und Comp, 1853) 97–100.

As a result, when it was first formulated the theory was not universally accepted in all German states. This hypothesis is supported by the discussion that took place in the committee that drafted the General German Commercial Code (*Allgemeines Deutsches Handelsgesetzbuch*) which came into force in 1871 and was written to be implemented in all German states and in Austria.[39] It was also drafted with a view to suiting the needs of those states who were not governed by the ALR or the ABGB. As usual in German and Austrian legal systems, the discussions of the drafting committee were officially recorded and published and unlike English explanatory notes these protocols were considered to be authority for the interpretation of the code.

The protocol reveals that the drafting committee discussed whether to insert a provision in the code that would classify securities as tangible goods which would have implemented the view put forward by Savigny and other academic commentators. The draftsmen decided against doing this because not all German states that were going to adopt the General German Commercial Code of 1871 (HGB) contained rules protecting the bona fide purchaser of tangible goods. Because such a purchaser of tangibles could not rely on a rule providing for the good faith acquisition of title in all German states, the theory that securities were tangibles was rejected. It would not have achieved the desired result; in those states where tangibles could not be acquired in good faith, the purchaser of securities would, like the purchaser of tangibles, have been subject to adverse claims. This was considered to be 'highly inappropriate' ('*höchst bedenklich*').[40] Rather than classifying securities as tangibles and thereby adopting the modern orthodox theory of securities, the draftsmen of the HGB went on to insert a provision that provided for the good faith acquisition of title to tangibles in general and of title to securities in particular. The purpose of specifically stating that securities were subject to the good faith acquisition rule was to protect purchasers against adverse claims irrespective of whether securities were classified as tangibles or as intangibles. The appearance of this rule in 1871 in all German states and in Austria coincided with Savigny's theory becoming the prevailing view. Whether or not there is

---

[39] L. Lutz (ed.), *Protokolle der Kommission zur Beratung eine allgemeinen deutschen Handelsgesetzbuches* (Würzburg: Verlag der Stahel'schen Buch- und Kunsthandlung, 1858) 432.

[40] Lutz, *Protokolle* 432, 440.

a causal link between the two we can observe that, by the end of the nineteenth century, the modern theory had become generally accepted.

The theory contends that rights issued in the form of securities are transformed from intangibles to tangibles upon issue of the securities. Classifying securities as tangibles helps to explain the rules by which they are governed. The metaphor that the rights materialise in the paper document operates as a theoretical explanation why the transfer of securities is not effected by way of assignment, but rather (like the transfer of tangibles) by way of delivery of the asset. The theory also helps to explain why the bona fide purchaser of securities is protected against adverse claims whereas the assignee of debt is not.

The theory became the basis upon which modern German law was drafted. The rules on securities and their transfer which are contained in the ALR/BGB reflect this theory and they will be analysed in chapter 10. In contrast, the Austrian rules on securities and their transfer were adopted in 1811 which was well before the modern theory had established itself. Securities and their transfers, as we have seen, are regulated in the section of the law on assignment in the ABGB. Notwithstanding this, modern Austrian law adheres to the theory because it helps to explain why securities, even though they are regulated in the context of the law of assignment, are not subject to the rules on assignment. It also explains why the purchaser of securities is protected by the ABGB against adverse claims arising out of unauthorised transfers whereas the assignee is not. Austrian law will be analysed alongside German law in chapter 10.

9.5 Summary of the analysis

Sections 9.1–9.4 show that German and Austrian legal doctrine struggled for the better part of the nineteenth century to find a generally accepted theoretical explanation for the rules governing securities. The problem was that the rules on assignment which were considered to govern securities and their transfer did not fully satisfy the needs of market participants in relation to securities transfers. Legal scholars tried to find a way through which the obstacles provided for by the law of assignment could be overcome.

A generally accepted theory emerged only after all the German states had rules on tangibles that suited the then prevailing market practice for bearer securities. The German doctrine on securities did not develop as a free-standing theory that could be applied independently of the legal rules governing other areas of the law. The doctrine relied on certain rules regulating the law of tangibles and it was not until the rules on tangibles contained a provision protecting the bona fide purchaser against adverse claims that the current orthodox view became generally accepted.

In chapter 10, it will be shown that once the theory that securities were tangibles had become the prevailing view, it set the limit within which market infrastructure, and the law regulating it, was able to develop further. It will be shown in chapter 11 that the theory that securities were tangibles shaped the type of infrastructure provider that emerged in both Germany and Austria. In addition, it will also be shown that the prevailing theory also determined the form in which paper documents were eliminated from the transfer process. When paper documents became too cumbersome to handle, Germany and Austria did not abolish them altogether but opted for immobilisation. In order to be able to maintain the existing legal analysis, paper documents had to continue to exist: rather than implementing a new legal framework for securities that did not require the existence of some tangible asset, law reformers in Germany and Austria preferred to adhere to the legal analysis already in place.

Before the implications of the modern theory for the legal and institutional development of the twentieth century are analysed, and in order to prepare the ground for the analysis of this development, the rules governing securities which are held directly will be examined, in chapter 10.

10 Paper transfers

Consistent with the prevailing theory adopted by German and Austrian law, transfers of securities in both are jurisdictions governed by the same rules on tangibles. In this chapter the rules on the transfer of ownership rights in securities will be analysed and the rules resolving unauthorised transfers examined (section 10.2). In addition, German and Austrian law have developed rules that protect the purchaser of securities against equities arising out of defective issues and these rules will be analysed in chapter 11. It will be assumed throughout that securities are held in the form of bearer securities directly by investors. The issues that arise when securities are held through intermediaries will be examined in chapter 11.

10.1 Transfer of ownership

Modern German and Austrian law apply the same rules to transfers of bearer securities as to transfers of tangible movables. In contrast to English law, which as we know distinguishes between ownership at law and ownership in equity, German and Austrian law have one unified doctrine of ownership which applies to all tangible assets and to securities. In subsection 10.1.1, German law will be analysed, followed by an analysis of Austrian law in subsection 10.1.2.

10.1.1 German Law

The BGB regulates the transfer of tangibles in ss. 929–936.

According to BGB section 929, the buyer becomes the owner if two requirements are satisfied. The buyer needs to acquire possession to the tangibles and the seller and the buyer need to agree that ownership is to be transferred to the buyer. There is no requirement for there to be a valid sales contract which underlies the transfer as long as the parties agree that, upon transfer of possession to the buyer, the buyer is to become the owner.

BGB, s. 929 does not explicitly state that it applies to bearer securities. The section of which the rule is a part, however, subjects bearer securities to the rules on tangible movables. The orthodox German view is that BGB, s. 929 applies to bearer securities.[1] As a result, the buyer of securities is considered to have become the owner when she has acquired possession to the securities certificates, provided that the seller and the buyer have agreed that ownership is to pass to the buyer. The requirement for the buyer to acquire possession of the securities certificates is, therefore, a crucial step without which the buyer will not acquire title to the securities. The requirement for possession is interpreted in two different ways, depending on whether the seller has authority to sell the securities.

When the seller has authority to sell the securities, the requirement for possession is interpreted in a way which is favourable to the buyer, who is considered to have acquired possession provided that she has complied with one of following options.

The buyer becomes the owner (1) if the seller delivers the securities to her. She also becomes the owner (2) if the securities are with a third party and if the seller assigns the right to claim the tangibles from the third party to her. Finally, the buyer is considered to have acquired possession (3) even if the securities remain with the seller provided that both parties agree that the seller now holds the tangibles not for herself, but possesses them on behalf of the buyer. There usually exists a contractual arrangement which, for example, appoints the seller a bailee of the assets.

This general rule, however, applies only if the seller was the owner or was authorised to sell the securities. If the seller was not so authorised, the alternatives for the buyer to acquire possession are more limited.

---

[1] Alfred Hueck and Claus-Wilhelm Canaris, *Recht der Wertpapiere*, 12th edn. (München: Franz Vahlen, 1986) 208; Wolfgang Zöllner, *Wertpapierrecht*, 14th edn. (München: Beck 1987) 175; Peter Marburger, in Norbert Horn (ed.), *J von Staudingers Kommentar zum Bürgerlichen Gesetzbuch Zweites Buch Recht der Schuldverhältnisse* (Berlin: Sellier–de Gruyter, 2002) s. 793, para. 19; Ulrich Meyer-Cording and Tim Drygala, *Wertpapierrecht*, 3rd edn. (Berlin: Luchterhand Neuwied, Kriftel, 1995) 6; Adolf Baumbach and Wolfgang Hefermehl, *Wechselgesetz und Scheckgesetz*, 22nd edn. (München: Beck, 2000) 4; Ingo Koller, 'Empfiehlt sich eine Neuordnung und Ergänzung des Wertpapierrechts im BGB?', in Bundesministerium der Justiz (ed.), *Gutachten und Vorschläge zu Überarbeitung des Schuldrechts*, vol. II (Köln: Bundesanzeiger Verlagsgesellschaft, 1981) 1439.

These circumstances will be analysed in section 10.2. In subsection 10.1.2, the Austrian rules governing transfers will be examined.

10.1.2 Austrian law

The Austrian rules on transfers of securities differ slightly from the German rules. Two differences stand out: the first is one of terminology; the second relates to the requirements that need to be satisfied for the buyer to become the owner of securities under Austrian law.

The first difference between Austrian and German law can be explained by the fact that the Austrian rules on securities transfers were adopted significantly earlier than the German rules. The ABGB came into force in 1811, almost a century before the current BGB, which entered into force in 1990.

When the ABGB was adopted, the modern theory on securities had not yet established itself. It was noted in section 9.1 that the ABGB does not use modern legal terminology but refers to bearer securities as 'debt notes that are issued to the bearer'.[2] For the same reason, transfers of bearer securities are not regulated in the section on tangible movables, but rather in the section on assignment.

ABGB, s. 1393 states that bearer securities are 'assigned' by way of delivery of the paper document. The transferee becomes the owner upon transfer of possession to the paper certificate to her.[3] Notwithstanding the difference in language, modern Austrian legal doctrine classifies securities as tangibles and this classification has been adopted to explain that the other rules contained in the section of the ABGB regulating assignment do not govern securities transfers. It has also been adopted to explain that there exist rules protecting the bona fide purchaser of securities against adverse claims.[4]

Like the BGB, the ABGB requires possession of the securities certificate to be transferred to the buyer for her to become the owner. As in German law, the acquisition of possession is a requirement for the buyer to become the owner of securities. The requirement for possession in Austrian law is interpreted in the same way as in German law. For possession to pass to the transferee it is not necessary that the certificates be physically delivered to her; it suffices that the seller

---

[2] ABGB, s. 1393 : 'Schuldscheine, die auf Überbringer lauten.'

[3] Günter Roth, *Wertpapierrecht*, 2nd edn. (Wien: Manz, 1999) 6–7; Helmut Koziol and Rudolf Welser, *Grundriss des Bürgerlichen Rechts*, vol. II, 12th edn. (Wien: Manz, 2001) 116.

[4] For this, see subsection 10.2.3.

agrees to hold the securities on behalf of the transferee. As in German law, the parties need to agree that upon transfer of possession to the securities, the transferee is to become the owner for ownership to pass to the transferee.

There exists a third requirement that needs to be satisfied in Austrian law for the buyer to become the owner of securities. In addition to the transfer of possession to the securities from the seller to the buyer and to an underlying agreement that the buyer is from then on to be the owner of the securities, there is a further requirement that needs to be satisfied for ownership to vest into the buyer. The transferee becomes the owner of the securities only if the transfer is governed by a valid contract. This requirement does not exist in German law. It is possible, in German law, for the sales contract to be invalid but for the transfer of ownership to have validly occurred. That can occur, for example, when the sales contract was made before possession to the securities was transferred to the buyer. In those circumstances it is possible for the sales contract to be made under a mistake which does not affect the later agreement made between the buyer and the seller to transfer ownership. The buyer would then have acquired ownership to the securities notwithstanding the fact that the sales contract was not valid. Under Austrian law, the position is different: the buyer does not acquire ownership if the sales contract is invalid.

10.1.3 Conclusions

German and Austrian law have the same approach to securities transfers. In both, securities are transferred by way of acquisition of the buyer of possession of the securities certificates. In both, it is not necessary for the buyer to receive physical delivery of the securities; it is sufficient if the buyer and the seller agree that the seller continues to hold the certificates on behalf of the buyer. In addition to the transfer of possession to the securities, both require that the buyer and seller agree that ownership passes to the buyer. Under Austrian law, but not under German law, it is also necessary for there to exist a valid sales contract between buyer and seller. This difference between Austrian and German law is significant in that the requirement for the buyer to become the owner is more onerous under Austrian than under German law. Notwithstanding this difference, however, German and Austrian law adhere to the same approach in relation to transfers of securities. In both, securities are classified as tangibles and transfers require possession of the securities certificates to pass to the buyer.

There are both differences and similarities in approach adopted by German and Austrian law compared to that of English law. Germany and Austria, on the one hand, and England, on the other, use different doctrinal mechanisms through which they analyse securities transfers. In German and in Austrian law, the buyer becomes the owner upon delivery of the securities certificates to her; it is not necessary for the issuer to become involved in securities transfers. English law, in contrast, seems to rely on the law of novation and requires the registration of the name of the buyer on the issuer register for legal ownership to pass to the buyer. Moreover, the two systems have implemented different doctrinal concepts of ownership. In German and in Austrian law, there is no distinction between law and equity; the buyer becomes the owner of securities upon acquisition of possession of the certificates. In English property law, there exists a distinction between ownership in law and ownership at equity. The buyer becomes the owner at equity upon delivery to her of the securities certificate;[5] she becomes the legal owner when her name is entered into the register of shareholders.[6]

Despite the difference in the legal doctrine applied by the respective systems in the context of securities transfers, they have in common that, under both regimes, the delivery of paper certificates causes the buyer to acquire proprietary rights. In England, paper certificates are documents of evidence only, but the delivery of the certificates appears to give rise to a constructive trust for the benefit of the buyer which causes the buyer to acquire equitable ownership. In German and Austrian law, paper certificates embody the entitlements and the delivery of the certificates causes the buyer to acquire full ownership of the entitlement.

10.2 Unauthorised transfers

10.2.1 Introduction

In both German and Austrian law, the bona fide purchaser of tangible movables is protected against adverse claims through provisions in the respective civil and commercial codes.

The German and Austrian rules differ from the English rules in several important aspects. Section 6.2 contained an analysis of the

---

[5] Subsection 2.4.6.   [6] See section 2.3.

English rules; the conclusion was that under the English law on estop-pel a bona fide purchaser has a claim against the issuer if she bought the securities relying on paper documents that were made out by the issuer. The issuer's liability is an indirect result of the English law of evidence. There exists a general principle that a person having represented some-thing to a third party who acted upon the representation cannot later claim that the matter represented was incorrect. This principle is applied to companies issuing certificates evidencing entitlements to registered securities. The certificates state that a certain person is the legal owner of a certain number of securities and this statement is considered to be a representation with which the company is fixed. If a third party buys securities in reliance on the certificates the company cannot then turn around and claim that the buyer is not the owner. This is because, having made the representation in the certificates, the company is unable to prove against the buyer that she did not purchase the securities from the owner. The company needs to treat the buyer as if she were the owner. At the same time, the company is also obliged to acknowledge the ownership rights of the person who owns the secur-ities and out of whose name they were unlawfully transferred. Both the original owner, who never lost her title, and the transferee who relied on securities certificates which were made out in the name of a person who was not the owner, can claim against the company. English law imposes the risk of unauthorised transfers at first instance on the issuer. The issuer may then be able to reimburse himself by claiming from other parties, in particular the person who instructed the issuer to transfer the securities out of the name of the owner.[7] Notwithstanding this, however, the issuer serves as the first point of call in cases of unauthorised transfers.

German and Austrian law approach unauthorised transfers differ-ently. The issuer does not carry the risk of unauthorised transfers; instead, the risk is imposed on the owner of the securities. Moreover, the liability of the owner is not a result of a representation made by the owner; it is rather a function of a legal presumption that the person who is able to transfer possession to the documents to the buyer is also authorised to sell. The German and the Austrian rules will be analysed in turn in subsections 10.2.2–10.2.3.

---

[7] See subsection 6.2.3.

10.2.2 German law

Unauthorised transfers of securities in German law are governed by the same set of rules as transfers of tangible movables. The BGB regulates transfers of tangible movables in ss. 929–936.

The conclusion of subsection 10.1.1 was that in German law the transferee becomes the owner if both parties agree that she should thereby become the owner and if she acquires possession to the certificates. This general rule, however, applies only if the seller was authorised to sell the securities. If the seller does not have authority to transfer ownership to the buyer, the buyer is nevertheless considered to become the owner if she satisfies the requirements of the rules on acquisition of ownership in good faith. Two requirements need to be fulfilled.

The first requirement is that the buyer act in good faith. Good faith is presumed unless the buyer knows – or, as a result of her gross negligence does not know – that the seller was not the owner. The HGB supplements the BGB rule on good faith by adding a rule that applies if the seller is a merchant. The transferee of a merchant is also assumed to have acted in good faith in circumstances where she did not believe that the seller was the owner, but where she believed that the seller had nevertheless authority to sell.[8]

The standard of good faith set by the HGB is identical to the standard set by the BGB. The transferee does not act in good faith if she knew – or, as a result of her gross negligence, did not know – that the transferee did not have authority to sell. Moreover, if the transferee is a bank, the bank does not act in good faith if the bearer securities were stolen, lost, or have otherwise disappeared and if the owner published a statutory announcement to that effect.

The second requirement is that possession to the tangibles be transferred to her by the seller or on her behalf.[9] The requirement for the acquisition of possession by the transferee in the context of unauthorised transfers is interpreted more narrowly than in the context of authorised transfers. The transferee acquires ownership in good faith upon the delivery of the certificates to her by the seller or by a third party on behalf of the seller. She also acquires ownership if the certificates are held by a third party and the seller assigns to her the right to claim the securities from them. Contrary to the position in cases of authorised transfers, the rules on acquisition of ownership in good

[8] HGB, s. 367.   [9] BGB, s. 935 (1) 2.

faith do not apply if transferor and transferee agree that the paper certificates should remain with the transferor.

German legal doctrine has attempted to explain this difference in the requirement for possession by pointing to an argument that has similarities with the rationale underlying the English rules. Some scholars argue that the buyer is protected because the physical delivery to her of a tangible movable entitles her first to assume that the transferor had authority to sell and secondly to act in reliance on that assumption. The same is said to be true if the seller is able to put her into a position to claim the movables from a third party. German and English law are similar in that in both jurisdictions the transferee's legal position changes because certificates are put to her. The certificates are deemed to contain information identifying the owner of the securities. In England, the certificates are deemed to refer to the owner's name. In Germany, the person who is in a position to cause the transferee to acquire possession of the certificates is deemed to be the owner. In both jurisdictions, paper securities play a crucial role in facilitating the protection of transferees against adverse claims.

This similarity is interesting to note, but should not mislead the reader into assuming that German and English law are otherwise identical. The rules governing the two jurisdictions differ in many aspects. There is no requirement in German law for the transferee to show that she acted to her detriment on a representation. Moreover, it has already been noted that the issuer does not carry the risk of unauthorised transfers. The risk of unauthorised transfers in German law is imposed on the owners of securities. Upon acquisition of ownership by the transferee, the owner loses her entitlement and this applies irrespective of whether the owner made a representation to the transferee.

The interests of the owner are normally protected by the rule that no acquisition of title in good faith occurs if the goods concerned were stolen, lost, or had otherwise disappeared without the owner's consent. This exception limits the application of the rule on good faith acquisition of ownership to cases where the owner entrusted a third party with the goods. If the person whom the goods were given to sells them without being so authorised or allows them to pass into the hands of a third person who sells the goods without authority from the owner, this falls back on the owner. The owner is saddled with the acts and omissions of the person with whom she leaves her possessions and therefore carries the risk of unauthorised transfers that occur. The exception discussed in this paragraph, however, does not apply to transfers of securities.

The rule that the owner carries the risk arising out of unauthorised transfers, even if she has not caused the bearer instrument to pass out of her immediate control, is explained by the fact that bearer securities are issued for the purpose of circulating in the market. The law recognises this purpose by adopting a rule that protects transferees against adverse claims in circumstances where the transferee of goods does not enjoy protection.[10] German law has taken a policy decision that the interest of the transferee in good faith and for value prevails over the interest of the owner of the securities. The fact that German law imposes the risk of unauthorised transfers on the owners of bearer securities causes owners to ensure that the securities are kept out of circulation. This need for the safekeeping of bearer securities caused the German and the Austrian market infrastructure to develop along a particular path.

10.2.3 Austrian law

The Austrian provisions protecting purchasers against adverse claims are similar to the German rules. Unauthorised transfers of bearer securities are subject to two provisions in the ABGB and to one provision in the Austrian Commercial Code. These provisions will be analysed in turn in this subsection.

The ABGB states in s. 371 that the owner of bearer securities loses the ability to enforce her ownership rights against a third party if the third party acquired the bearer securities in good faith.[11] The provision applies irrespective of whether the transferee acquired the securities for value.[12] It is, however, limited to fungible bearer securities.[13] Good faith is defined in ABGB, ss. 326 and 328. A purchaser does not

---

[10] Wolfgang Wiegand, in Karl Heinz Gursky (ed.), *J von Staudingers Kommentar zum Bürgerlichen Gesetzbuch Drittes Buch Sachenrecht* (Berlin: Sellier-de Gruyter, 2004) s. 935, para. 23.

[11] The ABGB does not use the term 'bearer securities' (*Inhaberpapiere*) but the term 'letters of debt issued to the bearer' (*auf den Überbringer lautende Schuldbriefe*). The modern view is that the two are equivalent (Eva Micheler, *Wertpapierrecht zwischen Schuld- und Sachenrecht: Zu einer kapitalmarktrechtlichen Theorie des Wertpapierrechts*, (Wien: Springer, 2004 53).

[12] Koziol and Welser, *Grundriss des bürgerlichen Rechts*, vol. I, 13th edn. (Wien: Manz, 2006) 336; Thomas Klicka, in Michael Schwimann (ed.), *Praxiskommentar edn. zum ABGB*, vol. II, 3rd edn. (Wien: Orac, 2004), s. 371, para. 4; Adolf Ehrenzweig, in Armin Ehrenzweig (ed.), *System des österreichischen allgemeinen Privatrechts*, vol. I/2, 2nd edn. (Wien: Manz, 1957) 190; Micheler, *Wertpapierrecht* 55.

[13] Micheler, *Wertpapierrecht* 54.

act in good faith if she knew – or, as a result of her negligence did not know – that the seller was not the owner. Any degree of negligence will suffice to cause the transferee to lose protection under the provision.

ABGB, s. 367 governs unauthorised transfers of tangible movables including bearer securities.[14] Other than ABGB, s. 371, the provision applies to infungible as well as fungible bearer securities. The transferee is, however, protected according to ABGB, s. 367 only if she acquires bearer securities for value. Moreover, ABGB, s. 367 applies only if the transferee purchased the bearer securities at a public auction, from a licensed tradesman, or from a person with whom the owner entrusted the bearer securities. Finally, the transferee acquires ownership only if she acts in good faith. As with ABGB, s. 317, any degree of negligence on the part of the transferee will cause her to fall foul of the requirement for good faith.

The Austrian Commercial Code also contains a rule protecting transferees against adverse claims. HGB, ss. 366–367 apply to transfers of goods and bearer securities which are explicitly referred to in HGB ss. 366 (5) and 367 effected by merchants. The rule governs tangible assets that are sold or pledged by a merchant; it does not apply to gifts. Other than ABGB, s. 371, HGB, s. 366 is not limited in its application to fungible securities. It applies to both fungible and non-fungible bearer securities. The provisions, moreover, require a standard of care more favourable to the transferee when determining whether she acted in good faith. The transferee does not act if good faith if she knows – or, as a result of her gross negligence did not know – that the transferor is not the owner or is not authorised by the owner. The transferee is therefore protected if she does not know as a result of negligence less severe than gross negligence that the transferor is not the owner or is not authorised by the owner. The rule, however, applies only if the securities were transferred by a merchant; it does not govern transactions between non-merchants.

Transfers from merchants are subject to the same rules in both Austrian and German law. The reason for this is that Austria adopted the HGB but not the BGB when the country was incorporated by Adolf Hitler into the German Reich in 1938. After the Second World War, Austria continued to apply the HGB alongside the ABGB.

---

[14] Koziol and Welser, *Bürgerliches Recht*, vol. I, 332–333.

10.2.4 Conclusions

Austrian and German law adopt the same doctrinal approach to unauthorised transfers. In both jurisdictions, the buyer of securities is protected against adverse claims by rules that are identical to the rules that govern tangible movables. There are, nevertheless, differences between the two countries. Austrian law protects the bona fide purchaser of fungible bearer securities even if she did not acquire the securities for value; German law does not have a provision of that kind. The protection of the transferee against adverse claims is limited to certain forms of possession in German but not in Austrian law. The standard of negligence for transfers from a person who is not a merchant according to the Austrian Commercial Code is more favourable to the transferee in German than in Austrian law.

In both German and in Austrian law, the risk of an unauthorised transfer is imposed on the owner of the securities. This leads to a need for the safekeeping of documents in both jurisdictions. The desire of owners to keep documents out of circulation has caused a certain type of market infrastructure to emerge in both Germany and Austria, a development which will be examined in chapter 11.

The doctrinal regime implemented in Germany and Austria differs significantly from the English doctrinal approach. Germany and Austria classify securities as tangibles. The risk of unauthorised transfers is imposed on the previous owner of the securities who loses her entitlement if a buyer acquires them in good faith. English registered securities are intangibles and the buyer of registered securities in England is protected against adverse claims through the law of evidence. Securities certificates give rise to an estoppel which allows the purchaser of securities to claim against the issuer. The risk of unauthorised transfers is, traditionally, imposed on the issuer rather than the owner of the securities, an approach slightly modified when USR 1995 and 2001 came into force. USR 2001 has shifted some of the risk associated with unauthorised transfers to the owner of the securities (see section 6.3). This has caused English law to become more like German and Austrian law, a similarity, however, which exists only at a functional rather than at a doctrinal level.

10.3 Defective issues

As in English law, securities under German and Austrian law are issued through a contract, entered into between the issuer and the investor who buys the securities when they are first issued and containing the terms of issue. In addition to the rules set up by the contractual arrangement between issuer and investor, their relationship may also be subject to statutory rules. In the case of shares, in particular, the German and Austrian laws on the joint stock company contain a number of rules regulating the rights and duties of shareholders and issuers.[15]

If the contract under which the securities were issued was defective, the issuer may be able to raise equities against the investor who first bought the securities. The question arises if the issuer is also able to raise these equities against any other investor who subsequently bought the securities on the market. German and Austrian law have rules that allow contractual parties also to raise equities that arose out of the contract against the original contractual partner against the person to whom an obligation was subsequently assigned. This rule, however, applies only when obligations are transferred by way of assignment. By classifying securities as tangibles, Austrian and German law are able to avoid the rules on assignment but even though the rules do not apply to transfers of securities, the question arises if the issuer is able to avoid liability by arguing that the rights embodied in the securities certificates can be exercised only subject to the contractual arrangement underlying the issue. The German and Austrian rules relating to defective issues will be examined in subsections 10.3.1 and 10.3.2. In both jurisdictions, the issuer's ability to raise equities against subsequent purchasers of securities is restricted.

10.3.1 German law

The BGB contains two provision restricting the issuer's ability to raise equities against the subsequent purchasers of securities.[16] German legal doctrine reads the two provisions together; the orthodox view is that, taken together, they enable the issuer to avoid liability if the certificates are forged. Other grounds permitting the issuer to avoid payment are: lack of capacity of the issuer upon issue, lack of authority of an agent

---

[15] There exists a doctrinal debate in German and in Austrian law as to whether purchasers of shares are protected against adverse claims. Some scholars propound the view that such protection exists only for debt securities, but not for shares. On the other hand, there exist good reasons to treat debt securities and shares alike (for an overview of the debate and for a view in favour of protecting shareholders against defective issues, see Micheler, *Wertpapierrecht* 168–171, 212–220).

[16] BGB, ss. 794, 796.

purporting to act on behalf of the issuer and coercion.[17] The issuer is also able to avoid liability if he has a claim arising out of his personal relationship with the holder of the bearer bond securities. Finally, the issuer can rely on all grounds that appear on the face of the certificates. This enables the issuer to refer to the content of the prospectus under which the securities have been issued provided that the certificates explicitly refer to that prospectus.[18]

Otherwise the position is that the person appearing as the issuer on a bearer bond certificate is liable if he has created securities certificates which have not been issued but which have nevertheless found their way into circulation. This applies irrespective of whether the certificates have been stolen, lost, or are otherwise circulating without having been duly issued by the issuer.

The statutory provisions giving rise to the issuer's liability in this context do not contain any further requirements; in particular, they do not explicitly require the bearer of the certificates to have acted in good faith upon acquisition. German legal doctrine has, nevertheless, introduced a subjective element on the part of the bearer that needs to be satisfied for the issuer to be liable in circumstances where he did not properly issue the bearer bonds.

The prevailing view is that the rule on issuer's liability as implemented by the BGB does not amount to strict statutory liability, but is to be classified as liability arising out of a representation made by the issuer.[19] The purpose of the statute is not to hold the issuer liable in all circumstances. The issuer is liable because he has created certificates that, on the face of them, appear to be validly issued. By printing such paper documents, the issuer represents that the rights which appear to be embodied in the certificates have been validly created. The issuer is bound by this representation but the issuer's liability is limited to circumstances where the bearer of the certificates relies upon the representation contained in the certificates.

---

[17] Marburger, J. von Staudingers Kommentar, s. 796, para. 3; Uwe Hüffer, in Peter Ulmer (ed.), Münchener Kommentar zum Bürgerlichen Gesetzbuch, vol. 5, 3rd edn. (München: Beck, 1997), s. 796, paras. 8–9.

[18] Marburger, J. von Staudingers Kommentar, s. 796, para. 7; see also Klaus Hopt, 'Änderung von Anleihebedingungen – Schuldverschreibungsgesetz, § 796 BGB und AGBG', in Steindorf Festschrift (Berlin: Walter de Gruyter, 1990) 362–363; in favour of a more generous approach, see Dieter Heckelmann, in Harm Peter Westermann (ed.), Ermann Bürgerliches Gesetzbuch, 10th edn. (Köln: Dr. Otto Schmidt, 2000) s. 796, para. 4.

[19] Ernst Jacobi, in Victor Ehrenberg (ed.), Handbuch des gesamten Handelsrechts, vol. IV/1 (Leipzig: O. R. Reisland, 1917) 286.

The issuer is, therefore, not liable if the contract under which the certificates have been issued is defective and if the certificates are still with the person to whom the securities have been first issued. The first purchaser from the issuer did not buy the securities in reliance on the representation made through the certificates, but subject to the contract which governs the issue. The issuer can raise all equities arising out of the defective contract against the first purchaser provided that she still holds the securities.[20]

The issuer is also not liable if the bearer of the securities knew – or, as a result of her gross negligence did not know – that the securities had not been validly issued.[21] In those circumstances, the bearer of the securities has not bought the securities in reliance on the representation contained in the certificates. A purchaser of securities which have not been validly issued, but who has, nevertheless acquired them in reliance on the securities certificate, cannot claim only against the issuer; she is also able to transfer the entitlement arising out of the certificates to a third party. The purchaser from such a transferee does not have to satisfy the subjective requirements.[22]

10.3.2 Austrian law

The ABGB does not contain rules that govern the issuer's liability in cases of defective issues. Austrian legal doctrine nevertheless accepts that the person who appears as the issuer on a securities certificate is liable to honour the rights incorporated in the document.

Different scholars have put forward different explanations for this.[23] The current prevailing view is that there exists a general legal principle that a person who makes a representation is liable to indemnify those who rely on it. This principle also applies to bearer securities.[24] The

---

[20] Marburger, *J. von Staudingers Kommentar*, s. 794, para. 1; Hüffer, *Münchener Kommentar*, s. 794, para. 4; Jacobi, *Handbuch des gesamten Handelsrecht* 284–285; Zöllner, *Wertpapierrecht* 41–42; Hueck and Canaris, *Recht der Wertpapiere* 34–35.

[21] Marburger, *J. von Staudingers Kommentar*, s. 794, para. 3; Jacobi, *Handbuch des gesamten Handelsrecht* 300–301; Hüffer, *Münchener Kommentar*, s. 794, para. 4.

[22] Zöllner, *Wertpapierrecht* 135; Micheler, *Wertpapierrecht* 93–94; for a different view on this point, see Lutz Sedatis, 'Absoluter und relativer Erwerb im Wertpapierrecht', in *Rehbinder Festschrift* (München: Beck, 2002) 741–758.

[23] See Micheler, *Wertpapierrecht* 77–87.

[24] Roth, *Wertpapierrecht* 17; Zöllner, *Wertpapierrecht* 37–39; Hueck and Canaris, *Recht der Wertpapiere*, 33–35; Baumbach and Hefermehl, *Wechselgesetz* 16–19; Locher, *Wertpapierrecht* (Mohr: Tübingen) 35; Jacobi, *Handbuch des gesamten Handelsrecht* 308–310; Ernst Jacobi, *Grundriss des Rechts der Wertpapiere im allgemeinen*, 3rd edn. (Leipzig: OR

issuer is liable if he has made out a certificate that appears to embody certain rights. Creating a piece of paper that looks like a validly issued bearer security amounts to a representation that the rights to which the paper document refer have been validly created.

As in German law, Austrian law does not consider the issuer to be liable if the bearer of the certificate is the person to whom the instrument was first issued. The issuer's liability is also limited to circumstances in which the bearer or the person from whom the bearer purchased the securities knew – or, as a result of her gross negligence did not know – that the securities were not validly issued.

10.3.3 Conclusions

Both German and Austrian law protect the good faith purchaser of securities against equities arising out of a defective issue. The issuer is unable to raise equities against a good faith purchaser of securities; the issuer's liability is explained by the fact that the securities certificates contain a representation of the issuer who represents that the securities have been validly created. A purchaser in good faith is able to rely on that and to enforce the rights referred to in the securities documents against this issuer.

The position adopted by German and by Austrian law has points of both similarity and difference with that in English law. In England, there exist two doctrinal tools through which the buyer of securities is protected against equities. The first doctrine which operates to protect buyers against equities is the doctrine of novation. The analysis presented in section 5.2 showed that transfers of English securities were, at least historically, analysed in terms of novation. Transfers by way of novation involve an agreement between the seller, the buyer and the issuer. The buyer of securities is protected against equities arising out of the original issue because her entitlement is based on the novation agreement rather than derived from the original agreement entered into between the issuer and the first buyer of the securities. This doctrine does not apply to German or Austrian securities.

The second doctrine through which buyers of securities are protected against equities in England is the doctrine of estoppel. English securities certificates constitute prima facie evidence that the rights to which they relate have been validly created. If a buyer acquires securities relying on

---

Reisland 1928) 58–60; Koller, 'Empfiehlt sich eine Neuordnung' 1438–1440; Micheler, *Wertpapierrecht* 80–87.

certificates made out by the issuer, the issuer is estopped from proving that the rights to which the securities refer have not been validly created. This is similar to the German and Austrian doctrine on the same point. All three jurisdictions classify securities certificates as containing a representation by the issuer that the rights they relate to have been validly created; the purchaser relying on this representation is protected against equities arising out of the original issue.

10.4 Summary of the analysis

In this chapter, the rules governing transfer of German and Austrian securities were analysed. The analysis was based on the assumption that securities are held directly without the assistance of an intermediary and leads to two conclusions. Germany and Austria, on the one hand, and English law, on the other, analyse securities and their transfers through different legal doctrines. Notwithstanding these differences, all three jurisdictions achieve outcomes that are, to some extent, similar.

In both German and Austrian law, securities are transferred by way of delivery of the securities certificate to the buyer. In addition, the buyer and seller need to agree that ownership is to be transferred to the buyer. Under Austrian, but not under German, law there exists a third requirement for ownership to be transferred to the buyer. For the buyer to become the owner of the securities under Austrian law, there needs to exist a valid sales contract between buyer and seller.

The German and the Austrian rules are different from the rules adopted by English law. Germany and Austria apply to transfers of securities the same rules that apply to transfers of tangibles. In contrast, England seems to rely on the law of novation when analysing securities transfers. As a result, in Germany and Austria the issuer is not involved in securities transfers. In relation to bearer securities, there is no requirement for the buyer's name to be entered on a securities register.

The rules adopted by Germany and Austria, respectively, are, however, also similar to the rules prevailing in English law. In all three jurisdictions the delivery of the certificate relating to securities is a requirement that can cause the buyer to acquire a proprietary right in the securities. In Germany and in Austria, the delivery of the certificate is necessary for the buyer to acquire full ownership of the securities; in English law the delivery of securities certificates can cause the buyer to acquire equitable ownership in the securities.

In German and Austrian law, the buyer is protected against claims relating to the fact that the seller was not authorised to sell the securities concerned. The rules protecting the buyer impose the risk of an unauthorised transfer upon the owner of the securities. The rules achieving this result are identical to the rules governing tangibles. The orthodox view is that the same rules that apply to tangibles also apply to securities because securities are to be classified as tangibles.

In England, buyers are also protected against unauthorised transfers, but under a doctrine different from German and Austrian law. England uses the rules on estoppel and the risk of an unauthorised transfer is primarily imposed on the issuer rather than on the owner of the securities.

In Germany and Austria, the buyer is protected against equities arising out of defective issues through a doctrine that is similar to the English rules on estoppel. Securities certificates are considered to contain a representation that the rights to which the certificates relate have been validly created. The issuer is bound by this representation and is unable to raise equities against the purchaser in good faith of securities.

This chapter also contained an analysis of the rules in Germany and Austria governing transfers of securities that are directly held. It was assumed throughout the chapter that investors keep securities certificates themselves and do not employ an intermediary. In chapter 11, the impact of the rules governing securities on the type of the institutional framework prevailing in Germany and Austria will be examined.

11 Impact on the institutional framework

In this chapter it will be shown that the German and the Austrian legal doctrine governing securities impacted upon the type of service provider that emerged in the German and Austrian market to service investors who wish to hold securities indirectly. It will also be shown that the process through which paper certificates were eliminated from the transfer process was shaped by the legal doctrinal framework that governed directly held securities. The market infrastructure for indirect holdings will be examined first.

11.1 Indirect holdings

The fact that German and Austrian bearer securities have come to be classified as tangibles has the advantage that the German and the Austrian rules on assignment do not apply to transfers. Transfers are instead subject to rules identical to those governing tangibles. As a result, the transferee is protected against adverse claims. The legal doctrine whereby protection against adverse claims is afforded to the buyer of securities has had a significant impact on the development of the institutional framework prevailing in Germany and in Austria.

The conclusion of section 10.2 was that the rules that protect the transferee of an unauthorised transferor against adverse claims cause the owner to lose her rights to the securities. Ignoring all other requirements for the moment, the transferee in good faith becomes the owner when she acquires possession to the securities. This rule has had a significant impact on the way in which investors hold securities certificates in Germany and in Austria. In contrast to England, where securities certificates do not need to be kept safely because the owner does not lose her rights if the certificates are stolen and then transferred to a third party, an investor under German and Austrian law needs to keep securities certificates out of circulation in order to prevent a third party from acquiring possession of – and, consequently, ownership of – bearer securities. Paper certificates need to be kept safe and this need for safekeeping facilitated an important development in Germany and Austria. It created a demand for depository services which was met by German and by Austrian banks, which developed the business of safe-keeping securities certificates for investors as a distinct branch of their commercial activities.

Rather than letting depository boxes or vaults to individual inves-tors, banks originally took the securities certificates and kept them for clients on an allocated basis. The banks kept individual files for each customer; the paper documents were not physically held by investors but were nevertheless appropriated to them. The German and the Austrian depository services for securities are an example of how legal doctrine can facilitate the emergence of certain types of infrastructure providers. In a similar way as the English law of novation facilitated the emergence of registrars in England, the German and the Austrian legal doctrine protecting purchasers against adverse claims facilitated the emergence of depositories in those countries.

11.2 Immobilisation

German and Austrian legal doctrine did not only play an important role in the emergence of securities depositories; it also shaped the process through which paper was eliminated from the transfer process.

In the context of German and Austrian legal doctrine, securities certificates perform two important functions. The first is that upon acquisition of possession to the securities certificate the buyer becomes the owner of bearer securities. The second is to provide for a legal explanation of the rules protecting the buyer against adverse claims arising out of unauthorised transfers. German and Austrian modern legal doctrine operates on the assumption that, in both countries, the bona fide purchaser can fend off adverse claims because securities are classified as tangibles. It has already been noted (p. 167) that this analysis is not historically true for Austrian law, where the provisions protecting bona fide purchasers were introduced before the modern theory had established itself. The modern theory is, nevertheless, seen as an explanation of the rules contained in the ABGB. The prevailing view is that, even if historically the explanation of these rules appeared well after they had been adopted, the rules still operate only because and if securities are classified as tangibles. For this to be the case, securities certificates need to be issued.

The theory that the classification of securities as tangibles explains the rules that govern their transfer in German and Austrian law is not only understood as providing an explanation of the rules governing securities, it is also understood as having a normative element. The orthodox German and Austrian view is that the special rules governing securities would not apply if securities were not classified as tangibles. This then leads to the conclusion that the existence of paper certificates is essential; if paper certificates ceased to exist, securities transfers would be subject to the rules on assignment.

This normative element of the prevailing German and Austrian theory played an important role when a need to eliminate paper documents from securities transfers appeared in both jurisdictions. This need emerged in the years after the First World War when both countries experienced an unprecedented economic crisis aggravated by rampant inflation. From the point of view of this book, the crisis triggered an important legal development. The crisis was, of course, disastrous for most industries, including the investment industry; securities prices fell sharply. The securities affected most by the decline of the market were those with fixed rates of return, whose prices dropped to a level that made it uneconomical for them to be kept on an allocated basis.

Holding them in separate files meant that they had to be taken out of their files when dividends were due so that the respective coupons could be separated from the main certificate or the attachment to it and presented to the issuer. Transfers involved the physical delivery of certificates. This was relatively easy to achieve when buyer and seller had holdings with the same bank but much more costly when the paper documents had to be physically moved between banks. Depository banks found that the cost of maintaining allocated client accounts exceeded the value of many of the instruments held.[1]

It became clear that the cost of holding securities indirectly had to be reduced and that this could be done only by reducing the need

---

[1] A. Metze, 'Das Giro-Effektendepot der Bank des Berliner Kassenvereins', *Zeitschrift für das gesamte Handelsrecht*, [1927] 376–377; Wilhelm Schütz, 'Die Änderung des Depotgesetzes und der Eigentumsvorbehalt bei Wertpapierlieferungen', *Bankarchiv* 23 (1923/24) 120; Ulrich Drobnig, 'Effektenverkehr', in Karl Kreuzer (ed.), *Abschied rom Wert papier? Dokumentlose Wertbewegungen im Effekten- Gütertransport- und Zahlungsverkehr* (Neuwied: Alfred Metzher Verlag, 1988) 17.

physically to handle paper certificates. This could have been achieved in different ways: in particular, it would have been possible for the market to adopt the same solution that was already in place for Government bonds. Government bonds at the time were not issued in paper form;[2] instead, a register of public debt existed and transfers were effected by means of an entry in that register. This transfer regime could have served as a role model for all other securities. It would have enabled German service providers to abandon securities certificates altogether. This, however, did not happen.

Instead, German and Austrian service providers adopted a solution that maintained securities certificates because securities were deposited with central depositories. Many years earlier, in 1850, the banks in Berlin had established a financial intermediary called the 'Kassenverein' which facilitated money transfers between its members.[3] Over time, the Kassenverein was also employed by banks to deposit securities they held in their own name.[4]

During the post-war crisis, the banks decided also to deposit client securities centrally with the Kassenverein and in order to save cost, the securities were to be kept on an unallocated basis. The Kassenverein was to keep records of the entitlements attributed to each of the banks, who in turn kept records of client entitlements. The securities were to be held by the Kassenverein as a bailee albeit with the name of the client owner being undisclosed to them. The identity of the client was, however, ascertainable through the depositing bank.

In 1925, the banks in Berlin approached their clients, asking them to approve of the new arrangement allowing banks to transfer client securities to the Kassenverein and agreeing for the securities to be kept there on an unallocated basis. The clients who felt unable to give their consent were advised that they had to expect a significant increase in fees for deposits kept on an allocated basis.[5]

---

[2] See below section 11.4.

[3] Georg Bruns, *Das Depotgeschäft* (Frankfurt am Main: Fritz Knapp Verlag, 1962) 35.

[4] Metze, 'Das Giro-Effektendepot' 377; Theodor Heinsius, Arno Horn and Jürgen Than, *Depotgesetz* (Berlin: Walter de Gruyter, 1975), s. 5, paras. 2–3; Claus-Wilhelm Canaris, in Hermann Staub (ed.), *Großkommentar zum Handelsgesetzbuch*, vol. III part 3, *Bankvertragsrecht*, 2nd edn. (Berlin: Walter de Gruyter, 1981), para. 1988; Dorothee Einsele, *Wertpapierrecht als Schuldrecht* (Tübingen: J. C. B. Mohr (Paul Siebeck), 1995) 12–13.

[5] Herbert Fürst, 'Sammeldepot an Effekten und Effektengiroverkehr', *Zentralblatt* [1928] 57; Metze, 'Giro-Effektendepot' 377–378; Georg Opitz, *Fünfzig depotrechtliche Abhandlungen* (Berlin: Walter de Gruyter, 1954) 426–428.

Banks in Frankfurt am Main, Dresden, Essen and Stuttgart followed the example of the banks in Berlin and created their own central depositories. Austria also created a central depository.[6] The result was that a handful of regional depositories held a significant proportion of securities in Germany, linked with each other through accounts.[7] Each depository serviced the banks and clients linked to it by acting as a central depository for securities physically located with it but also by acting as an intermediary for securities kept with any of the other depositories.[8]

When securities were transferred, they no longer had to be physically moved; rather, they were transferred through book entry. If both buyer and seller kept securities accounts with the same bank, that bank would effect the transfer by debiting the seller's account and crediting the buyer's account. If buyer and seller kept accounts with different banks linked to the same depository, the seller's bank would ask the depository to transfer the securities to the account of the buyer's bank, which would then credit the securities to the buyer's account. Transfers of securities between buyers and sellers who held their accounts with banks linked to different depositories would be effected through the accounts of both depositories. The depository to which the seller was indirectly linked would transfer the securities from the account of the seller's bank to the account of the depository to which the buyer's bank was linked. Then the depository of the buyer's bank would credit the securities to the account of the buyer's bank, which would in turn credit the buyer's account.

The result was that transfers could be effected without the need physically to handle securities certificates which made a significant reduction in cost. At the same time, securities certificates were not abolished altogether and the fact that securities certificates continued to exist was considered to be of significant importance. The common belief was that for clients to continue to hold proprietary rights in securities and for buyers to be protected against adverse claims, securities certificates had to continue to exist because otherwise securities could not be classified as tangibles and the law of assignment would automatically apply to them. This common belief followed from the

---

[6] Eva Micheler, *Wertpapierrecht Zwischen Schuld und Sachenrecht: Zueiner Kapitalmarktrechtlichen Theorie des Wertpapierrechts* (Wien: Springer, 2004), 144.

[7] Carl Heumann, 'Die Entwicklung des Effekten Giro-Verkehrs: Notwendigkeiten und Möglichkeiten', (1927/28) 27 *Bankarchiv* 223.

[8] Metze, 'Giro-Effektendepot' 377–378.

theory that had become generally accepted as explaining the rules governing securities.

Banks felt that they would have been unable to persuade clients to accept the new arrangement if the legal regime governing the way they held securities had been changed. Rather than creating a new regime from scratch that would afford the same protection to clients as the existing rules, German banks preferred to operate within the existing legal framework. In order the facilitate the changeover, the banks commissioned a legal opinion by two leading specialists in the field, Georg Opitz and Hans Schultz, who devised a solution that was based on the existing legal rules. They concluded that clients continued to have possession of the certificates albeit mediated through a chain of intermediaries and on an unallocated basis, but that that was sufficient for them to retain ownership to the securities certificates.[9]

Because clients continued to have possession of the documents, transfers continued to be analysed in terms of possession. The theory that was developed at the time, and that continues to apply today, is that when securities are transferred there occurs a change of possession of the underlying documents. German legal doctrine and case law maintain that upon credit of the securities to the transferee's account the transferee acquires possession of the underlying documents. This is the case notwithstanding the fact that the certificates are not physically moved during the transfer. This analysis allows lawyers to continue to apply the rules governing transfers of tangibles.

Because securities and their transfer are considered to remain subject to the law of tangibles, lawyers are also able to argue that the rules on good faith acquisition of title continue to be applicable to protect transferees against adverse claims. In order to facilitate the changeover to a more economical market practice, German lawyers developed the law in a path-dependent fashion: they redefined the German concept of possession.

It is important to note that the ability to continue to apply the rules on tangibles to securities and their transfers determined the design of the new market infrastructure. Banks did not create a new market infrastructure independently of existing legal rules; the reform was carried out with the declared aim of remaining within the existing legal framework. The banks took the view that they would succeed in convincing their clients to accept a modernised transfer regime only if the legal analysis remained the same.

---

[9] Opitz, *Fünfzig depotrechtliche Abhandlungen* 1.

11.3 Global certificates

German and Austrian market practice continued to develop along the path it had previously adopted. German and Austrian bearer securities are traditionally issued in the form of individual certificates. The issuer produces one certificate for each unit of every type of security issued. These certificates need to be protected against forgery; issuers therefore need to be careful about the quality of the paper and the type of printing they use and incur significant expense in arranging for the production of individual certificates.

Once most certificates had been deposited in a central depository, it became apparent that individual certificates had ceased to perform their original purpose of circulating between market participants. A large number of individual paper certificates were produced, only to be stored with a central depository. Issuers realised that the cost involved in producing certificates could no longer be justified and the depositories found that individual certificates consumed a significant amount of space and required maintenance, both of which caused unnecessary expense.

The issue of cost first arose during the Second World War. At the time, paper was a rare and expensive commodity and it seemed wasteful to print individual certificates only for them to disappear in a vault.[10] It would have been possible to re-think the transfer regime that governed securities and to fully dematerialise securities transfers. This, however, was not done. Issuers rather resolved to issue one global certificate instead of individual ones.

Global certificates can be issued in two forms. They can be issued as temporary global certificates giving the investor a right to have, if she so wishes, individual certificates issued to her. They can also be issued as permanent global certificates denying the investor a right to individual certificates. Both types of global certificates began to replace individual certificates in Germany and Austria during the Second World War.

Today most issues of debt securities are represented by a permanent global certificate. Shares and other equity securities tend to be represented by a temporary certificate giving owners the right to request the issue of individual certificates.[11]

---

[10] Paul Fleischmann, 'Wertpapiere im totalen Krieg', [1943] *Bankarchiv* 9; Fritz Fabricius, 'Zur Theorie des stückelosen Effektengiroverkehrs mit Wertrechten aus Staatsanleihen', (1963) 162 *Archiv für die civilistische Praxis* 460.

[11] Micheler, *Wertpapierrecht* 252–260.

This changeover from individual to global certificates is significant from a legal point of view because it is no longer possible to allocate particular certificates to particular owners. It cannot be said that individual owners have a legal relationship such as possession with a particular number of securities. German and Austrian law overcame the allocation problem in a fashion consistent with the path previously adopted. Rather than creating a new doctrinal solution German and Austrian legal doctrine expanded the scope of application of the rules of possession. The current orthodox view is that if securities are issued in the form of global certificates, investors have joint possession of, and are co-owners of, the underlying certificate.

This analysis makes it possible for German and Austrian lawyers to continue to apply the rules on tangibles to transfers of securities. Securities are for all practical purposes transferred by way of book entry. From the point of view of German and Austrian legal doctrine, however, the transfer involves a change in possession of the underlying document. The transferee is considered to acquire joint possession of, and a co-ownership right of, the underlying global certificate upon credit of the securities to her account. Investors do not own individual certificates but are nevertheless deemed to have a proprietary relationship with a tangible securities certificate.

The prevailing view is that the assumption that investors continue to hold and transfer possession to a tangible certificate is necessary to allow German legal doctrine to continue to rely on the rules of good faith acquisition of ownership rights to tangibles in order to protect transferees against adverse claims.[12]

11.4 Government bonds

German Government bonds are perhaps the most striking example of the impact of legal doctrine on institutional development.

On 31 May 1910, Germany passed a special law on the register of public debt (*Reichsschuldbuchgesetz*).[13] Based on that law, German Government bonds were not issued in the form of bearer or any other kind of paper certificates. Instead, the German state created a register in which the names of the owners of the securities were entered.

---

[12] Micheler, *Wertpapierrecht* 161–171.
[13] *Reichsgesetzblatt* 1910, I 840; Hans Lessing, 'Das Reichsschuldenbuch', (1915/16) 15 *Bankarchiv* 293.

Ownership rights to public debt securities were transferred by way of entry in that register.[14]

The German register for public debt created a paperless transfer system for securities. This register was established before the German economy slid into the financial crisis that dominated the 1930s; the transfer system for Government bonds at the time was less costly than the transfer system for private sector securities. It did not require intermediaries to maintain files for individual customers from which securities certificates had to be physically moved to effect a transfer.

Germany already had a paperless transfer mechanism in place when it became clear that the transfer procedure for paper securities was too expensive. Given that a model for paperless transfers already existed it is surprising that the German banks did not build on that model when they introduced reform. They did not introduce a central register of securities; they rather chose to create a central depository. They felt constrained by existing legal doctrine, as we have seen; they wanted to create a transfer system which would continue to operate on the basis of the rules on tangible movables.

Legal doctrine not only caused Germany not to take a path of reform that could well have generated more benefits than the system that was actually implemented, it also affected the development of the law relating to public debt securities. German banks not only held private sector securities for their clients, they also offered services in relation to Government bonds. Over time, transfers of Government bonds were integrated with transfers of other securities.[15] This was done by entering the name of the central depositories on the register of Government bonds. The central depository would act as a trustee for the benefit of the banks, which in turn would act as trustees for their clients.

At first, it was unclear how transfers of Government bonds were to be analysed. In 1937, Government bonds were explicitly made subject to the law on securities deposits. *Depotgesetz* 1937, s. 42 states that the rules of the *Depotgesetz* can, by way of a statutory instrument, also be made applicable to merchants who hold public debt securities as trustees for clients (see

---

[14] For an account of the historic background of the German register for public debt, see also Berthold Wagner, '50 Jahre Bundesschuldenverwaltung', [1999] *Wertpapier Mitteilungen* 1949.

[15] Georg Opitz, *Depotgesetz*, 2nd edn. (Berlin: Walter de Gruyter, 1955) 435–436; Einsele, *Wertpapierrecht* 15–17; Bruns, *Das Depotgeschäft* 45–47; Klaus Peters, *Wertpapierfreies Effektensystem* (Göttingen: dissertation, 1975) 74; Fabricius, Zur Theorie des stükelosen Effektengiroverkehrs, 456.

subsection 12.1.2). Statutory instruments to that effect were enacted in 1940 and in 1942[16] and these rules continue to be applied today.[17]

The effect of this statutory intervention is that Government bonds are considered to be governed by the rules on tangibles, notwithstanding the fact that no paper certificate representing the instrument exists.

Orthodox German legal doctrine justifies the application of the rules on tangibles by way of a legal fiction, which is that as a result of the statutory incorporation of Government bonds into the system for transfers of bearer securities, Government bonds are deemed to be tangible movables[18] and their transfers governed by the rules on tangibles movables.

When Government bonds are credited to the transferee's account, this is legally analysed in the following terms. The transferee is deemed to have acquired possession of the certificates, the existence of which is also deemed. The transferee is also protected against adverse claims by the rules on tangible movables.

This development of German law exemplifies two phenomena. The first is that law develops by legal doctrine refining existing concepts rather than by creating new solutions from scratch. The example of Government bonds shows that German legal doctrine, when faced with the choice, preferred to operate a legal fiction to adopting a transfer system that would require the creation of a new legal basis. The second is that the legal doctrine steered the German market infrastructure towards immobilisation and prevented the development of a paperless central register for government securities from developing. The central register for Government bonds was instead integrated into the immobilised transfer system which requires legal doctrine to operate on the basis of fictitious documents. That route, however, is perceived to be safer than creating a paperless transfer system from scratch.

---

[16] Verordnung über Verwaltung und Anschaffung von Reichsschuldbuchforderungen vom 5.1.1940 (*Reichsgesetzblatt* 1940, I 3); Verordnung über die Behandlung von Anleihen des Deutschen Reiches im Bank- und Börsenverkehr vom 31.12.1940 (*Reichsgesetzblatt* 1941, I 21); Zweite Verordnung über die Behandlung von Anleihen des Deutschen Reiches im Bank- und Börsenverkehr vom 18.4.1942 (*Reichsgesetzblatt* 1942, I 183).

[17] *Bundesanleihegesetz* dated 29.3.1951 and Art. 2 *Depotgesetznovelle* 1972; Wolfgang Gößmann, in Herbert Schimansky, Hermann-Josef Bunte and Hans-Jürgen Lwowski (eds.), *Bankrechts-Handbuch*, vol. II, 2nd edn. (München: Beck, 2001), s. 72, para. 68; Peters, *Wertpapierfreies Effektensystem* 21–23; Peter Scherer, in Karlheinz Boujong, Carsten Thomas Ebenroth and Detlev Joost (eds.), *Handelsgesetzbuch*, vol. II (München: Beck/ Verlag Franz Vahlen, 2001), s. 42 DepotG, para. VI 586.

[18] Fabricius, 'Zur Theorie des Stückelosen Effectengiroxerkehrs' 463–464; Opitz, *Fünfzig depotrechtliche Abhandlungen* 538, 722.

11.5 Summary of the analysis

In this chapter, two conclusions were drawn from the discussion of the impact legal doctrine has had on the institutional setup of market infrastructure providers.

The first was that the German and Austrian rules protecting purchasers against adverse claims arising out of unauthorised transfers created an incentive for investors to prevent documents from disappearing out of their possession. This created a demand for depository services in the German and Austrian market. This demand was met by the German and Austrian banks, which developed specialised depository services. The second was that the doctrinal framework that governed paper transfer of securities had an impact on the way in which paper certificates were eliminated from transfers in Germany and Austria. The legal doctrine underlying securities in both jurisdictions is based on the normative assumptions that the special rules that govern transfers of securities are applied because securities are tangibles. From that legal scholarship derives the conclusion that if securities are not classified as tangibles, these special rules cannot be applied. Instead, securities transfers would have to be governed by the law of assignment. To prevent this from happening, it would be possible to draft a special regime that applied to securities transfer irrespective of how they were classified. It would also have been possible for German and Austrian law to build on the rules that were in place for Government bonds for which no paper certificates existed.

This option was, however, not adopted. Instead, securities certificates were eliminated from the transfer process by putting them out of circulation (immobilisation) rather than by abolishing them (dematerialisation). The prevailing view was that it was of crucial importance that the legal analysis which governed paper securities continued to be applied even in an environment in which paper certificate had ceased to perform their original function of transferring the entitlement embodied in them. As a result, the German and Austrian market put in place central depositories.

Following the analysis of the process that led to immobilisation in Germany and Austria contained in this chapter, chapter 12 will focus on the legal analysis of immobilised securities.

12 Immobilisation and its legal analysis

The conclusion of chapter 11 was that after German law had adopted the analysis that bearer securities constituted tangible movables, legal doctrine continued to develop the law of securities in the context of such movables. This played an important role in shaping the market infrastructure of both Germany and Austria: both countries developed a market infrastructure based on securities depositories rather than on owner registers.

Chapter 11 also referred to the fact that transfers of deposited securities are deemed to involve a transfer of possession of the underlying documents from the transferor to the transferee. The chapter also concluded that the rules on the good faith acquisition of title continued to be applied to protect transferees against adverse claims.

In this chapter, the legal analysis underlying transfers of deposited securities will be examined further. It will be shown that, over time, the legal analysis which was originally based on the BGB and the ABGB became the subject of special legislation.

12.1 Genesis of the statutory regime

12.1.1 1896 German statute

The first German statute specifically addressing securities was enacted in 1896.[1] At the time, German banks held a significant number of securities certificates on behalf of their clients which were mostly kept on an unallocated basis. Problems arose in 1891 when the banking system faced a

---

[1] Austria enacted legislation similar to the German legislation in 1924. For an analysis of the Austrian rules, see Micheler, *Wertpapierrecht zwischen Schuld- und Sachenrecht: Zu einer kapitalmarktrechtlichen Theorie des Wertpapierrechts* (Wien: Springer, 2004) 138–140.

major financial crisis. Some banks discovered that there were shortfalls in securities; they did not possess sufficient securities to meet all their clients' claims. It became clear that German law did not sufficiently protect investors holding securities indirectly through bank depositories.

German law solved the legal issues that arose in a path-dependent manner. Since the starting point was that the securities were tangibles, it was only natural for the law to analyse issues arising out of deposited securities in terms of bailment.

In German law, there are two types of bailment – entitled regular deposit (depositum regulare) and irregular deposit (depositum irregulare) – respectively. If assets are kept in a regular deposit, the depositor keeps her proprietary rights to the assets. If they are kept in an irregular deposit, title to the assets is transferred from the depositor to the depositee. The depositor has contractual rights only to have securities of the same kind and quantity returned to her. In normal circumstances, this difference would not be of great practical significance. As long as the depositee is financially in the position to satisfy claims raised against her, proprietary as well as contractual claims can be successfully enforced. This changes, however, with the depositee approaching insolvency. In the depositee's insolvency contractual claims are of no significant value whereas, provided the asset is still with the depositee, proprietary claims will be satisfied in full.

One of the problems that arose during the German bank crisis at the end of the nineteenth century was that some banks had used ambiguous documentation.[2] Investors generally seemed to have assumed that their securities were kept on the basis of a regular deposit, with the result that they would enjoy proprietary rights and be protected in the banks' financial crisis.[3] Some banks had used terms that could also be read as providing for a depositum irregulare giving investors only contractual rights. In the litigation that followed the bank crisis, the courts had to square the imprecise wording contained in the relevant banking documentation. The judges struggled to reach consistent results and found themselves, at times, reaching different conclusions in cases that appeared to be similar on the facts.[4]

---

[2] Bum, JBl 1924 93 (93); Bettelheim, JBl 1924 193 (193.ff.).
[3] Hofmannsthal, *Bankhaftungsgesetz* 30.
[4] Compare OGH 16 November 1921, Ob II 825/21 SZ 3/110 with OGH 23 November 1921, Ob I 819/21 SZ 8/115. In beiden Fällen wurden Wertpapiere als Kaution für Spekulationsgeschäfte bei einem Kommissionär hinterlegt. Im ersten Fall entschied das Gericht, dass ein Pfandbestellungsvertrag vorlag. Eine zu besichernde Forderung

Another problem was that there were cases where investors could rely on clear terms providing for a regular deposit, but were nevertheless unable to enforce their property rights. The reason was that, at the time of a bank's insolvency, the customer files did not contain the securities belonging to the respective customers. There were two reasons for this.

The first was that it had become common practice for banks to use deposited securities for their own purposes.[5] The banks did not do this with the intent to defraud; rather, they wanted only to make temporary use of the assets with which they were entrusted. They had the intent to return the securities after they had been used, and had, at the time, no reason to believe that they would be unable to completely restore their clients' securities holding. Customers had been unaware that their securities had been taken out of their files and it was unclear if the banks, in using the securities, were acting in breach of their obligations to the customers.

The second reason leading to shortfalls of securities was that some banks outsourced some of their services relating to securities to other banks. Provincial banks would, for example, not keep client securities themselves but rather deposit them with better-equipped and more centrally located banks. Client securities were also delivered by provincial banks to banks in business centres for the purpose of corporate actions. Provincial banks would, for example, not themselves claim dividends for client securities but ask banks located closer to the issuer to do this for them. For the purpose of claiming dividends, the dividend coupons that were attached to the securities certificate had to be presented to the issuer and were therefore delivered to the bank employed to claim dividends.

The banks who delivered securities or dividend coupons to other banks did not in all cases disclose that they were client securities that did not belong to them. Under the standard documentation at the time, the depositee had a lien over deposited goods securing claims she had against the depositor. When banks entrusted other banks with client securities without notifying them of their clients' proprietary interest the depositee banks were protected by the rule on the bona fide acquisition of title. Because they did not have notice of the adverse client interest they

---

bestand nicht. Der Hinterleger konnte die Papiere, die in der Konkursmasse noch vorhanden waren, absondern. Im zweiten Fall entschied das Gericht, dass die hinterlegten Papiere als Vorauszahlung geleistet wurden. Der Hinterleger hatte nur einen schuldrechtlichen Anspruch auf Rückgabe der Anzahlung.

[5] Drucksachen des Reichstags 9. Legislaturperiode IV. Session 1895/97 Nr 14 abgedruckt, in Georg Opitz, *Depotgesetz*, 2nd edn. (Berlin: Walter de Gruyter, 1955) 465–466.

acquired a lien over client assets even though the depositor banks were not entitled to create a proprietary interest in their favour.[6]

Another issue was that proprietary claims could be satisfied only if the securities held by the banks were actually appropriated to the client accounts. Legal doctrine tried to construe an argument whereby clients should be able to enforce property rights against assets of the same kind held by the banks on an unappropriated basis; there was, however, no legal basis for that view.[7]

All these and other legal uncertainties,[8] which became apparent during the banking crisis, caused the legislature to intervene by reacting in a path-dependent fashion. It enacted special rules governing bailment of securities. In 1896, the law 'On the duties of merchants safekeeping securities for others' was adopted.[9] The statute did not affect the general law of bailment; it created a special regime for securities only. The 1896 statute required depositories to appropriate securities to client accounts, and provided for other safeguards; it has been amended and renamed in the meantime but continues to influence the modern law. Some of the provisions in the act currently in force can be traced right back to the 1896 Act.

12.1.2 Depotgesetz 1937

The conclusion of subsection 11.2 was that, starting in 1925, German banks changed their system of holding securities. Instead of maintaining securities on an allocated basis they persuaded clients to agree to having their securities kept in bulk and on an unallocated basis. This changeover was supported by a legal opinion written by two leading German scholars.

In 1937, the German legislature decided to replace the 1896 statute with a modernised version and enacted the 'Law on the deposit and the acquisition of securities',[10] referred to as the *Depotgesetz* 1937. It builds on the 1896 statute and clarifies several legal issues that were discussed at the time with a view to ensuring that investors had proprietary rights in the securities held in deposits rather than contractual rights against the intermediary.[11]

---

[6] Bum, JBl 1924 93 (93).   [7] Bum, JBl 1924 93 (94).
[8] Bettelheim, JBl 1924 193 (194).
[9] *Gesetz betreffend die Pflichten der Kaufleute bei Aufbewahrung fremder Wertpapiere vom 5. Juli 1896*, RGBl 1896 183.
[10] *Gesetz über die Verwahrung und Anschaffung von Wertpapieren vom 4. 2. 1937*, RGBl 1937, I 171.
[11] Schubert, *Ausschussprotokolle* 497ff. 502.

The explanatory material accompanying the *Depotgesetz* 1937 states that the legislature also intended to give statutory support to the transfer system which was already in operation.[12] Until then, the central depositories established by the German banks operated on the basis of the general terms of business of the banks involved. The *Depotgesetz* 1937 permitted the creation of central depositories by way of statutory instruments. Following the adoption of the *Depotgesetz* 1937 statutory instruments were enacted that conferred the status of a central depository on the already existing institutions.

The *Depotgesetz* 1937 applied in Germany and in Austria, which was incorporated into the German Reich in 1938 and it continued to apply in both countries after the Second World War. Both countries have in the meantime amended the Act and currently apply a revised and updated version.

12.2 Relationship between clients and their intermediary

It has already been noted that deposited securities and their transfers are governed by the law relating to tangible movables. This also has implications for the analysis of the relationships between investors and intermediaries.

In section 10.3 it was shown that intermediaries started to appear first in Germany and in Austria, driven by a need for the safekeeping of the certificates representing bearer securities. This need arose because the rules protecting buyers against adverse claims imposed the risk of an unauthorised transfer upon the owner of the securities. In German and in Austrian law owners lose all their entitlements when a third party in good faith acquires the securities and receives possession of the certificates.

In Germany, the function of an intermediary is traditionally performed by banks. The conclusion of section 11.1 was that banks at first held securities on an allocated basis for individual clients. The relationship between clients and banks therefore came to be analysed in terms of bailment: clients were considered to be the owner of the securities, banks were considered to be bailees.

The reforms of the 1930s and subsequent reforms changed the ways in which securities were held by intermediaries, in two ways. The first was that securities were transferred from individual files attributed to

---

[12] Schubert, *Ausschussprotokolle* 497 558.

individual customers to holdings in bulk on an unallocated basis. The second was that customer securities were transferred into the vaults of central depositories. The banks with whom clients had their immediate relationship ceased to have immediate physical control over the certificates.

Multi-layered intermediated holding structures have also emerged. Some banks which hold client accounts do not themselves hold accounts with the central depositories, but use other banks to act as their intermediary; in those cases it is possible for there to be several intermediary banks between the client and the central depository.

Alongside these changes in banking practice, the *Depotgesetz* regulates the relationship between clients, their securities and their intermediaries. On every level of this intermediated structure, the account holder is, in principle,[13] entitled to claim delivery of the securities to her. This claim has priority over the claims of the general creditors in the intermediary's insolvency.[14]

Banks maintain records only of the securities held by their immediate account holder. Based on these records, they have no means of identifying to whom the securities held by the account holder ultimately belong. Clients can therefore claim only as against their immediate intermediary; this intermediary will then claim from its immediate intermediary which, in turn, will claim from its immediate intermediary until the claim has reached the central depository which will deliver the certificates to its immediate account holder who will pass them on up the chain.

Account holders are not entitled to request the delivery of securities carrying the same numbers as those they originally handed over to their intermediary which then passed the securities certificates down the chain for them to be kept with the central depository.[15] Moreover, claims against intermediaries are subject to the rules on shortfalls. If a shortfall arises with an intermediary because securities have, for example, been misappropriated, all clients of that particular depository bear the

---

[13] There is no such entitlement if the securities are held in the form of a permanent global certificate. There is also no such entitlement if the securities concerned are Government bonds for which no certificates exist.

[14] German *Depotgesetz*, s. 8, 7 (1); Austrian *Depotgesetz*, s. 5 (2), 6.

[15] Siegfried Kümpel, *Bank- und Kapitalmarktrecht*, 3rd edn. (Köln: Verlag Otto Schmidt, 2004) para. 11.217; Theodor Heinsius, Arno Horn and Jürgen Than, *Depotgesetz* (Berlin: Walter de Gruyter, 1975), s. 7, para. 10; Einsele, in MünchKommHGB, DepotG, Rz 83; see also OGH 20.4.1926 Ob I 335/26 SZ 8/122.

shortfall on a pro rata basis. No attempt is made to determine to whom the shortfall should be attributed. Moreover, in contrast to the position in general German and Austrian property law, clients do not lose their entitlement if the whole bulk of client securities is sold, but later replenished. The effect of this rule is best explained by reference to an example.

If the depository holds 1,000 units of a particular security in bulk for its clients and if that bulk consists of contributions of 250 made by clients A, B, C and D, the four clients hold equal co-ownership interests in the bulk. If the intermediary misappropriates the total of the 1,000 units, and then acquires 1,000 units of the same security for client E, these securities would be considered to belong to E under general German and Austrian property law rules. The *Depotgesetz* modifies this outcome in favour of A, B, C and D and to the disadvantage of E. To satisfy the claims of all clients, the depository would need to have 2,000 units. In most cases the depository will be able restore the bulk to this size; if the depository is unable to do this, the shortfall of 1,000 units is attributed to all the clients of the depository which holds securities of that type. As a result, E receives half of the remaining 1,000 units. A, B, C and D each receives 1/8 of the remaining 1,000 units.[16]

The rules on shortfalls apply to all intermediaries that form part of the chain connecting the ultimate client with the central depository. If any one of the intermediaries concerned does not have sufficient securities in its account and is unable to make up for the shortfall out of its own resources, the claim of the account holder of this intermediary will be reduced on a pro rata basis. This also reduces the entitlements of those account holders further up the chain which hold their entitlements through the intermediary at the level at which the shortfall occurred. This, consequentially, also reduces the entitlements of those retail clients routing their entitlements albeit indirectly, but nevertheless, through the affected intermediary.

The *Depotgesetz* does not only modify the entitlements of clients in cases of shortfalls. It also gives clients preferential rights over securities held by the depository in its own name. In the insolvency of the depository, the securities held by it are separated from the assets available for distribution to the general creditors of the depository. These securities are available to satisfy the claims of clients whose securities have been misappropriated by the depository and of clients who have not yet been

---

[16] Iro, *Bankvertragsrecht*, I 10/48.

credited with a co-ownership interest but who have parted with 90 per cent or more of their consideration.[17]

The later rules of the *Depotgesetz* are more than a modification of the general rules of property law: the German and the Austrian legislature have taken the policy decision that client interests are superior to those of the general creditors of the depository. Interestingly, however, this policy decision gives clients preferential rights only in circumstances where the depository owns securities in its own name. This can be explained by the fact that whether or not securities are credited to a client account is outside the client's control. Whether or not a client has a proprietary interest in securities held by the intermediary should therefore not depend on a credit effected on the books of the client's intermediary.

In summary, clients have a preferential claim to request delivery of securities to them. That claim is, however, enforceable only as against a client's immediate intermediary which pursues the claim further down the chain. Clients are not entitled to request delivery of specific securities certificates and their entitlement is subject to the rules on shortfalls.

The services provided for by German and Austrian intermediaries have changed from services relating to the safekeeping and maintaining of paper certificates to services involving the maintaining of securities accounts. The *Depotgesetz* has put in place rules that have modified the claims of clients from claims to individual certificates to claims for the delivery of securities, the amount of which is subject to the rules on shortfalls.

Notwithstanding these changes in both the pattern through which securities are held and in the legal rules governing the entitlements of clients, German and Austrian law continues to analyse the relationship between clients and intermediaries in terms of bailment. Rather than identifying a new set of legal rules that would more appropriately reflect the change in the nature of the service provided by the intermediaries, German and Austrian law has modified its concept of bailment to accommodate the multi-layered structure which is in place today.

The intermediary with which the retail clients hold securities is referred to as a bailee (*Verwahrer*). All other intermediaries are referred to as indirect bailees (*Zwischenverwahrer*). All intermediaries, including the central depository, are deemed to hold the securities on behalf of ultimate clients the identity of whom is known only to the intermediary which holds the ultimate client account. This analysis applies

---

[17] *Depotgesetz*, s. 32; Austrian *Depotgesetz*, s. 23.

notwithstanding the fact that there can be multiple intermediary banks between the central depository and the ultimate retail client through whose accounts securities are held.

12.3 Co-ownership

In section 12.2 it was shown that the German and Austrian *Depotgesetz* regulates the claim of clients against their intermediaries. The claim of clients is not subject to the general rules of the German BGB or of the Austrian ABGB on co-ownership; it is subject to the *Depotgesetz*. In this section it will be determined if the claim regulated by the *Depotgesetz* can be classified as a co-ownership claim, but first the German and Austrian law concepts of ownership and of co-ownership will be explained.

Under the general rules of German and Austrian property law, owners continue to hold ownership in specific securities as long as they can identify them. If an owner keeps a record of the serial numbers of the securities certificates that belong to her, she is able to claim the securities from a third party with whom the certificates happen to be found.[18]

Co-ownership arises under the general rules of German and Austrian property law when fungibles are mixed in a way which makes it impossible to determine which particular items belong to each of the individual owners. In such circumstances, the owners whose fungibles form part of the bulk have co-ownership rights in the bulk. The size of their co-ownership interest is determined by the size of their contribution to the bulk.[19] Other than in English law, co-owners do not jointly hold an interest in every single unit that forms part of the bulk. Co-owners under German and Austrian law are entitled to a fraction of the whole bulk and in cases of shortfalls the shortfall affects all co-owners on a pro rata basis.

---

[18] This claim is subject to the rules on good faith acquisition of title. The owner will have lost title and will not be able to claim the securities if the third party has acquired them in good faith.

[19] For German law: BGB, s. 948; Wolfgang Wiegand, in Karl Heinz Gursky (ed.). J von, *Staudingers Kommentar zum Bürgerlichen Gesetzbuch, Drittes Buch Sachenrecht* (Berlin: Sellier–de Gruyter, 2004), s. 957, para. 7; Gerd-Hinrich Langheim, in Norbert Horn (ed.), *J von Staudingers Kommentar zum Bürgerlichen Gesetzbuch, Zweites Buch Recht der Schuldverhältnisse* (Berlin: Sellier–de Gruyter, 2002), s. 742, para. 18. For Austrian law: ABGB, s. 415; Holzner, JBl 1988 564 (569, 570f, 632f); *ibid.*, JBl 1995 521 (521f); Thomas Klicka, in Michael Schwimann (ed.), *Praxiskommentar zum ABGB*, vol. II, 3rd edn. (Wien: Orac, 2004) section 415 para 8; OGH 10.4.1997, 6 Ob 2353/96f SZ 70/63; OGH 3.12.1969, 5 Ob 253/69 SZ 42/181.

German property law does not have rules on following or tracing of ownership or co-ownership interests. If an asset is misappropriated, the owner continues to have ownership rights in the asset and is able to claim it from any third-party holder provided that the asset still exists and has not been acquired by a third party in good faith. If the asset has ceased to exist, or if a third party has acquired an overriding ownership interest, the previous owner loses her proprietary entitlement.

The operation of these rules is best illustrated by way of an example. If a warehouse keeper holds grain for several customers in a silo and misappropriates the entire content of that silo by selling it to a third-party purchaser, it is likely that the buyer will acquire ownership of the grain in good faith. As a result, the customers lose their co-ownership interest in the grain. Because German and Austrian law, traditionally, do not have rules on following or tracing, the customers do not have a proprietary interest in the proceeds received by the warehouse keeper. If the proceeds are later used by the warehouse keeper to acquire grain of the same type, the customers continue to have no proprietary entitlement to that grain. The customers can claim damages or restitution against the warehouse keeper who misappropriated the grain, but these claims are not proprietary. Once a third party has acquired ownership in good faith, customers do not have a proprietary interest in any other asset held by the person who misappropriated the grain, or any other third person.

The *Depotgesetz* is based on the assumption that investors, through a chain of indirect bailees, hold an interest in the underlying securities documents which are maintained by the central depository which also acts as a bailee on behalf of the ultimate investor. Investors are presumed to have an interest in the underlying documents. Nevertheless the *Depotgesetz* significantly modifies this general property law regime. This is because the interest of the ultimate investor is enforceable only through the claims available under the *Depotgesetz* and these claims differ significantly from the claim available to owners and co-owners under general German law.

The first difference is that investors whose securities are held in bulk under the *Depotgesetz* are not considered to be owners of particular securities. This applies irrespective of whether investors are able to prove that securities carrying certain numbers belong to them. Even if investors are able to identify their certificates, they are not entitled to delivery of them. Under general German and Austrian property law, they would be entitled to claim the certificates.

The second difference between the claim put in place by the *Depotgesetz* and the German and the Austrian general property law is that investors are unable to claim securities directly from the central depository which keeps the certificates in its vaults. Again, this applies even if an investor is able to prove her entitlement in relation to certificates carrying specific numbers. Under general rules of German and Austrian property law, owners would be entitled to claim securities provided that they were able to identify the numbers of the certificates to which their interest relates.

The third difference is attributable to the rules on shortfalls implemented by the *Depotgesetz*. Like general rules of property law in Germany and Austria, the *Depotgesetz* allocates the risk of shortfalls proportionally between all clients. The difference is, however, that the rules of the *Depotgesetz* apply even to cases where it can be identified to whom the securities which had disappeared belonged. The *Depotgesetz* prohibits courts from attributing the shortfall to specific investors; whenever there is a shortfall that is not remedied by the intermediary it will be attributed to each of the investors holding the particular type of securities on a pro rata basis. Under general property law rules, the court would first work out to which clients the disappeared securities belonged. Such an identification is easily carried out – for example, by determining at which point in time investors bought securities. If the shortfall occurred before a specific client had securities credited to her account, her securities would not have been in the pool at the time when the shortfall arose and she would therefore not have the bear the shortfall under the general property law regime. The loss would be imposed on the clients who held securities in the pool at the time of the shortfall and would be attributed pro rata between all clients only if such an allocation of loss was impossible. The *Depotgesetz* requires pro rata allocation in all cases.

Moreover, the rules of the *Depotgesetz* apply from the moment at which the securities certificates are delivered to the depository. This applies irrespective of whether the securities which belong to a particular client continue to be attributable to her. According to the general rules, co-ownership would not arise if particular securities could be attributed to individual clients. For co-ownership to arise under the general property law regime it is necessary for the securities to be mixed with other securities of the same type in a way that makes it impossible for them to be identified as the securities of a particular contributor. The *Depotgesetz* advances the point in time at which a client's ownership interest in particular units of a security is replaced by a co-ownership interest in all the client securities of that type held by the intermediary. This is a significant change in the entitlements of the client; if the intermediary goes insolvent after securities have been delivered to him, the client will be affected by a shortfall in the securities held by the depository even if she can identify the securities she delivered.[20]

These modifications have caused a debate in German law on whether the proprietary claim available to clients against their immediate intermediary can still be classified as a claim enforcing a co-ownership interest, or whether it is an independent statutory proprietary claim.[21] There also exists the view that the claims available under the *Depotgesetz* are so different in nature to what would ordinarily be classified as a proprietary claim by German law that the claim cannot be classified as proprietary.[22]

Nevertheless, the orthodox German and Austrian view is that ultimate investors are co-owners of the certificates deposited with the central depository. The concept of ownership normally requires there to be appropriation. Ownership and co-ownership can normally exist only if there are assets which can be identified and attributed to the individuals holding title. The *Depotgesetz* removes the link between investors and particular certificates.

The co-ownership analysis also applies where securities are not represented through individual certificates held in bulk but also where they are issued through a global certificate and where Government bonds are transferred through the central depository. In the former case, the investors are considered to be the co-owners of the global certificate. In the latter case, no certificates exist. German law nevertheless deems the existence of a certificate, of which the investors holding Government bonds are deemed to be the co-owners.

---

[20] *Depotgesetz*, s. 6; Austrian *Depotgesetz*, s. 5; Heinsius, Horn and Than, *Depotgesetz*, s. 7, para. 3; Wolfgang Gößmann, in Herbert Schimansky, Hermann-Josef Bunte and Hans-Jürgen Lwowski (eds.), *Bankrechts-Handbuch*, vol. II, 2nd edn. (München: Beck, 2001), s. 72, paras. 82–83, 96–98; Einsele, *Wertpapierrecht als Schuldrecht* (Tübingen: J. C. B. Mohr (Paul Siebeck), 1995) 24; Jürgen *Than*, in Obst and Hintner 847; Scherer, *Handelsgesetzbuch*, s. 6 Dorothee DepotG, para. VI 361.

[21] For the debate see *Siegfried Kümpel*, 'Der Bestimmtheitsgrundsatz bei Verfügungen über Sammeldepotguthaben – zur Theorie des Bruchteilseigentums sui generis', [1980] *Wertpapier Mitteilungen* 430; Heinsius, Horn and Than, *Depotgesetz*, s. 8 Rz 1–3; Claus-Wilhelm Canaris, in Hermann Staub (ed.), *Großkommentar zum Handelsrechts*, vol. II, part III *Bankvertragsrecht*, 2nd edn. (Berlin: Walter de Gruyter, 1981), para. 2120; Micheler, *Wertpapierrecht* 177–181.

[22] Einsele, in MünchKommHGB, DepotG, Rz 83.

12.4 Transfer of co-ownership

12.4.1 Introduction

The conclusion of subsection 10.1.1 was that, in German law, the buyer acquires ownership to securities if two requirements are met: the seller and the buyer need to agree that ownership passes to the transferee; the buyer also needs to acquire possession to the securities certificates. It was also pointed out in subsection 10.1.1 that under German and Austrian law a wide concept of possession has been adopted. For the buyer to acquire possession it is not necessary that the certificates be physically moved: for possession to pass to the buyer, it is sufficient for the seller to assign her right to the buyer to claim the securities from a third party.

12.4.2 Depotgesetz

These rules also apply to transfers of securities if they are maintained with the central depository. The German and Austrian *Depotgesetz* does not disapply the general property law in this respect; it only adds a rule which is important mainly from the perspective of retail clients. The provision applies if an investor instructs an intermediary to purchase securities for her provided that the intermediary acts in one of two ways. The rule governs a purchase if the intermediary, when carrying out the transaction for the client, acts either as a commission agent or buys the securities in its own name, but on behalf of the client. In both cases, the investor acquires a co-ownership interest in the securities kept in bulk with the central depository when the securities are credited to her on the books of the intermediary which carried out the purchase in her behalf.[23]

The rule implements a special regime for intermediated purchases of securities. Its doctrinal significance lies in the fact that the point in time at which the buyer of securities acquires ownership can be determined without reference to the rules on possession. In practical terms, the rule creates certainty for retail clients. It determines when they acquire a co-ownership interest irrespective of whether the intermediary has itself received a credit of the securities on its own account further up the chain.[24] If intermediaries credit securities to the account of a client

---

[23] *Depotgesetz*, s. 24; Austrian *Depotgesetz*, s. 17.

[24] If the intermediary purchasing securities on behalf of clients receives the client securities before it credits them to the client's account, the client acquires property rights at the point in time at which the intermediary receives the securities (Micheler, *Wertpapierrecht* 205–209).

before they have themselves received a corresponding credit on their own account further down the chain, the client credit will very probably be conditional upon the intermediary itself receiving credit of the securities. In cases where an unconditional credit to the client account is effected prior to the credit on the intermediary's account, however, the client will be considered to be a co-owner from the time when the credit on her account was effected. In such cases, the securities held by the respective intermediary on behalf of its clients are considered to belong to all its clients. Until the intermediary has received a corresponding credit there will not be sufficient securities in the client pool held by the intermediary to satisfy the claims of all its clients. Should the shortfall prove to be permanent, all the clients of that intermediary will share it on a pro rata basis.

The rule applies only to purchases carried out through intermediaries; it does not apply if investors purchase securities in their own name and have them transferred to their securities accounts. It does not, for example, apply if banks or other financial service providers purchase securities for their own accounts. In those cases, the point in time at which the purchase acquires a co-ownership interest in the securities is determined by applying the general rules, which will be analysed below.

12.4.3 German property law

The analysis in subsection 10.1.1 led to the conclusion that two requirements needed to satisfied for a buyer to become the owner of securities under German law. These requirements will now be analysed in turn.

The first requirement for ownership to pass is that both parties need to agree that the transferee is to become the owner. German law distinguishes between the sales contract, which creates an obligation of the seller to transfer ownership to the buyer, and an additional agreement, which effects the transfer of ownership to the buyer. This second agreement can be concluded at the same time as the sales contract is made: this will be the case, for example, where a tangible item is sold for cash and delivered to the buyer on conclusion of the sales contract. If the parties agree to postpone completion to a point in time after the sales contract has been entered into, the agreement to transfer ownership will be concluded at this later time. Contracts for the sale of securities are not normally completed on conclusion of the sales contract; there is frequently a time lag between the sales contract and the delivery of the securities and the purchase price.

Moreover, if a sales contract for securities has been made on the stock exchange, the buyer and seller do not communicate directly and do not know each other's identity. The parties continue to deal on an intermediated basis after the sales contract has been concluded and throughout the completion process. The orthodox view, therefore, is that the parties conclude the agreement which transfers ownership to the buyer through their intermediaries. The seller is said to make the respective offer to transfer the securities to the buyer upon instructing the central depository either itself or through an intermediary.[25] For an agreement to arise, the buyer then needs to accept the offer. However, the buyer does not accept the offer herself, and there is a debate among German scholars as to who acts as the buyer's agent in this context. Some scholars write that the offer is accepted by the central depository which acts on the buyer's behalf,[26] others that, in a chain of intermediaries, the buyer's intermediary accepts the offer on her behalf.[27] For the purposes of this book there is no need to investigate this question further; it suffices to note that the completion of a sales transaction involves an agreement which is additional to the sales contract and which causes the buyer to acquire ownership. This agreement is entered by intermediaries on behalf of the buyer and seller. It is worth noting that both offer and acceptance are not concluded in the ultimate buyer's name; the respective acting intermediary is considered to act as an agent for an undisclosed principal.[28]

The second requirement for ownership to be transferred to the buyer is that the buyer needs to acquire possession of the securities certificates. When securities are kept in a bulk with a central depository, no documents will be physically delivered to the buyer. The securities certificates are also not transferred to a file which would be attributable

---

[25] Kümpel, *Bank- und Kapitalmarktrecht*, para. 11.371–4; Einsele, *Wertpapierrecht* 59.

[26] Rögner, in Christian Huber (ed.), *Bankrecht* (Baden-Baden: Nomos, 2001) 336f; in 2003, the German central depository introduced settlement through a central counterparty. Since then, the offer is said to be accepted by that central counterparty rather than by the central depository (Kümpel, *Bank- und Kapitalmarktrecht*, para. 11.382–7; Norbert Horn, 'Die Erfüllung von Wertpapiergeschäften unter Einbeziehung eines Zentralen Kontrahenten an der Börse', [Sonderbeilage 2/2002] *Wertpapier Mitteilungen* 11);

[27] Gößmann, *Bankrechts-Handbuch*, s. 72, para. 108; Heinsius, Horn and Than, *Depotgesetz*, s. 6, para. 84; Canaris, *Bankvertragsrecht*, para. 2019; Einsele, *Wertpapierrecht* 63.

[28] Kümpel, *Bank- und Kapitalmarktrecht*, para. 11.393–9; Heinsius, Horn and Than, *Depotgesetz*, s. 6, para. 84; Einsele, *Wertpapierrecht* 48–50; Rögner, in Huber (ed.), *Bankrecht* 336–337; Horn, 'Die Erfüllung' 11; for a different view see Canaris, *Bankvertragsrecht*, para. 1891.

to the buyer; they remain at the same location in the vaults of the central depository.

Transfers are effected by way of book entry on the accounts of the transferee and of the transferor if they both hold accounts with the same bank. If they hold accounts with different banks, the bank of the transferor will transfer the securities to the bank of the transferee, which will in turn credit the transferee's account. If both intermediary banks are directly linked with the central depository, the transfer will involve the following debit bookings. There will be a debit on the transferor's account on the level of her intermediary bank and a debit on the intermediary bank's account on the level of the central depository. Corresponding to these debit bookings there will be two credit bookings. On the level of the central depository, the securities will be credited to the account of the transferee's intermediary. On the level of the transferee's intermediary bank, the securities will be credited to the transferee's account.

German law classifies these book entries in terms of the law of possession. The analysis develops the concept of possession, starting from the assumption that the possession of physical documents is a legal relationship between a person and a tangible. Possession normally involves a person physically holding particular identifiable tangible movables. In the context of deposited securities, German law has modified this basic concept of possession in two ways. The first is that investors in securities which are kept in bulk do not have a relationship to individual certificates. They are co-owners of the bulk. This also means that they jointly hold possession of the bulk as a whole. They do not individually have possession of individual certificates but each investor has what could be called 'co-possession' of the whole bulk of securities. When securities are transferred this involves the transfer of that possessory interest rather than a transfer of possession to specific documents. The second modification involves the assumption that possession or co-possession is a legal relationship which is capable of being subjected to a division of labour. The ultimate possessor can arrange her relationship with the tangible such that some elements of co-possession are exercised by a different person on her behalf. The analysis distinguishes between holding direct and holding indirect co-possession of securities certificates. It also introduces the concept of holding co-possession, directly or indirectly, on behalf of a third party.

In the analysis, the central depository holds direct possession of the documents, but does so on behalf of the ultimate investor. The intermediaries further up the chain hold indirect co-possession of the documents and also act on behalf of the ultimate investor. The ultimate investor is classified as holding indirect co-possession of the documents, but acts on her own behalf. Outsourcing some of the elements of co-possession to the central depository and the intermediaries, the ultimate investor is nevertheless considered to satisfy all the legal requirements necessary to give her co-possession of the securities certificates.

Direct co-possession manifests itself in the physical holding of the securities document. Indirect co-possession manifests itself in the book entry on the account maintained with the central depository or an intermediary further up the chain. For co-ownership to be transferred to the buyer it is sufficient for her to acquire indirect co-possession as long as the intermediaries further down the chain, who are presumed to mediate possession on behalf of the respective end investor, continue to remain in place.

When securities are credited to the account of a buyer, the buyer acquires indirect co-possession of the securities certificates. This causes the chain of intermediaries which previously mediated co-possession in favour of the seller to mediate co-possession in favour of the buyer. By acquiring indirect co-possession, the buyer also gets the benefit of the mediated elements of possession performed by the intermediaries. The indirect co-possession of the buyer, taken together with the mediated elements of possession, causes the buyer to acquire a complete co-possessory relationship between herself and the securities documents.[29] Having acquired co-possession of the underlying documents, the buyer also becomes the co-owner of the certificates.

12.4.4 Global certificates and Government bonds

Subsection 12.4.3 focused on securities for which individual certificates are maintained in bulk with the central depository. Transfers of securities represented by a global certificate and Government bonds for which no certificate exists, but which are nevertheless transferred through the central depository, will now be examined. Global certificates will be analysed first.

If a securities issue is represented by a global certificate which is held through the central depository, the investors holding securities of that

---

[29] Alfred Hueck and Claus Wilhelm Canaris, *Recht in der Wertpapiere*, 12th edn. (München: Franz Vahlen, 1986) 16; Ulrich Drobnig, Dokumentenloser 'Effektenverkehr', in Karl Kreuzer (ed.), *Abschied von Wertpapier? Dokumentenlose Wertbewegungen im Effeckten-, Gütertransport- und Zahlungsverkehr* (Neuwied: Alfred Metzner Verlag, 1988) 28; Horn, 'Die Erfüllung' 9–10.

issue are considered to be co-owners of the global certificate. They are also considered to hold joint possession of the document. The analysis is otherwise identical to the analysis in relation to individual certificates maintained in bulk: the buyer becomes the owner if she has agreed with the seller that ownership passes to her and if she has acquired possession of the securities concerned.

Concerning the requirement for possession, investors are considered to be co-owners of the global certificate; they also hold joint possession of it. Individual investors therefore hold co-possession of the certificates indirectly mediated the chain of intermediaries and the central depository. Co-possession is transferred to the buyer by way of credits to securities accounts.

This analysis applies irrespective of whether the certificates are temporary or permanent global certificates. The only difference between securities held in the form of individual certificates or in the form of temporary global certificates, on the one hand, and securities held in the form of permanent global certificates, on the other, is that in the case of permanent global certificates investors can transfer their entitlement only through intermediaries attached to the central depository; they are unable to request delivery of individual certificates.

12.4.5 German Government bonds

No certificates are issued for German Government bonds; the central depository nevertheless offers services relating to the holding and transfer of these securities. If securities are kept through the central depository, it appears as the holder on the register relating to Government bonds. Otherwise transfers are effected through entries on the accounts maintained by the central depository on behalf of intermediaries and by the intermediaries on behalf of the ultimate clients. These entries are identical to the entries that are carried out for securities for which paper certificates exit.

The legal analysis that applies to transfers of Government bonds is also identical to the analysis of transfers of securities represented by paper. Notwithstanding the fact that no paper certificate exists, Government bonds are considered to be governed by the rules on tangible movables. Transfers are analysed in terms of possession of a document the existence of which is deemed. Rather than implementing a solution that would reflect modern transfer practice, German legal doctrine prefers to further develop and expand the legal analysis that was already in place. From the lawyer's point of view, operating rules based on a legal fiction are preferable to creating new rules whose application might create legal uncertainties.

12.4.6 Austrian law

The Austrian rules on transfers of indirectly held securities are similar to the German ones. For the purposes of this book and in the context of this subsection it suffices to point to one difference between Austrian and German rules.[30] This difference has already been mentioned in subsection 10.1.2, but should be remembered here. In addition to the requirements that need to be satisfied in German and Austrian law, Austrian law imposes a third requirement. The buyer becomes the owner only if there exits a valid sales contract between herself and the seller. This third requirement needs to be satisfied irrespective of whether securities are held directly or indirectly. Otherwise in this context the Austrian rules are similar to the German ones.

12.4.7 Conclusions

The analysis adopted by German and Austrian law relies on the rules of possession and develops them further to accommodate transfers of tangibles that appear only on the books of intermediaries. This allows German and Austrian law to continue to uphold the analysis that securities are tangible assets that are transferred according to the rules on governing tangible movables. This analysis applies to securities for which individual certificates are maintained in bulk, to securities for which there exist temporary or permanent global certificates and also to German Government bonds for which no certificates are issued. The analysis presented here gives an example of how legal doctrine perpetuates itself: lawyers adhere to existing legal concepts and law evolves consistently with pre-existing legal doctrine.

The doctrinal analysis adopted by German and Austrian law differs significantly from that adopted by English law. German and Austrian intermediaries are bailees; they do not have a proprietary interest in the securities they hold for clients. English intermediaries are trustees and hold either legal or equitable title to client securities. In Austria and in Germany clients are deemed to have a property relationship with the underlying securities documents; there is no such thing in English law.

Nevertheless the outcomes produced by the two approaches are similar at a functional level. Investors have property rights under both regimes:

---

[30] For a detailed analysis see Micheler, *Wertpapierrecht* 187–209.

this gives them a preferential status in the insolvency of the intermediary. Moreover, despite the fact that investors under German and
Austrian law have a claim to the underlying securities, this claim is
enforceable only indirectly through the chain of intermediaries that
operates between the ultimate client and the central depository. The
claim is subject to the rules on shortfalls; the extent to which it can be
satisfied is determined by the entitlements held by the intermediaries
forming part of the chain.

There exists a slight difference in terms of outcomes achieved by the
two approaches. In German and Austrian law the buyer of indirect securities usually becomes the owner when the securities are credited to her
account. In England, equitable ownership usually vests in the buyer
when the three requirements for certainty have been satisfied. This is
frequently before the securities are credited to the client's account.

12.5 Unauthorised transfers

12.5.1 German law

The *Depotgesetz* does not contain special rules dealing with adverse
claims. German and Austrian legal doctrine apply the general rules of
property law contained in their respective civil and commercial codes.

These rules protect the bona fide purchaser of tangible movables. The
conclusion of subsection 10.2.2 was that they apply also to bearer
securities. To be protected against adverse claims the buyer needs
to satisfy two requirements; she needs to show that she acted in good
faith; she also needs to have possession of the tangible movable transferred to her.

In subsection 10.2.2 it was shown that the rationale underlying the
German rules on this point is that the delivery of a tangible movable to
the buyer entitles her to assume that the seller had authority to sell. The
buyer is also entitled to assume that the seller had authority to sell if she
has had assigned to her the right to claim the securities from a third
party by the seller. The rules on good faith acquisition of title are,
traditionally, explained as being a reflection of the ability of the seller
to effect delivery of a particular item. If the seller is able to bring an asset
into the physical possession of the buyer, the buyer is entitled to assume
that the seller also had authority to sell.

This underlying explanation causes some German scholars to propound the view that the buyer of a co-ownership interest is not protected

by the rules on good faith acquisition of title.[31] A co-ownership interest is not capable of being physically delivered to the buyer. When the buyer acquires co-possession, no aspect of the transfer process indicates which fraction of the ownership right to the bulk belonged to the buyer. The physical delivery of particular items amounts to a representation entitling the buyer to assume that the seller had authority to sell, but the acquisition of co-possession does not represent to the buyer the fraction of the bulk to which the seller's assumed authority relates.

The exclusion of co-ownership interests from the application of the rules on the good faith acquisition of ownership does, however, not concern transfers of co-ownership interests held in securities that are deposited according to the *Depotgesetz*. The general view of German legal doctrine is that co-ownership interests in deposited securities can be acquired in good faith. The policy reason supporting this is that the transfer system which is supported by the *Depotgesetz* would not be able to operate efficiently if transferees could be subjected to adverse claims.[32] Investors can choose to hold and transfer securities either in the paper form or through intermediaries connected with the central depository. When securities are transferred through the physical delivery of paper documents, the transferee is protected against adverse claims. Intermediaries would be unable to persuade clients to take advantage of their custody and transfer services if clients did not receive equivalent protection when deposited securities are transferred. It is in the interest of the German securities market to eliminate paper from the transfer process; as a matter of legal policy, the law should support this legitimate market interest and protect buyers acquiring securities through the paperless transfer system against adverse claims.

---

[31] Canaris, *Bankvertragsrecht*, paras. 2026–2027, 1994; Einsele, *Wertpapierrecht* 105–106; Opitz, *Depotgesetz* 313; Heinsius, Horn and Than, *Depotgesetz*, s. 24, para. 26; Horn, 'Die Erfüllung' 11.

[32] Kümpel, *Bank- und Kapitalmarktrecht*, para. 11.411–11.412; Canaris, *Bankvertragsrecht*, para. 2026; Hueck and Canaris, *Wertpapiere* 16; Ingo Koller, 'Der gutgläubige Erwerb von Sammeldepotanteilen an Wertpapieren im Effektengiroverkehrs', [1972] *Der Betrieb* 1905; Heinsius, Horn and Than, *Depotgesetz*, s. 6, para. 91; Fritz Fabricius, 'Zur Theorie des stückelson Effektengiroverkehrs' 482; Ulrich Meyer-Cording and Tim Drygala, *Wertpapierrech*, 3rd edn. (Berlin: Luchterhand Neuwied, Kriftel, 1995) 23; Harm Peter Westermann, 'Das Girosammeldepot im deutschen Recht', (1985) 49 *Rabels Zeitschrift für ausländisches und internationales Privatrecht* 231; Drobnig, 'Dokumentenloser Effektenverkehr' 30; Ingo Koller, 'Empfielt sich eine Neuordnung und Ergänzung des Wertpapierrechts im BGB', in Bundesministerium der Justiz (ed.), *Gutachten und Vorschläge zu Überarbertung des Schuldrechts*, vol. II (Köln: Bundesanzeiger Verlagsgesellschaft, 1981) 1504.

The doctrinal argument supporting the application of the rules on the good faith acquisition of ownership to co-ownership interests in deposited securities is that in the case of deposited securities, there exists a method of representing to the buyer the fraction of the bulk to which the interest of the seller relates. The credit on the account of the buyer amounts to a representation which entitles the buyer to assume that the seller was authorised to sell.[33] Credits on securities accounts maintained according to the *Depotgesetz* have this particular legal quality because the banks effecting these credits are subjected to a special regulatory regime.[34] As a result, the rules on the good faith acquisition of title apply.

12.5.2 Austrian law

The conclusion of subsection 10.2.3 was that the Austrian rules on the good faith acquisition of ownership to securities differ slightly in detail from the German ones. These differences do not, however, have an impact on the analysis of transfers of deposited securities in Austrian law. Like German legal doctrine, Austrian legal doctrine maintains that a co-ownership interest is, in principle, not protected by the rules on the good faith acquisition of title.[35] Co-ownership interests in deposited securities are, however, exempt from that principle. As in German law, the credit on a securities account is presumed under Austrian law to amount to a representation that entitles the purchaser to assume that the vendor had authority to sell.[36]

12.5.3 Conclusions

Both German and Austrian law apply the rules on the good faith acquisition of tangible movables to transfers of securities which are held through intermediaries connected to the central depository. Both legal systems adapted these rules. The current doctrinal position is that the credit on a securities account is a representation entitling the

---

[33] Canaris, *Bankvertragsrecht*, para. 2027; Koller, 'Der gutgläubige Erwerb von Sammeldepotanteilen an Wertpapieren im Effektengiroverkehrs', [1972] Der Betrieb, 1857 1905–1906; Heinsius, Horn and Than, *Depotgesetz*, s. 6, para. 91; Horn, 'Die Erfüllung' 11–12, 14–15.

[34] Canaris, *Bankvertragsrecht*, para. 2027; Heinsius, Horn and Than, *Depotgesetz*, s. 6, paras. 40, 91.

[35] Gert Iro, in Peter Avancini, Gert Iro and Helmut Koziol, *Österreichisches Bankvertragsrecht*, vol. II (Wien: Manz, 1993), paras. 7/124, fn. 338, 7/153.

[36] Iro, *Bankvertragsrecht*, II, para. 7/154.

buyer to assume that the seller had authority to sell. It is important to note that the prevailing view in both systems is that the rules on the good faith acquisition of title can be applied only because securities are classified as tangible movables; the orthodox view is that if that classification were to change, the buyer would not be protected against adverse claims.

In contrast, English law has yet to find a way in which the rules governing unauthorised transfers certificated transfers can apply to unauthorised transfers of uncertificated transfers.[37] There is, however, every reason to believe that the courts will find a solution consistent with the path adopted by English law.

12.6 Defective issues

The conclusion of section 10.3 was that under both German and Austrian law there is a rule that causes the issuer to be liable if she has created bearer certificates that appear to carry certain rights. This amounts to a representation with which the issuer is fixed even if she did not validly issue the certificates. The issuer is liable to a bearer who relied on the certificates and acquired them without knowing that they had not been validly issued. In both jurisdictions, the issuer is liable because the bearer relied upon paper certificates.

Both German and Austrian law encounter difficulties when analysing securities that have been issued defectively and that are transferred through the central depository and the intermediaries attached to them.[38] The problem is that transfers through the central depository are effected through book entry; the certificates are kept in a vault and the purchaser does not rely on a representation contained in them when she buys the securities.[39] It is nevertheless possible to fix the issuer with a representation. If the issuer provided the central depository with a global certificate or otherwise caused the securities to be transferable through the central depository, this amounts to a

---

[37] See section 6.3.
[38] Interestingly, a similar problem arises in England, where the rules on defective issues developed in relation to certificated securities and where it is yet unclear how these rules apply to uncertificated transfers (chapter 5).
[39] Meyer-Cording and Drygala, Wertpapierrecht 22; Andreas Zahn and Stephan Kock, 'Die Emission von unverbrieften Schuldtiteln durch die Europäische Zentralbank', [1999] Wertpapier Mitteilungen 1963–1964; Ulrike Meyer-Panhuysen, Die fehlerhafte Kapitalerhöhung (Köln: Dr. Otto Schmidt 2003) 39–41, 53.

represenation. The issuer is liable to those who purchased securities relying on the fact that the securities were transferable through the current German and Austrian depository system.[40]

12.7 Summary of the analysis

In this chapter, the German and Austrian rules governing transfers of indirectly held securities have been analysed. Unlike England, which has opted for dematerialising securities transfers, Germany and Austria opted for immobilising them. The relationship between intermediaries and investors is traced in terms of bailment in both German and Austrian law. Investors are considered to be co-owners of the indirectly held securities; they are also considered to hold co-possession of the securities certificates deposited with the central depository. This contrasts with the position adopted by English law, where the relationship of investors holding securities indirectly is governed by the law of trusts.

A co-ownership interest in indirectly held securities is transferred by way of a book entry on the books of the intermediary with which the securities are held. This book entry is legally classified as involving a transfer of possession to the securities certificates from the seller to the buyer.

Purchasers of indirectly held securities are protected against adverse claims arising out of unauthorised transfers by the same rules that protect purchasers of directly held securities in German and Austrian law. Notwithstanding the fact that investors hold a co-ownership interest in a bulk of securities held with a central depository, the buyer in good faith can rely on the rules protecting the purchaser of a tangible against unauthorised transfers. The position in English law is less clear. The rules that govern transfers of certificated securities had not been abolished when uncertificated securities were introduced in England. It is, however, unclear if, and to what extent, the rules that protect purchasers of certificated securities also offer protection to purchasers of uncertificated securities.

In spite of the different doctrinal approach prevailing in England, on the one hand, and in Germany and Austria, on the other, there exists one important similarity. All three jurisdictions have found a way of eliminating paper from the process of transferring securities; at the

---

[40] Micheler, *Wertpapierrecht* 242–246.

same time, neither of the jurisdictions has created a new legal regime from scratch to support securities transfers that are effected without the need to move paper certificates. Instead in all three jurisdictions the existing rules governing paper transfers were modified to accommodate paperless transfers. Moreover, the analysis presented in chapters 4 and 11 leads to the conclusion that the legal rules governing paper transfers had significant impact on the institutional setup that was put in place to handle paperless transfers.

13 Evidence of convergence?

The analysis of German and Austrian law contained in this book has focused on bearer securities since almost all German companies issue them. This, however, has changed in recent years. A few large German listed companies have replaced bearer with name shares, a change caused by globalisation.[1] The reason for the change was that the companies concerned wanted to be able to list directly on the New York Stock Exchange (NYSE). The NYSE, however, lists only name shares. In order to be able to issue the same type of share to investors in the US and to German investors, the German issuers decided to issue name instead of bearer shares on both the American and the German stock market. The German legislature supported this changeover by reforming the law of name shares which is traditionally contained in the German Joint Stock Companies Act (*Aktiengesetz*).

This Act requires German companies which issue name shares to maintain a register of shareholders. At the same time, the law relating to this register was also updated. Interestingly, the changes that were effected included a change in German legal terminology. Before the reform, the share register was referred to as a 'share book' (*Aktienbuch*). That term was abandoned in the course of the reform and replaced by the term 'share register' (*Aktienregister*). This change in terminology is noteworthy in the context of this book because the explanatory notes to the revised statute explicitly state that the terminology was

---

[1] Peter Hommelhoff and Christoph Teichmann, 'Namensaktie, Neue Medien und Nachgründung – aktuelle Entwicklungslinien im Aktienrecht', in Dietrich Dörner, Dieter Menhold, Norbert Pfitzer and Peter Oser (eds.), *Reform des Aktienrechts, der Rechnungslegung und der Prüfung*, 2nd edn. (Stuttgart: Schäffer-Poeschel, 2003) 106–107.

chosen in order to more closely reflect the English term 'registered share'.[2]

The German settlement system also supported the German companies' move away from bearer and towards name shares by introducing a facility which made it is possible for retail investors to have their names entered into the share register notwithstanding the fact that they held the shares through a chain of intermediairies. This development is an example of convergence. German law was changed in order to become more like the perceived prevailing international standard, with a view to enabling German issuers to compete on a global market.

It is important to note, however, that the reform did not change the legal doctrine that was already in place. Bearer shares were replaced with name shares in order to comply with American market practice. The share register was renamed to reflect English-language usage. None of this, however, affected the doctrinal analysis of the share transfers. The reform was carried out in line with prevailing German property law doctrine and did not change the legal nature of German shares. It also left the analysis of the transfer process unaltered. German name shares, like German bearer shares, are considered to be tangibles. In order for them to be transferred within the German settlement system they are endorsed to the bearer. This endorsement transforms name into bearer shares and their transfer is then governed by the same rules that govern all other bearer securities. The certificates for name shares are deposited with the central depository. As with bearer shares, the rules on possession of these securities certificates determine the point in time when the buyer becomes the owner of name shares, and notwithstanding the change in name, an entry on a German share register does not cause the shareholder concerned to become the owner of the shares.

---

[2] *Bundestag Drucksache* 14/4051 10, also published in [2000] *Zeitschrift für Wirtschaftsrecht* (ZIP) 939.

14 Conclusions on German and Austrian law

The focus of part II of the book was the German and the Austrian law of securities. Securities are classified as tangibles in both German and Austrian legal doctrine and their transfers are governed by the same rules as transfers of tangible assets. This analysis is supported by the theory that the paper certificates which are traditionally issued for securities embody the entitlements to which they relate. The analysis appeared in the later part of the nineteenth century and became the orthodox theory prevailing in both Germany and in Austria after the German states and Austria had adopted rules protecting the bona fide purchaser against unauthorised issues.

Under both German and Austrian law, the buyer needs to acquire possession to the securities certificate in order to become the owner of the certificate and of the entitlement to which it relates. The buyer of securities is protected against adverse claims arising out of unauthorised transfers in the same way as the buyer of tangible movables; there also exists a rule protecting the buyer against claims arising out of defective issues.

In both German and Austrian law, the rule protecting the buyer of securities against unauthorised transfers imposes the risk of such transfers upon the owner of securities who loses her entitlement when a buyer in good faith and for value acquires possession to the securities documents. As a result, a need exists for the safekeeping of documents in both German and Austrian law, which facilitated the emergence of depositories in both jurisdictions.

The theory underlying securities and their transfers in both German and Austrian law has had a significant impact on the way in which paper certificates were eliminated from securities transfers in both countries. The theory is held to state a normative principle that the

rules protecting investors against adverse claims arising out of unauthorised transfers apply only because securities are classified as tangibles. If securities were classified as intangibles, investors would not be
protected against unauthorised transfers. When the handling of paper
certificates became too cumbersome, the German market considered
it prudent not to adopt a new regime from scratch; it decided rather
that the legal analysis previously in place should remain unchanged.
Securities continued to be classified as tangibles but the paper documents representing the securities were immobilised. The German and
Austrian markets built a new transfer system around the incumbent
legal analysis.

A central depository exists which stores securities certificates for
most German listed securities. Clients usually hold securities through
subdepositories which maintain accounts with the central depository
and the relationship between clients and their depositories is analysed
in terms of bailment. Depositories are not considered to hold property rights in client securities; they only mediate possession between
their clients and the securities certificates which are maintained by
the central depository. Investors are considered to be co-owners and
co-possessors of the securities held with the central depository.
Ownership of these securities is transferred by way of book entry
which is, however, doctrinally classified as involving a transfer of
co-possession from the seller to the buyer. The buyer is protected
against adverse claims that may arise out of unauthorised transfers or
out of defective issues.

After this brief summary of the analysis contained in part II of the
book, the conclusions drawn from the complete analysis of English,
German and Austrian law will be presented in part III.

PART III

Conclusions

15 Legal development as a path-dependent process

The analysis contained in this book has shown the impact of legal doctrine on legal development. English, German and Austrian law have historically developed in a path-dependent fashion. The path along which that development took place was shaped by legal doctrine: in all three jurisdictions, the legal environment that existed when securities were first issued determined their legal nature.

A distinction needs to be made between the factors that cause change to the law and the form in which the law absorbs the need for change. The need for reform is triggered by causes which also lie outside the law, and these causes are not analysed in this book. The book is rather based on the assumption that politics, economics, culture, social and commercial norms can bring about a need to change legal rules. Once a need for the law to accommodate change has emerged, however, the reform process has historically been shaped by legal doctrine. The legal systems analysed in this book did not construct new rules from scratch; rather, they modified the existing legal doctrine. Moreover, the lawyers charged with participating in reform by drafting the underlying legal rules favoured reform that required little modification of existing rules over reform that required significant change.

This pattern of change is inherent in the law. One reason explaining why lawyers prefer to modify existing rules rather than drafting new rules is that legal rules are necessarily incomplete: it is impossible to draft law that anticipates all the factual issues that will appear in the future. Irrespective of how carefully a legal document has been worded, it will be interpreted by the judiciary in the light of circumstances that may not have been foreseen by its drafters.

Keeping this in mind, the lawyers drafting new rules are faced with the somewhat conflicting need to implement their clients' demands with precision, reflecting the needs of their clients as closely as possible; this requires them to select legal concepts that produce reliable results. In order to achieve that, they rely on legal concepts that are frequently used and have been tested in court on many occasions. The more frequently a legal concept has been used, the easier it is to predict how it will operate in the context of a proposed new legal structure and the principles that determined the legal concept prior to the reform will continue to govern the concept in the context of the new structure. These principles also bind judges and all others who will interpret the new rules in the future.

Market participants may be happy to take commercial risk, but they put a high premium on achieving legal certainty. The result is that the lawyers advising them apply existing legal concepts to accommodate new developments rather than adopting new solutions that create more efficient, but less tested, results. Legal practice needs to deliver predictable results[1] and this discourages experiments with new techniques.

The same is true for the legislature. The lawyers drafting new legislation need to implement government policies as precisely as possible. Moreover, they need to be able to predict the way in which a proposed new set of rules will be applied by legal practice, and how it will be interpreted by the courts. This requirement for certainty and predictability leads them to use familiar doctrinal tools rather than experiment with more straightforward but unfamiliar and untested legal techniques.

This analysis applies irrespective of whether a particular jurisdiction uses rules or standards to regulate a particular matter. Rules are drafted with a view to regulating a particular field in a high degree of detail; standards are worded in general and abstract terms and leave discretion to those who implement the law. Even if the legislature decides to use standards, those drafting them nevertheless anticipate that a particular standard will operate in a way that is consistent with pre-existing legal doctrine.

Another phenomenon identified by the analysis in the book is that once a path has been adopted by legal doctrine, that path is not reversed. Whenever legal rules make it impossible for lawyers to achieve a desired outcome directly, an attempt will be made to reach it indirectly. Once a solution has been found to overcome a certain rule that is perceived to create an obstacle to market participants, legal practice adheres to this solution even though the rule around which it was originally created may

---

[1] For an account of the influence of transactional lawyers on legal development, see also R. C. Nolan, 'Property in a Fund', 120 (2004) *LQR* 108–136.

have long disappeared. Once the indirect route has become standard practice, lawyers will not deviate from it even if a direct route has become available and even if it is more efficient.

The fact that in England there exist registered securities and an English law of registered securities is an example of this phenomenon. When securities first emerged assignment or any other way of transferring securities directly between investors was not available. Legal practice reverted to an indirect route and applied the law of novation, and the underlying logic has shaped the legal nature of English securities and the regime governing their transfer ever since. The analysis did not change when assignment became generally possible; English market practice continued to issue registered securities and develop the law consistently with the legal doctrine that was already in place.

When securities first became widespread in Germany and Austria, the assignment of debt was possible. The rules on assignment, however, made it difficult to issue securities to the bearer and did not protect purchasers against adverse claims. In order to avoid these disadvantages German and Austrian legal doctrine searched for some time to find an alternative to the law of assignment that would better serve the needs of market participants. As soon as all German jurisdictions had developed rules on tangibles giving protection against adverse claims, it became the generally accepted theory that securities were tangibles and that their transfers were governed by the law of tangibles. This analysis has remained the basis of all legal development ever since. Even when the handling of paper certificates became too cumbersome, and law reform eliminating paper became necessary, the reform was structured around the dogma that securities were tangibles.

All three jurisdictions have eliminated the need to physically move paper certificates from the transfer process. The point in time at which this took place was determined by circumstances outside the law. But, the law – and, in particular, the legal doctrine governing securities prior to the reform – determined the way in which law reform was carried out.

England eliminated paper in the late twentieth century. The reform was triggered, among other factors, by an unprecedented increase in securities volumes caused by the privatisation of previously state-controlled enterprises. This book does not further analyse the reasons that led to the need for reform in English law; it rather focuses on the way in which the reform was carried out. The reform process was determined by the legal doctrine already in place in England, so England eliminated paper from securities transfers by creating dematerialised securities.

Before dematerialisation, securities were classified as intangibles and transfer procedures were modelled around the law of novation. After dematerialisation, the previous principles of analysis continued to apply. Securities were still classified as intangibles and the transfer procedure governing dematerialised securities replicated the transfer procedure that had been in place before. Dematerialisation also did not affect the analysis of securities that were held indirectly through intermediaries. The analysis before dematerialisation was that intermediaries held securities on trust for investors and this analysis applied irrespective of whether securities were held in certificated or uncertificated form.

Germany and Austria experienced the need to eliminate paper from transfers of securities in the 1930s. Until then, German and Austrian securities had been transferred by physical delivery of paper certificates but the circumstances of the 1930s made it necessary to reduce the need for paper certificates to be moved. The book does not explain the historical, political and economic reasons that led to this need for reform; the focus of the analysis is the method through which paper was eliminated, a method determined by incumbent German and Austrian legal doctrine. Even though the drafters of the 1930s' reform could have built on a law enacted in 1910 which made it possible for Government bonds to be issued and held as dematerialised securities,[2] the reform did not take advantage of that model. Rather, the reform was carried out consistently with the legal rules that had been in place before. Before the reform, securities were considered to be tangibles and securities held through intermediaries were analysed through the law of bailment. The drafters of the reform did not change the principles of this analysis; rather they modified the law of bailment to accommodate securities maintained on an unallocated basis. Securities continued to be classified as tangibles. The analysis remained intact notwithstanding the fact that individual certificates were replaced by global certificates and was also extended to Government bonds for which no certificates existed.

Legal doctrine causes the law to develop path-dependently. Law changes and adapts to new demands and circumstances but change is effected by adapting existing legal concepts rather than by introducing new ones. Legal systems have a certain limited set of doctrinal tools which they apply whenever a new challenge to the law appears and this has a self-perpetuating effect. New legal problems are solved by those

---

[2] For an analysis German Government bonds, see section 11.4.

who apply the law by making use of those existing concepts that are most developed and therefore safest to use. When lawyers absorb change they dig deeper into existing soil, rather than branching out into new fields.

Another reason why lawyers drafting new rules have, historically, not carried out law reform by creating new rules from scratch is that legal rules need to operate within the network of other legal rules in place in a particular jurisdiction. If law reform is carried out in particular area of the law, this can have a knock-on effect on other areas and such effects can lead to unintended consequences.

To give a few examples, if the legal nature of securities changed in a particular jurisdiction it may become impossible to enforce claims against securities because the rules on enforcement do not accommodate the new nature of the instruments and the form in which they are transferred and held. Likewise, it is possible for enforcement problems to arise in the context of insolvency law. The law of succession is another area of the law which could be affected by a reform of the law of securities. The law of succession contains different rules depending on what type of asset is concerned; if a new asset is created it is possible that none of the categories inherent in the law of succession will apply to that asset. Another area of the law affected by a change in the law of securities is tax law. If the legal nature of an asset changes it is possible for tax rules or exceptions to them to cease to apply to the asset in its new legal form.

If rules relating to securities are created from scratch, the drafters of the new legal regime will be able to anticipate some of the knock-on effects such a change will have on other areas of the law but it is also likely that they will overlook other areas. To avoid unintended consequences those drafting law reform prefer to stay as closely as possible within the already existing legal framework rather than drafting new rules from scratch.

Another context in which problems are likely to arise is private international law. If a legal system changes its doctrinal approach to securities, the private international law rules in place in other jurisdictions may cause the classification of the instruments to change, which may have undesired consequences in the context of international transactions. Undesired consequences of this type cannot be prevented by the jurisdiction carrying out the law reform; they would require the legislature of other jurisdictions to intervene.

The importance of legal doctrine in applying and developing the law, and the tendency of market participants to adopt a risk averse attitude to legal uncertainty, causes legal development to progress consistently with pre-existing legal doctrine. Incumbent legal doctrine shapes the thinking process of the legal experts assisting those in charge of creating new transactional solutions, or designing new governmental policies. Lawyers are accustomed to using a limited set of doctrinal tools; they use them with great skill and are able to assist the business community and the government to achieve the economic and policy outcomes they desire. They are, however, restricted by existing legal doctrine.

To be sure, this book does not promote the view that law and legal doctrine are independent of economical, political, cultural, sociological, or other influences: it rather assumes that all these influences are present. They trigger legal development; they also cause the law to produce certain outcomes. But the form in which outcomes are produced is determined by the legal doctrine prevailing in the jurisdiction concerned.

For example, the level of protection prescribed by mandatory legal rules for the benefit of retail investors may differ according to the political, economic, or cultural climate prevailing in a particular country. A jurisdiction which places a high premium on investor protection may chose to protect all investors who hold securities through intermediaries against the intermediary's insolvency by giving them proprietary rights in all circumstances. A jurisdiction which adopts a more liberal approach to investor rights would leave the decision as to whether investors who hold securities through intermediaries enjoy proprietary or contractual rights to the parties concerned and would leave them to put in place the respective arrangements.

The form in which these different levels of investor protection are implemented, however, is independent of politics, economics, culture, or other factors; it is a function of the legal doctrine prevailing in the respective jurisdiction. To modify the level of investor protection in England in the context of the previous example, the law of trusts would be amended. Germany and Austria would, in the circumstances, modify the rules governing bailment contained in the *Depotgesetz*.

The first thesis put forward in this book is that law and legal development cannot simply be explained as a function of external influences. Legal doctrine is a factor in its own right that determines the form of future development. In addition, legal doctrine influences market infrastructure. The relationship between legal doctrine and market infrastructure will be examined in chapter 16.

16   Legal doctrine and market infrastructure

The first conclusion derived from the analysis contained in this book is that legal doctrine determines the form of future legal development. Having determined the influence of incumbent legal doctrine on future legal doctrine, a second observation can be made.

It has already been noted in section 1.2.1 that a view exists that incumbent institutions have an influence on the development of future institutions. Mark Roe makes the point that the shareholder structure prevailing in one jurisdiction exercises an influence to prevent change which would be efficient from an overall market perspective, but which would cause incumbent power-holders to lose influence. Roe refers to this phenomenon as 'structure-driven path-dependence'. In addition to structure-driven path-dependence, rule-driven path-dependence also exists. Rule-driven path-dependence occurs because law determines the framework within which institutions act. Law is, however, subject to politics and also to institutional pressures. Institutions will use their influence to cause the law to suit their own political objectives. In Mark Roe's analysis, institutions come first; they are themselves a function of politics or even historical accidents. Law is a secondary indirect factor which facilitates political influence and can be modified to any desired degree.

The analysis contained in this book sheds further light on the relationship between law and institutions. It confirms the theory that the institutions prevailing in a jurisdiction influence future development. In England, for example, the process of eliminating paper from securities transfers was beset with difficulties because of institutional lobbying.[1] The first attempt to put in place reform had to be abandoned and

---

[1] See section 3.2.

the Bank of England had to step in to take over the reform process. Institutional pressures operated to delay market infrastructure reform.

When institutional pressures were overcome and the Bank of England succeeded in dematerialising securities transfers, the legal form in which dematerialisation was carried out was determined by the legal doctrinal rules governing securities prior to dematerialisation. Law in this context did not operate as a factor which could have been modified to any degree at the discretion of political institutions. Legal doctrine rather set the boundaries within which institutions felt compelled to remain. This does not prejudice the outcome of change, but it determines the form which the rules facilitating reform take. Legal doctrine does not prevent England from replacing registrars with a central register; but legal doctrine requires English law to organise securities transfers around a register in which the names of securities holders are entered.

Moreover, the type of institutions that have emerged in England, Germany and Austria can be explained by the legal doctrinal rules in place in all three jurisdictions. In England, there exist registrars which administer securities transfers on behalf of issuers. For uncertificated securities the issuer register is kept centrally by CREST, which serves as the registrar for some, but not all, purposes. The existence of this particular branch of the financial services industry can be explained by the fact that English securities are registered securities which require the issuer to maintain a record of the names and certain particulars of securities holders. The analysis presented in this book showed that the involvement of the issuer in securities transfer historically occurred because securities were originally transferable only by novation. The legal doctrinal rules that were in place when securities were first issued in England caused a certain financial infrastructure to arise.[2]

The same observation is true for German and Austrian law.[3] In both jurisdictions, legal doctrine protects transferees against adverse claims by limiting the entitlements of previous owner. This created a need for investors to keep securities documents safe, which in turn led to the emergence of a financial services provider offering depository services.

The second thesis advanced in this book is that law not only receives impulses from politics, economics, culture, social and commercial norms that trigger future legal development. Law also sends impulses to other subsystems of society: legal doctrine can determine the form of market infrastructure prevailing in a jurisdiction.

---

[2] See chapter 4.   [3] See section 10.3.

17   Implications for convergence

The conclusion of the analysis contained in this book is that the form of legal development in England, Germany and Austria has historically been determined by the legal doctrine in place prior to the reform process. The historical legal analysis serves as evidence that law changes consistently with incumbent legal doctrine. Once a legal system adopts a particular legal doctrine to govern an area of the law, changes to the law that become necessary afterwards will be carried out by modifying that particular legal doctrine rather than by adopting a new doctrinal regime. This, over time, causes legal rules to become increasingly refined and specialised.

This has implications for convergence. It becomes impossible for any particular legal system to implement the same rules in place in another legal system even if these rules happen to create a regime that is more efficient, politically preferred and more compatible with social, commercial and cultural norms. If one jurisdiction, for example, responded to the market practice of having transfers of securities administered by a service provider who acts as an intermediary by developing its law of bailment, that jurisdiction will adapt and transform the rules governing bailment to accommodate changes in market practice. The law of bailment will change to accommodate the requirements set by market practice. Every change in market practice will cause the law of bailment to evolve and to move further away from its original starting point. Over time, the law of bailment will reach a level of sophistication that makes it impossible to transplant the rules that have evolved in one jurisdiction into another even if the two systems originally had identical rules of bailment.

This argument goes beyond efficiency. The costs of changing over to a new regime are quantifiable in money terms; the legal uncertainty attached to a set of rules can be priced. In theory, therefore, a jurisdiction would adopt the regime for which the anticipated benefits outweighed the cost arising out of the legal uncertainty attached to the rules that needed to be adopted to support the regime. Convergence would occur if the competitive advantage of a certain set of rules compensated the anticipated cost of adopting an unfamiliar legal regime. This, however, can happen only in so far as rules are adopted that are compatible with the legal doctrine in place in a particular jurisdiction.

Globalisation will not change this pattern of legal development. Assuming that market forces will bring the laws of different jurisdictions closer together, this will concern only the outcomes produced by different legal rules. At a formal level, the different legal doctrinal approaches in place worldwide will continue to determine the legal concepts implemented in support of these outcomes. It is not possible for a jurisdiction to start from scratch, or to replace its existing doctrine with a completely different type of legal doctrine.

In order to illustrate this conclusion it is helpful to carry out an thought experiment based on an assumption. The assumption is that a changeover by Germany and Austria to the regime in place in England would create an economically more efficient regime for both Germany and Austria. This would take into account the costs involved in changing over to a new regime – which, it is assumed, are outweighed by the gains in efficiency generated by the new regime. In addition to improving economic efficiency, the changeover would also be desirable from the perspective of political, social and commercial norms and culture. Based on this assumption, the question arises whether it would be possible for Germany or Austria to reform its law by implementing a statute whose wording was identical to USR 2001.

The first observation to make on this point is that a wholesale adoption of USR 2001 would be possible only alongside statutory reform that would also implement the rules of company law that dealt with the English share register and share certificates. In addition, the reform would have to implement rules that create the same effect as the English case law governing the acquisition of legal title to securities. The concept of ownership at law, as opposed to ownership in equity, would have to be introduced into Germany or Austria. The same would be true for the rules on defective issues and unauthorised transfers. For Germany and Austria to have regimes identical to the English one both countries would also have to adopt the English rules on holdings through intermediaries, which would require both jurisdictions to create a statutory regime replicating English trust law.

None of this will occur. English securities law relies on legal concepts that were created in the context of the parallel jurisdictions of law and equity. It is governed by principles that derive their origin from case law developed over centuries. It is impossible to draft legal rules from scratch that would accurately replicate English property and trust law in an environment that does not have the benefit of being able to rely on the underlying case law. Law reform of this type is bound to cause major difficulties. It would be impossible to predict the implications a reform of this type would have on other areas of the law.

For further illustration of the role of legal doctrine in the context of convergence of legal systems, it is helpful to reverse the assumption on which our experiment thought is based. Assuming that, taking into account the cost of the changeover, the most efficient solution for England would be to adopt the current German or Austrian regime and that a change to that effect would also be supported by political forces and by the constraints created by social and commercial norms and culture, the question arises whether it would be possible for England to adopt rules that were identical to the German or Austrian *Depotgesetz*.

A reform of this type would require England also to put in place rules of bailment and rules relating to tangible movables that are identical to German or Austrian rules. In relation to indirect holdings, English law would have to implement the German concept of indirect co-possession; this would require England first to draft rules that would modify the English property law which has evolved from the distinction between law and equity to accommodate a unitary concept of ownership and rules of possession that are able to operate a concept of constructive possession. The German and Austrian *Depotgesetz* is based on principles of property law that are worded in fairly abstract terms, whose understanding has been refined over centuries. It forms part of a network of rules that cannot be replicated in the context of English law. It would be impossible to draft rules that make it possible for England to adopt a statute identical to the German or Austrian *Depotgesetz*.

Legal doctrine sets limits to convergence. Law reform has historically been carried out consistently with incumbent legal doctrine, a historical pattern of legal change that is likely to continue in the face of current pressures for convergence. Convergence will not cause the rules of one jurisdiction to become a global model which is adopted verbatim around the world. Even if we assume that the Companies Act of a particular jurisdiction has mapped out the best governance model for companies operating in globalised economies, this Act will not become the global law of the company. The Act shaped by the legal doctrine of that jurisdiction could not be absorbed entire in other jurisdictions: convergence can occur only at a functional level.

The analysis presented in this book leads to the conclusion that even if economic, political and cultural factors supported convergence of law, legal doctrine would determine the form in which such convergence occurred. In other words this means that even if it were cost-efficient, politically and culturally acceptable for a jurisdiction to change to a new legal framework, the change would occur only if the proposed new rules sat squarely with the doctrinal rules already in place in this context in the jurisdiction concerned.

This does not mean that convergence is impossible. Convergence is possible, but only at a functional level. It is possible for English, German, and Austrian law to change their respective regimes in a way that makes them more like each other. Our comparison between English and German law has shown that rules with a different doctrinal background are able to produce similar results. German rules governing transfers of paper securities are, for example, doctrinally different from English rules governing transfers of certificated securities. Notwithstanding these differences in legal doctrine, the delivery of securities certificates causes the buyer to acquire a property interest in both jurisdictions. The same is true for the rules protecting investors against adverse claims arising out of unauthorised transfers. In English legal doctrine, adverse claims are contained in the law of evidence and, more recently, in USR 2001. In German and Austrian law, the law of property protects buyers against adverse claims. The two approaches traditionally differ in how they allocate the risk of unauthorised transfers; nevertheless, they both afford effective protection to the buyer. Moreover, it is possible for the outcomes produced by each of these approaches to be modified. In England, for example, the implementation of USR 2001 has modified the allocation of the transfer risk associated with unauthorised transfers, with the result that the outcome produced by English legal doctrine is now more like the outcomes produced by German and Austrian legal doctrine.

Concerning the protection against equities arising out of defective issues of securities, both the English and the German and the Austrian approaches apply similar concepts and achieve similar outcomes.

When regulating property rights in indirectly held securities, English legal doctrine applies the law of trusts, German and Austrian legal doctrine the law of bailment and a sophisticated theory of co-ownership and indirect co-possession. Notwithstanding these significant differences, both approaches make it possible for investors to hold proprietary rights in indirectly held securities. The rights of investors have priority in the insolvency of the intermediary; they also have priority over charging orders granted in favour of unsecured creditors of the intermediary.

The book also refers to examples of functional convergence which have occurred in the context of globalisation. In England, the 2001 reform of the USR changed the law so that full legal ownership is vested in the transferee when the securities were transferred on the records maintained by CREST. Before this reform, legal title vested in the transferee at a later point, when the register maintained by or on behalf of the issuer was amended. The reform was triggered by a desire of the English market to bring its settlement regime in line with perceived best international practice but the form in which it was carried out was determined by incumbent English legal doctrine.[1]

In Germany, the law of name shares was reformed in 2001. The reform was demanded by issuers, who wanted to be able to issue name shares to international investors. A number of issuers wanted to list their securities directly on the NYSE, which does not accept bearer shares. German law also enables issuers to issue name securities, but the legal rules supporting name shares was somewhat outdated. Germany reformed the respective provisions contained in the *Aktiengesctz*, giving German law a more modern regime of name shares. It did, however, involve only peripheral changes; it did not cause German legal doctrine to become more like English or American legal doctrine since the changes were carried out consistently with pre-existing German legal doctrine.

International law reform projects, which are in a position to see beyond the legal framework adopted by any particular jurisdiction, also propose reform on a functional rather than on a formal level. Both UNIDROIT and the EU Legal Certainty Project have opted for functional convergence, and these law reform initiatives will be examined in the sections 17.1 and 17.2.

---

[1] See section 3.4.

17.1 UNIDROIT draft Convention

UNIDROIT is in the process of adopting a Convention on the substantive rules regarding intermediated securities. A first draft of that Convention was published in May 2005 and in March 2006 an updated version of that draft was adopted (known as the Convention). The successive drafts of the Convention were prepared by a drafting committee, a group of lawyers from several jurisdictions: Japan, the UK, Canada, Belgium, Chile, a 'Nordic' country, France, Germany, Luxembourg, Switzerland and the US.[2]

The draft of the Convention was written with a view to providing a standard model for securities that are held and transferred through intermediaries. Article 3 states that, in the implementation, interpretation and application of the Convention, regard is to be had to its purpose, to its international character and to the need to promote uniformity and predictability in its application. It can thus be inferred that one of the aims of the Convention is to create uniform legal rules.

Analysis of the Convention shows that it does not promote formal convergence of legal rules: the drafters are not proposing rules that should be implemented in an identical wording across jurisdictions. The Convention also does not attempt to provide an exhaustive legal framework governing securities held through intermediaries. It explicitly allows for the application of domestic (non-Convention) law. Domestic law applies in matters that are subject to the Convention but that are either not expressly settled in the Convention or that cannot be settled in conformity to the general principles on which the Convention is based.[3]

The Convention promotes functional rather than formal convergence. It does not require legal systems to classify securities as either tangibles or intangibles. It also does not distinguish between bearer, name, or registered securities. It rather regulates securities, in whichever form they may have been issued, that are held through accounts. In doing so, the Convention connects to the common denominator of both English and German law and, it can be speculated, of all the legal systems that were represented on the drafting committee. In both English and German law, securities are held through intermediaries and entitlements of investors are recorded on accounts kept by them. By regulating investor rights by reference to these accounts, the

---

[2] UNIDROIT 2006, Study LXXVIII Doc. 42 ii.   [3] Art. 3 (2), Draft Convention.

Convention avoids having to interfere with the respective legal analysis of the nature of the securities: it does not regulate their proprietary doctrinal analysis.

17.2 EU Legal Certainty Project

The EU has put forward a law reform project which aims to determine whether the differences in the legal regimes governing securities and their transfers provide for obstacles to the emergence of a single European securities market. Like the UNIDROIT in its current draft Convention, the Legal Certainty Group has opted for functional rather than formal convergence.

The Legal Certainty Group first carried out a survey of the existing legal frameworks of all the EU member states; the laws of Japan, the US and Canada were also analysed. The information collected by the Legal Certainty Group, however, was not used as a basis for an economic analysis. It did not compare the relative efficiency of these existing legal frameworks nor determine whether there existed a set of legal rules that would be more efficient in economic terms than any of the rules currently in place.

The members of the Group, having analysed the different legal regimes, instead used their professional judgement to determine whether or not reform harmonising the law across Europe would be necessary. They also used their professional judgement, rather than economic legal analysis, when explaining the options available for a harmonised regime.

Select bibliography

Since the key works on English law and governance with which this book is concerned, such as Roe, *Political Determinants of Corporate Governance* (2003), can easily be consulted, this bibliography cites primarily works in German which are less easily accessible.

Baumbach, Adolf and Wolfgang Hefermehl, *Wechselgesetz und Scheckgesetz*, 22nd edn. (München: Beck, 2000)

Binding, J., 'Der Vertrag als alleinige Grundlage der Inhaberpapiere', *Zeitschrift für das gesamte Handelsrecht und Wirtschaftsrecht* 10 (1866) 400

Bluntschli, Johann Caspar, *Deutsches Privatrecht*, vol. 2 (München: Literarisch-artistische Anstalt, 1854)

Bornemann, Friedrich Wilhelm Ludwig, *Systematische Darstellung des Preußischen Civilrechts mit Benutzung der Materialien des Allgemeinen Landrechts*, vol. 1, 2nd edn. (Berlin: Jonas, 1842)
Darstellung des Preußischen Civilrechts mit Benutzung der Materialien des Allgemeinen Landrechts, vol. 3, 2nd edn. (Berlin: Jonas, 1843)

Brunner, Heinrich, in Wilhelm Endemann (ed.), *Handbuch des deutschen Handelsrechts*, vol. II (Leipzig: Fues's Verlag, 1882)

Bruns, Georg, *Das Depotgeschäft* (Frankfurt am Main: Fritz Knapp Verlag, 1962)

Canaris, Claus-Wilhelm, in Hermann Staub (ed.), *Großkommentar zum Handelsgesetzbuch*, vol. III, part 3, *Bankvertragsrecht*, 2nd edn. (Berlin: Walter de Gruyter, 1981)

Coing, Helmut, *Europäisches Privatrecht, 19. Jahrhundert*, vol. II (München: Beck, 1989)

Commentar zum allgemeinen Landrecht für die preußischen Staaten, vols. 1, 2 (Breslau: Hamberger, 1804) (no author)

Dabelow, Christoph Christian von, *System des gesammten heutigen Civil-Rechts*, vol. I, 2nd edn. (Halle: 1796)

Danz, Wilhelm August Friedrich, *Handbuch des heutigen deutschen Privatrechts* (Stuttgart: Löflund, 1797)

Drobnig, Ulrich, 'Dokumentenloser Effektenverkehr', in Karl Kreuzer (ed.), *Abschied vom Wertpapier? Dokumentenlose Wertbewegungen im Effekten-, Gütertransport- und Zahlungsverkehr* (Neuwied: Alfred Metzner Verlag, 1988) 11

Eichhorn, Carl Friedrich, *Einleitung in das deutsche Privatrecht mit Einschluss des Lehensrechts* (Göttingen: Vandenhoeck und Ruprecht, 1823)

Einert, Carl, *Über das Wesen und die Form des Literalcontracts wie dieser zur Zeit der Justinianischen Gesetzgebung ausgebildet gewesen und Vergleichung desselben mit dem Wechsel* (Leipzig: Tauchnitz, 1852)

Einsele, Dorothee, *Wertpapierrecht als Schuldrecht* (Tübingen: J. C. B. Mohr (Paul Siebeck), 1995)

Engelmann, Arthur, *Das Preußische Privatrecht in Anknüpfung an das gemeine Recht* (Breslau: Koebner, 1883)

Fabricius, Fritz, 'Zur Theorie des stückelosen Effektengiroverkehrs mit Wertrechten aus Staatsanleihen' (1963), 162 *Archiv für die civilistische Praxis* 460

Fleischmann, Paul, 'Wertpapiere im totalen Krieg', [1943] *Bankarchiv* 9

Fürst, Herbert, 'Sammeldepot an Effekten und Effektengiroverkehr', *Zentralblatt* [1928] 57

Gengler, Heinrich Gottlieb Philipp, *Lehrbuch des deutschen Privatrechts*, vol. I (Erlangen: Verlag von Theodor Bläsnig, 1854)

Glück, Christian Friedrich, *Ausführliche Erläuterung der Pandekten*, vol. XVI, 2nd edn. (Erlangen: Palmsche Verlagsbuchhandlung, 1844)

Goldschmidt, L., *System des Handelsrechts*, 4th edn. (Stuttgart: Verlag von Ferdinand Enke, 1892)

Gönner N. Th., *Von Staatsschulden, deren Tilgungsanstalten und vom Handel mit Staatspapieren* (München: Fleischmannsche Buchhandlung, 1826)

Gößmann, Wolfgang, in Herbert Schimansky, Hermann-Josef Bunte and Hans-Jürgen Lwowski (eds.), *Bankrechts-Handbuch*, vol. II, 2nd edn. (München: Beck, 2001)

Heckelmann, Dieter, in Westermann, Harm Peter (ed.), *Ermann Bürgerliches Gesetzbuch*, 10th edn. (Köln: Dr. Otto Schmidt, 2000)

Heumann, Carl, 'Die Entwicklung des Effekten Giro-Verkehrs. Notwendigkeiten und Möglichkeiten', (1927/28) 27 *Bankarchiv* 223

Hommelhoff, Peter and Christoph Teichmann, 'Namensaktie, Neue Medien und Nachgründung – aktuelle Entwicklungslinien im Aktienrecht', in Dietrich Dörner, Dieter Menhold, Norbert Pfitzer, and Peter Oser (eds.), *Reform des Aktienrechts, der Rechnungslegung und der Prüfung*, 2nd edn. (Stuttgart: Schäffer-Poeschel, 2003)

Hopt, Klaus, 'Ideelle und wirtschaftliche Grundlagen der Aktien-, Bank- und Börsenentwicklung im 19. Jahrhundert', in Helmut Coing and Walter Wilhelm (eds.), *Wissenschaft und Kodifikation im 19. Jahrhundert Band V* (Frankfurt am Main: Vittorio Klostermann, 1980)

'Änderung von Anleihebedingungen – Schuldverschreibungsgesetz, § 796 BGB und AGBG', in *Steindorf Festschrift* (Berlin: Walter de Gruyter, 1990) 341

Horn, Norbert, 'Die Erfüllung von Wertpapiergeschäften unter Einbeziehung
    eines Zentralen Kontrahenten an der Börse', [Sonderbeilage 2/2002]
    Wertpapier Mitteilungen 11
Hueck, Alfred and Canaris, Claus-Wilhelm, *Recht der Wertpapiere*, 12th edn.
    (München: Franz Vahlen, 1986)
Hüffer, Uwe, in Peter Ulmer (ed.), *Münchener Kommentar zum Bürgerlichen
    Gesetzbuch*, vol. 5, 3rd edn. (München: Beck, 1997)
Iro, Gert, in Peter Avancini Gert Iro and Helmut Koziol, *Österreichisches
    Bankvertragsrecht*, vol. II (Wien: Manz, 1993)
Jacobi, Ernst, in Victor Ehrenberg (ed.), *Handbuch des gesamten Handelsrechts*,
    vol. IV/1 (Leipzig: O. R. Reisland, 1917)
Jacobi, Ernst, *Grundriss des Rechts der Wertpapiere im allgemeinen*, 3rd edn. (Leipzig:
    O. R. Reisland, 1928)
Klaus, Peters, *Wertpapierfreies Effektensystem* (Göttingen: dissertation, 1975)
Klicka, Thomas, in Michael Schwimann (ed.), *Praxiskommentar zum ABGB*, vol. II,
    3rd edn. (Wien: Orac, 2004)
Koch, Christian Friedrich, *Allgemeines Landrecht für die Preußischen Staaten, Erster
    Teil, Erster Band*, 4th edn. (Berlin: Guttentag, 1862)
Koller, Ingo, 'Der gutgläubige Erwerb von Sammeldepotanteilen an
    Wertpapieren im Effektengiroverkehrs', [1972] *Der Betrieb*, 1857
    'Empfiehlt sich eine Neuordnung und Ergänzung des Wertpapierrechts im
    BGB?', in Bundesministerium der Justiz (ed.), *Gutachten und Vorschläge zu
    Überarbeitung des Schuldrechts*, vol. II (Köln: Bundesanzeiger
    Verlagsgesellschaft, 1981)
Koziol, Helmut and Rudolf Welser, *Grundriss des Bürgerlichen Rechts*, vol. II, 12th
    edn. (Wien: Manz, 2001)
    Grundriss des bürgerlichen Rechts, vol. I, 13th edn. (Wien: Manz, 2006)
Kümpel, Siegfried, *Bank- und Kapitalmarktrecht*, 3rd edn. (Köln: Verlag Otto
    Schmidt, 2004)
    'Der Bestimmtheitsgrundsatz bei Verfügungen über Sammeldepotguthaben –
    zur Theorie des Bruchteilseigentums sui generis', [1980] *Wertpapier
    Mitteilungen* 422
Langheim, Gerd-Hinrich, in Norbert Horn (ed.), *J. von Staudingers Kommentar zum
    Bürgerlichen Gesetzbuch, Zweites Buch Recht der Schuldverhältnisse* (Berlin:
    Sellier–de Gruyter, 2002)
Leske, Franz, *Vergleichende Darstellung des Bürgerlichen Gesetzbuches für das Deutsche
    Reich und der Landesrechte, Band III, Das Bürgerliche Gesetzbuch und das Preußische
    Allgemeine Landrecht* (Berlin: Liebmann, 1900)
Lutz, L. (ed.), *Protokolle der Kommission zur Beratung eine allgemeinen deutschen
    Handelsgesetzbuches* (Würzburg: Verlag der Stahel'schen Buch- und
    Kunsthandlung, 1858)
Marburger, Peter in Norbert Horn (ed.), *J. von Staudingers Kommentar zum
    Bürgerlichen Gesetzbuch, Zweites Buch Recht der Schuldverhältnisse* (Berlin:
    Sellier–de Gruyter, 2002)

Metze, A., 'Das Giro-Effektendepot der Bank des Berliner Kassenvereins', *Zeitschrift für das gesamte Handelsrecht*, [1927] 377

Meyer-Cording, Ulrich and Tim Drygala, *Wertpapierrecht*, 3rd edn. (Berlin: Luchterhand Neuwied, Kriftel, 1995)

Micheler, Eva, *Wertpapierrecht zwischen Schuld- und Sachenrecht: Zu einer kapitalmarktrechtlichen Theorie des Wertpapierrechts* (Wien: Springer, 2004)

Mittermaier, C. J. A., *Grundsätze des gemeinen deutschen Privatrechts*, vol. II, 7th edn. (Regensburg: Manz, 1847)

Mühlenbruch C. F., *Die Lehre von der Zession der Forderungsrechte*, 3rd edn. (Greifswald: Ernst Mauritius, 1836)

Niebauer, Anton, 'Die Begebungspraxis bei Österreichischen Staatsanleihen', *Bankarchiv* 6 (1906/1907) 35

Nolan, R. C., 'Equitable Property', 122 (2006) LQR 232–265
'Property in a Fund', 120 (2004) *LQR* 108–136

Ofner, Julius (ed.), *Der Urentwurf und die Beratungsprotokolle des Österreichischen Allgemeinen Bürgerlichen Gesetzbuches*, vol. 2 (Wien: Alfred Hölder, 1889)

Opitz, Georg, *Depotgesetz*, 2nd edn. (Berlin: Walter de Gruyter, 1955)
Fünfzig depotrechtliche Abhandlungen (Berlin: Walter de Gruyter, 1954)

Poschinger, Heinrich von, *Beitrag zur Geschichte der Inhaberpapiere in Deutschland* (Erlangen: Deichert, 1875)
Die Lehre von der Befugniß zur Ausstellung von Inhaber-Papieren (München: Lindauer, 1870)

Rögner, Herbert, in Christian Huber (ed.), *Bankrecht* (Baden-Baden: Nomos, 2001)

Roth, Günter, *Wertpapierrecht*, 2nd edn. (Wien: Manz 1999)

Savingy, Friedrich Carl, *Das Obligationenrecht als Theil des heutigen römischen Rechts*, vol. II (Berlin: Bei Veit und Comp, 1853)

Scherer, Peter, in Boujong, Karlheinz, Carsten Thomas Ebenroth and Detlev Joost (eds.), *Handelsgesetzbuch*, vol. II (München: Beck/Verlag Franz Vahlen, 2001)

Schumm, C., *Die Amortisation verlorener oder sonst abhanden gekommener Schuldurkunden nach gemeiner deutscher Praxis mit Berücksichtigung deutscher Partikulargesetze, besonders im Betreff der auf Inhaber (au porteur) gestellten Staats- und öffentlichen Kreditpapiere* (Heidelberg: Mohr, 1830)

Schütz, Wilhelm, 'Die Änderung des Depotgesetzes und der Eigentumsvorbehalt bei Wertpapierlieferungen', *Bankarchiv* 23 (1923/1924) 119

Sedatis, Lutz, 'Absoluter und relativer Erwerb im Wertpapierrecht', in *Rehbinder Festschrift* (München: Beck, 2002)

Seuffert Johann Adam, *Praktisches Pandektenrecht*, 2nd edn. (Würzburg: Verlag der Stahel'schen Buchhandlung, 1848)

Siebel, Ulf, *Rechtsfragen internationaler Anleihen* (Berlin: Duncker und Humblott, 1997)

Theodor, Heinsius, Arno Horn, and Jürgen Than, *Depotgesetz* (Berlin: Walter de Gruyter, 1975)

Thöl, Heinrich, *Das Handelsrecht in Verbindung mit dem allgemeinen deutschen Handelsgesetzbuch*, vol. I, 4th edn. (Göttingen: Verlag der Dieterichschen Buchhandlung, 1862)

Trumpler, H., 'Zur Geschichte der Frankfurter Börse', *Bankarchiv* 9 (1909/ 1910), 100

Unger, Josef, *Die rechtliche Natur der Inhaberpapiere* (Leipzig: Breitkopf und Härtel, 1857)

Wagner, Berthold, '50 Jahre Bundesschuldenverwaltung', [1999] *Wertpapier Mitteilungen* 1949

Wayna, Josef von, *Antwort auf die Stock-Jobbery, und der Handel mit Staatspapieren nach dem jetzigen Zustande, politisch und juristisch betrachtet* (Wien: Gerold, 1821)

Weitz, Eric, *Prussian Civil Code, excerpts translated from Allgemeines Landrecht für die Preussischen Staaten* (Berlin, 1821)

Westermann, Harm Peter, 'Das Girosammeldepot im deutschen Recht', (1985) 49 *Rabels Zeitschrift für ausländisches und internationales Privatrecht* 214

Wiegand, Wolfgang, in Karl Heinz Gursky (ed.), *J. von Staudingers Kommentar zum Bürgerlichen Gesetzbuch, Drittes Buch Sachenrecht* (Berlin: Sellier–de Gruyter, 2004)

Zahn, Andreas and Stephan Kock, 'Die Emission von unverbrieften Schuldtiteln durch die Europäische Zentralbank', [1999] *Wertpapier Mitteilungen* 1955

Zimmerman, Reinhard, 'Savigny's Legacy: Legal History, Comparative Law, and the Emergence of a European Legal Science', (1996) 112 *LQR* 575

Zöllner, Wolfgang, *Wertpapierrecht*, 14th edn. (München: Beck, 1987)

Index